POLAR WIVES

Polar

The Remarkable Women behind
the World's Most Daring Explorers

KARI HERBERT

Foreword by **JON BOWERMASTER**

GREYSTONE BOOKS
D&M PUBLISHERS INC.
Vancouver/Toronto/Berkeley

Greystone Books
An imprint of D&M Publishers Inc.
2323 Quebec Street, Suite 201
Vancouver BC Canada V5T 4S7
www.greystonebooks.com

Cataloguing data available from Library and Archives Canada
ISBN 978-1-926812-62-5 (pbk.)
ISBN 978-1-926812-63-2 (ebook)

Editing by Barbara Pulling
Cover design by Naomi MacDougall and Heather Pringle
Text design by Heather Pringle
Cover photograph of Jo Peary © Herbert Collection;
photograph of the *Fram* © Fridtjof Nansen / National Library of Norway
Author photograph © Herbert Collection
Printed and bound in Canada by Friesens
Distributed in the U.S. by Publishers Group West

We gratefully acknowledge the financial support of the Canada Council for
the Arts, the British Columbia Arts Council, the Province of British Columbia
through the Book Publishing Tax Credit and the Government of Canada through
the Canada Book Fund for our publishing activities.

Greystone Books is committed to reducing the consumption of old-growth forests
in the books it publishes. This book is one step towards that goal.

For my loving parents

CONTENTS

POLAR WIVES

Jon Bowermaster

FOREWORD

I HAVE HAD the good fortune to spend years of my life exploring some of the most remote corners of the planet, including many long months in the Arctic and the Antarctic. I've seen the ends of this earth by both classic and modern means, sailing a small boat to Antarctica and flying by Twin Otter to the South Pole, travelling by dogsled through the High Arctic and landing by Russian helicopter at the North Pole.

Some of my favourite cold expeditions have followed in the footsteps of Ernest Shackleton. I've been near to the spot where the *Endurance* went down, which is now mostly open ocean. I've stood on the beach on Elephant Island where Shackleton and his men jerry-rigged the *James Caird* for the highly dubious crossing to South Georgia Island. At South Georgia I've climbed the same route he and his five companions were forced to undertake after landing on the far side of the island, away from help. And I've stood at the Boss's grave at Grytviken and toasted him with whisky there, as is the ritual.

Yet despite those retracings, and despite having read everything I could about Shackleton's life, expeditions, motivations, dreams and disappointments, the most enduring question I've had about the man has long gone unanswered: During those two years and eight months that he was gone from England, without any word back to his home or homeland, what must Mrs. Shackleton have been thinking?

Now, thanks to Kari Herbert's exhaustive research, I have answers. Emily Shackleton—described here as "the epitome of the long-suffering polar wife"—was doing what the partners of adventurers have always done: making do, taking care, longing for and—somehow—abiding the long absence of the man she loved.

Was the inevitable suffering, made torturous by unknowns, worth it? In her case, seemingly yes. But each polar partner's experience is different, whether centuries ago or today.

All of the women in this book possessed a strength and perseverance perhaps not so common for their times. These were unique individuals—an acclaimed singer, a poet and a seasoned adventurer among them—who in spite of the social constraints of their respective eras were in many respects the equals of their more public partners.

Many things about leading an adventurous life have changed in the nearly one hundred years since Shackleton sailed for Antarctica on his penultimate voyage south. The very definition of exploration has evolved. New lands and trade routes are not still out there to be discovered; except for the ocean's great depths, this globe has been largely mapped. It is also now possible for those who travel to even the most remote, forsaken corners of the world to do something that Ernest Shackleton—like Robert Falcon Scott, Robert Peary, John Franklin, Fridtjof Nansen and even Wally Herbert—was incapable of doing: calling home.

Imagine how life would have been made easier for Emily Shackleton—or Kathleen Scott, Jo Peary, Eleanor Anne Franklin, Jane Franklin, Eva Nansen or Marie Herbert—if her partner had simply had a satellite telephone.

Of course technology is no cure for the ache and non-stop worry that comes with the territory whenever a partner goes "out there" for long periods. Judging from Kari Herbert's work, the one who leaves and the one who stays behind share that empty feeling. That will always be hard.

Kari Herbert's writing about the lives of polar wives will forever change the way we think about adventurers and their mates. To paraphrase from a tribute paid to Ernest Shackleton at the memorial held after his too-early death at forty-seven, Emily survived his absences because she knew and understood him best... and thus loved him most.

INTRODUCTION

A FLIMSY TENT clung to a desolate beach in northwest Greenland, surrounded by boulders and flattened alpine flowers. It was the height of summer, 1891. Beyond the sheets of rain, black basalt cliffs towered above the canvas shelter like a petrified wave crested with a vast ice cap that stretched to the horizon and beyond.

In the shelter a man lay strapped to a plank. His wife smoothed his brow, leaning over him in full plaid skirts and a neatly tailored woollen jacket. Farther up the beach, the five other members of the expedition struggled to secure the materials needed to build their headquarters; the wind whipped shouts and expletives from their mouths almost before they were uttered.

Alone in the tent with her incapacitated husband, Jo Peary shuddered as the nearby icebergs ground together. One of the ropes holding the tent to the shore suddenly snapped, sounding like the report of a pistol, but nothing could be done. Far more pressing was the torrent of water rushing through the tent from the swollen glacial stream. Perched tailor-fashion on provision boxes, her legs and skirts heavy with mud, Jo tried in vain to dam the surging water so that it would not soak her patient, then tried to rescue equipment and supplies before they were swept away. Unable to hear or be heard over the shrieking wind, the thrumming of the remaining guy ropes and the urgent flapping of the canvas, Jo wrestled with the fear that at any moment they might be torn from their tiny base. "It was," she later recalled, "a most wretched night."

There was no chance of her going back to her comfortable home in Washington, D.C. Earlier that day Captain Richard Pike, master of the whaling steamer *Kite*, had given the order for his ship to weigh anchor and head south with haste. He had delivered another expedition to the same area ten years earlier, and he recognized the signs of a tempest. The *Kite* had to leave immediately or face being crushed by the mountainous icebergs driven at speed toward one another by wind and waves.

Far above the storm clouds, the sun continued its lazy sweep over the tundra. It had not set for almost three months, and it would be another two before the High Arctic slipped into the first dark hours that would lengthen into a four-month winter night. It was here that Jo and a small band of men would live and travel for the next twelve months.

EXACTLY EIGHTY YEARS later, my mother, Marie Herbert, stood on the deck of a supply ship holding me, her ten-month-old daughter, in her arms and surveying this same High Arctic fjord with trepidation. Herbert Island, just across the water from where Jo Peary had once lived, was to be our home for the next two years. In "the euphoria of wedlock," my father, the polar explorer Wally Herbert, had proposed that she join him on his next journey to the North. She was delighted. As the future wife of a polar explorer, she had accepted the inevitability of separation while her husband continued his work in the inhospitable regions of the world. This was the opportunity of a lifetime and, as she recorded later, she reckoned that there would be time enough later to repent. Since their first meeting my father had enthused about the Arctic, but she was now confronted by a scene far from the magical place she had imagined. Herbert Island was a razor-back ridge of featureless rock, my mother later recalled: "No light shone on it or was reflected back. The bleak monotony of it was broken only by the scars and scratches of the cutting winds which had swept it clean. There seemed no space for man or beast on this barren rock: and this was where I had brought my baby to live ... My vision blurred. I thought I would choke. I could say nothing."

FOR JO PEARY and my mother, encountering the northern wilds was an initiation into a life that years earlier they could scarcely have imagined. They had joined what could loosely be termed the "polar wives' club"—a curiously isolated band of women whose focus was propelled to the far reaches of the known world by the force of their husbands' ambition.

Although of different eras, origins and backgrounds, the seven women whose stories are retold in this book shared the belief that their men had vital life missions to complete. Unlike the mythical figure of Penelope—to whom almost all would be compared—who waited impotently for some sign that her lover was to return safely, each of these women encouraged her husband to seek out the unknown. To varying degrees, these polar wives embodied a range of roles beyond those normally expected: manager, publicist, mother figure, fundraiser, nurse, counsellor and, most important, muse. Driven by love, pride and a fierce loyalty, each developed a bond with her husband that transcended time, place and expectation.

It is almost universally accepted that the pioneering polar explorer is a particular breed of man: he is brave and bold and carries with him a conviction, or delusion, that he was born to succeed. Intolerable physical hardship and privation for such men are simply necessary hurdles on the quest for achievement; they are part of the job description for an explorer. The wife of a polar traveller must be the equal of her husband in character, if not ambition, to endure the challenges that haunt every polar family, whether the men are abroad or at home. Invariably the question is posed: What would make a woman choose a husband who is likely to be away for years at a time, and who—if he returns at all—comes home a changed man, mentally or physically scarred by his experiences? It is a question that has often been asked of my mother. There is no easy answer, for the relationship between each polar explorer and his wife and family is unique. That makes their stories all the more compelling.

My father was one of the last of the old-school pioneers: travelling by dog sledge through virgin wilderness, navigating by the stars and using techniques of polar survival learned from the Inuit of northwest Greenland and from men who had travelled with the likes of the polar heroes Scott and Shackleton. Like them, my father faced blizzards that could suffocate and disorient even the most experienced traveller; he fought malnutrition and starvation and stepped out into the unknown with echoes of the scornful accusation that he was embarking on a journey that was impossible, even downright suicidal, ringing in his ears. As did many of those polar travellers before him, he trusted to providence when the odds seemed to be stacked too high, the dangers too great.

At the height of his career my father completed what is often called "the Last Great Journey on Earth"—the crossing of the Arctic Ocean via the North Pole. This epic sixteen-month slog over continually shifting, breaking sea ice not only was the first expedition to cross the top of the world, but is now generally accepted to have been the first to have reached the North Pole by surface crossing. Although I did not witness this particular achievement, I often saw my father in his element in the polar wilds, and on several occasions I clutched the hand of my mother as he left us, heading out on another expedition to the North.

I grew up watching my father chasing his dreams, my mother alongside him whenever possible, applauding his vision even when it meant periods of great loneliness, financial strain and concern for his safety. Even given the numerous trials that my parents faced over the years, theirs was an enviable marriage in many respects, one built on tremendous respect, friendship and a shared love of adventure. Unusually, my father was not the only one to travel. Frequently he supported my mother when she was driven by wanderlust, and then it would be my father, my sister and me keeping the home fires burning.

It was only when I started cutting my own trail in life that I realized our experiences as a family were often far from "normal." I began to acknowledge the affinity we shared with the men and women at the heart of the greatest polar stories, and I found myself intrigued by the coincidences of experience that seemed to link us. From my fascination with this personal aspect of polar history, this book was born.

These stories begin in a time popularly known as the heroic age of exploration: a period spanning the late Georgian, Victorian and Edwardian eras that was dominated by great personalities and numerous geographical firsts. The stories culminate two and a half centuries later, just before the development of global communications fundamentally changed the way travellers operated in the field. Put simply, the subjects of this book were unfamiliar with GPS and satellite telephones.

The explorers of the heroic age were the superstars of their time, the heralds of a new era, in which the conquest of nature was seen as the last great battle for control of human reality. On these men were pinned hopes for the creation of order in an otherwise chaotic existence. These men of empire, whether British, American or Norwegian, felt invincible, and where better to form myths of modern-day knights than at the extremities of the known world.

As the outlines of the world's continents rapidly came into focus, the race was on for the attainment of the most elusive places: the Northwest Passage and the North and South Poles. Novelists, poets and artists stimulated the public's imagination with their tales of suspense and adversity in the great frozen wilderness. But for women in this time of great endeavour, freedom was not so easy to come by. Constricted by the gentilities and pruderies of their age, some in the late nineteenth century sought an escape: if not physically, then mentally. A French writer once said: "It is enough to love a man, to have him accomplish for you, all the conquests he has failed to make; to have him fulfill, for you, a purpose for which he himself has known only failure." Although this statement would excite a strong reaction today, for some of the early women in this book it rang true. Creative expression was often their only means of exploration, visualizing exotic scenes of crystalline ice and assigning to the polar regions a romanticism that in reality did not exist.

The stories of the brave men conquering the Poles were intoxicating, and to take tea or dance with a polar explorer could be a woman's highlight of the year. These were fearless lions who would face the great, sublime forces of nature and return battle-scarred. Marriage, a profound journey in itself, appeared all the more exciting when there was the prospect of experiencing by proxy some of the most dangerous and beautiful places on earth.

For the explorers, a resilient wife was an important—perhaps the most important—member of an expedition team. It was essential that the wife of a polar pioneer match her husband's spirit—the relationship could not survive otherwise. The women had to be understanding, adaptable, intelligent and confident; the success or failure of expeditions often depended on their foresight and support. Privately, these women were the inspiration for many great journeys. An achievement such as the discovery of a Northwest Passage or the attainment of the North or South Pole would not only guarantee fame and perhaps wealth for the explorer but also provide a lasting legacy for his wife and children.

Perhaps surprisingly, even when their husbands were in the field at the same time, there was little interaction among the polar wives. Ever loyal, these women were often as competitive as their men. Routes, sponsors and contacts were jealously nurtured and protected; the little correspondence that existed between the women was polite but guarded. Although they might have been some comfort to one another, they preferred to handle similar challenges alone.

In no small way, the women themselves have dictated how this book should be arranged. In an attempt to give deeper insight into these turbulent lives, I have arranged the book in a series of episodes, rather than creating chronological biographies. In this way, the distinct personality of each woman, I hope, will come alive. If I am thought to give too much place to the men, it must be remembered that the lives of these women were bound to their husbands. Seeing the inner world of these explorers through the eyes of the ones who loved them best will also, I hope, add a new dimension to these brave but often flawed polar heroes.

Readers may wonder why I have not included the wives of other great figures of exploration, such as Marie, the wife of Frederick A. Cook, a rival claimant to the North Pole, or Oriana, wife of the explorer Edward Wilson, who died with Scott after reaching the South Pole in 1912. Modern women such as Ginny, the childhood sweetheart and soulmate of Sir Ranulph Fiennes, have also been fundamental to the success of their husbands. Although these women all deserve to be acknowledged, to include their stories would require more space than I have here; the life stories of the women featured have already, by necessity, been cut dramatically.

My book draws heavily upon original sources and descendants' accounts. Some of the handwriting—for example, that of Jane Franklin—was at times almost illegible; other letters had been written across horizontally, then overwritten vertically and diagonally, which made my research immensely challenging. Punctuation, particularly in letters written in high emotion or in private journal entries, was naturally idiosyncratic. Wherever possible I have kept the original punctuation, except for rare instances where the meaning of the letter would have been lost. Likewise, I have kept original spellings intact.

In the traditional historical biographies, most of these women's fascinating stories have been eclipsed by those of their husbands. Emily Shackleton in particular has almost completely faded from view, largely because she destroyed many of the letters between herself and her husband. I have relied on Shackleton's own words in many instances to illuminate the woman he loved; in posterity, he shines light on the companion who lived so resolutely and loyally in his shadow.

The women in this book were constant beacons to their life partners. Even when they were thousands of miles away, their husbands could imagine their voices beyond the screams of polar storms, urging them forward, willing them to succeed even if the journey was through a frozen hell with little hope of return. Here, these voices are finally heard.

PART ONE

A RESTLESS COMPANION

I

Jo Peary

CALL OF THE LODESTAR

Of course, if I feel so inclined,
I can go out and sit on an iceberg until I
freeze to it, and let the wind and snow
beat upon me, even starve myself; but my tastes
do not run in that direction.

JO PEARY

O<small>N THE AFTERNOON</small> of June 6, 1891, an attractive brunette clasped the hand of her husband and turned to smile at the press gathered on board the greasy little whaling steamer *Kite*, moored at her dock in Brooklyn. On the quayside, crowds strained to catch a glimpse of the elegant young woman who was to be the first female member of an expedition to the Far North. Shouts of encouragement peaked over murmurs of concern as the press and family members were ushered off the ship, leaving the unworldly Mrs. Peary on board among a wild-looking band of men. Elegantly dressed and with a gentle, youthful demeanour, Josephine Peary looked starkly out of place. According to the *New York Times*, the decks of the *Kite* were stained with the "oil and fat of a hundred whales and ten times that many seals." Precariously perched above was a crow's nest lined with furs, ready to keep any observer warm

against the bitter polar storms. In the hold were four big Newfound-
land dogs, which Robert Peary hoped to use as supplementary pulling
power, along with teams of huskies. The cook, a British whaler, confided to the *Times* reporter that he saw the addition of these dogs in
purely culinary terms:

> They're the best h'eatin' in the world . . . Many's the time I've h'eat
> Esquimau dogs, but they has the taste of wolf in 'em, and you can't
> get it out. American dogs, on the contrary, is good h'eatin' seven
> days in the week, an' you can take your last look at them there in
> the hold, for you'll never see 'em again or my name h'aint Tom
> Andy.

It was with such rough companions that Jo would be confined
for the next twenty-three days in narrow, cramped quarters during
their passage to Whale Sound, preceding a further fourteen months
of isolation upon the shores of North Greenland. The "party will
abandon all the airs of its former self the moment it makes its home on
the *Kite*," the newspaper sagely noted.

Jo, however, was radiant. Whereas many women of her time were
still living through their men by proxy, she would fully embrace
the adventure and make it as much her own as it was her husband's.
Yet her motivation for joining his expedition was love rather than
heroism. "I felt that my place was at his side," she told her daughter
years later. "As long as he was willing to have me along, and I was not
a hindrance to his plans, I wanted to be with him." In turn, Robert
Peary did not question her courage and resilience—they both knew
that there was no room on a polar expedition for any persons, male or
female, who could not look after themselves.

For Peary, the clamour of the press, the cannon shot and whistles
and the scores of steamers, yachts and pleasure boats spilling over
with handkerchief-waving passengers were a positive omen not only
for the expedition but for his place in the world, and with Jo at his
side he felt invincible. To his mother he wrote, "Now I feel that all is

written in the irrevocable book that I have been selected for this work, and shall be upheld or carried safely and successfully through." This vehement belief in the importance of his life mission was something that Jo would have to support and ultimately defend.

JOSEPHINE CECILIA DIEBITSCH was born in Washington, D.C., on May 22, 1863, to Prussian immigrants, Herman von Diebitsch and Magdelena Schmid; Magdalena was a descendant of the family that owned the well-known German publishing firm Tauchnitz. Herman and Magdelena had independently fled the carnage of the Revolution of 1848, hoping to make a new life in the United States, where they had met and fallen in love. Herman Diebitsch dropped the *von*—the sign of nobility—from his name and searched for a suitable job. To his disappointment, although he was fluent in French, German, Russian and English and had a sound knowledge of Latin and Greek, he found it impossible to secure a position of any merit. Manual labour was the only option available to him in a land suspicious of foreigners. For several years Herman and his gentle wife, who had once enjoyed a life of rare privilege, struggled to provide for their family. In quick succession, child after child was born and then buried. Out of twelve children, Josephine—known as Josie or Jo—was the eldest of just four who lived into adulthood. Sun-drenched childhood days on a farm in Maryland were overshadowed by poverty, grief and a father who, embittered by the crash of his fortunes, had become withdrawn and deeply unhappy.

By the time she met her future husband, however, the prospects for Jo's family had improved. Significantly, Jo's father had been awarded the position of head clerk of the Smithsonian Institution in Washington. Jo was determined to avoid the hardships her parents had endured. Headstrong, clever and hard-working, she sailed through her exams before persuading her father to allow her to attend a business school, where she became valedictorian of her class. By the time she was nineteen, she had worked for two years at the census bureau and then taken over the duties of her increasingly frail father at the

Smithsonian, which, particularly given that she was working at the same salary, was a rare accomplishment for her time. It was this confident young woman to whom, in 1882, Lieutenant Robert E. Peary of the Civil Engineer Corps of the U.S. Navy was irresistibly drawn.

Jo had had no shortage of suitors, a situation that she found amusing but rather tiresome. Her first impression of Peary at the popular dance hall Marini's in Washington was that he was an "old man." Tall and rake-thin with piercing blue eyes, this intense-looking gentleman nine years her senior was a world away from the carefree young men who had usually pursued her. When Peary first called upon her, Jo left the entertaining to her widowed mother, believing that they would have much more in common. Her apparent lack of interest exasperated and intrigued Peary. She would soon discover that little would deter her new suitor once he had set his sights.

AN ONLY CHILD, Robert Edwin Peary was born in Cresson, Pennsylvania, on May 6, 1856, to Charles Nutter Peary and his wife, Mary Webster Wiley. The newlyweds had left their home state of Maine to seek a new life in the sweeping, forested landscape of the Alleghenies, where Charles quickly secured work in the shook trade—the manufacture of staves for barrels which would be sent to the West Indies and returned to the United States filled with rum or molasses. When Mary discovered she was pregnant, they were overjoyed. But before long their future together was shattered: aged just thirty, Charles was struck down with pneumonia and died shortly after. Inconsolable, the gentle, pious Mary Peary immediately packed up their modest possessions and with Bertie moved back to Maine. From that moment on she devoted her life to her only child.

Overprotective and fearful that her son's natural high spirits were an early sign of "deep-rooted depravity," Mary brought her son up as she would a daughter, teaching him needlepoint and insisting that he wear a sunbonnet when he went outside, to protect his fair skin. Ironically, her efforts to protect him from the more boisterous side of life only made him want to experience it more fully. Mercilessly teased for both his bonnet and his lisp, which would plague him even as an adult in moments of anger or excitement, he became increasingly mischievous. He would throw stones at windows just to hear the tinkling sound of the glass shattering, took great delight in frightening girls with a variety of tricks and—unspeakably shocking for his God-fearing mother—learned a wide vocabulary of oaths and expletives, which he used to great effect when the minister came to visit.

By his early twenties Peary was steadily gaining confidence in both his work and his social life and was beginning to extricate himself from his mother's well-meaning but cloying protection. Obsessed with the desire to improve himself, he swam every day for at least a mile—one hundred feet of it underwater—frequented the theatre and took dance classes.

"I feel myself overmastered by a resistless desire to do something," he wrote to his mother at the time. "I do not wish to live and die without accomplishing anything or without being known beyond a narrow circle of friends. I wish to acquire a name which shall be an 'open sesame' to circles of culture and refinement anywhere. A name which shall make my mother proud & which shall make me feel that I am peer to anyone I may meet." He also needed someone other than his mother by his side—someone who could match his spirit and be comfortable in the company of the great and the good. It was clear from their first meeting that Jo Diebitsch was of a very different calibre than any girl he had so far encountered.

Courting Jo was one of the most significant decisions that Peary would ever make. She would become his fiercest advocate and guiding light. Yet, although the attraction between them was intense, their courtship became an excruciatingly long affair. Peary's hankering for fame, which in time would become an obsession, coloured their relationship from the start. He believed that if he could only discover a route for a trans-isthmus canal—a cut through unexplored jungles and swamps that would provide a navigable waterway between the Atlantic and the Pacific—then he would be guaranteed not only wealth but also a place in history. Marriage would have to wait.

Peary's time in Nicaragua was harrowing. He and his men hacked through impenetrable undergrowth and spent hours wading through murky water that reached to their necks. It was here that he learned some of his most valuable lessons in leadership by "singing with them, yelling at them, and at the last moment, giving them a drink of Gin all around, which brought them yelling into camp at 6:05 p.m."

Peary was a complicated suitor, and his early relationship with Jo was punctuated by misunderstanding and confusion. One moment he could be attentive and adoring, the next cold and unreachable. Her innocent inquiries about his work only amplified his frustration at his lack of progress. His work in the jungle was gruelling, and the men under his command were slow and thick-headed. Peary fumed that they couldn't cut a trail in the woods if their lives depended on it. Emaciated and irritable, he longed to return to Jo. "My Smiling Eyes," he wrote as his leave neared:

> Sweetheart I am coming home, can you realize what it means. Coming home. The very sunlight glistens "sweetheart", the breezes whisper "sweetheart" the perfume of the flowers throbs "sweetheart". I already feel & yet cannot realize that I shall feel your warm, throbbing embrace, shall look into your clear starry eyes, shall feel your eager lips pressed to mine... I must come to your arms at once. Do you understand?

Peary returned to Washington intermittently, and on one occasion, in a favourite bookshop, he found a slim booklet entitled *Conjectures on the Inland Ice of Greenland*. Struck with a powerful sense of destiny, Peary went on to read all he could find on the subject of the mysterious island. Perhaps the Arctic, not Nicaragua, was the place where he could make his name. The following year, on a self-financed expedition, he attempted a crossing of Greenland's unexplored ice cap. After penetrating the inland ice for just a hundred miles, he was forced to turn back. Nevertheless, Peary believed that he had found his calling. On February 27, 1887, he wrote to his mother:

The trip means to me, my mother, first an enduring name and honor, second certainty of being retained in the Navy... third, social advancement, for with the prestige of my summer's work, and the assistance of friends whom I have made this winter, I will next winter be one of the foremost in the highest circles in the capital, and make powerful friends with whom I can shape my future instead of letting it come as it will... Remember, mother, I *must* have fame, and I cannot reconcile myself to years of commonplace drudgery and a name late in life when I see an opportunity to gain it now.

The urgency he felt to establish his name was only increased by the news that the young Norwegian Fridtjof Nansen had beaten him in crossing the ice cap of Greenland. Peary agonized over whether he could marry and still continue his life's quest. Love, and the legacy he envisioned for himself, finally made the answer clear.

On a stiflingly hot day in August 1888, Peary married his Jo at home in a simple service. "If you will only love me half as much as I do you I know we shall be the happiest people in the world," she wrote in a joyful love note. Shortly after, they took a train to Sea Bright, New Jersey. To the bride's infinite surprise, Peary's mother, Mary, accompanied them on their honeymoon, then moved into the newlyweds' marital home and appeared to have no intention of leaving. After two months Jo gave her husband an ultimatum: either his mother returned to her own home or Jo would leave for good. She also advised him that she wished to join him on his expeditions: "I have said so many times that you shall not go away without me again that [my sister] sings 'chestnuts' as soon as I begin & I am afraid you will too when you read it so often, but don't forget my sweetheart I mean it every time." Three years later she waved goodbye to her family and headed with her husband to the Far North.

JUST AS the ship's cannons were fired to mark the Fourth of July 1891, the *Kite* became icebound. Fog pressed in around the small vessel, and hoarfrost encrusted the rigging so that it looked like a phantom ship. Their forced imprisonment made the crew despondent, but the otherworldliness of it elated Jo Peary. Then, all at once, the *Kite* lurched violently. A large piece of ice had struck the rudder, slamming the iron tiller against her husband's leg. "How I got to him I do not know," she reported, "but I reached him before anyone else, and found him standing on one foot looking pale as death." The bones in his right leg were fractured between the knee and the ankle. For the remainder of their journey north, Peary was strapped to a table in his cabin, wincing in pain as the boat butted its way through thick pans of ice.

Peary's injury jeopardized the entire expedition. The nine fare-paying scientists on the ship, whose financial contributions represented a significant part of the expedition budget, demanded that the captain return south immediately. Landing and abandoning a crippled explorer and his gentle wife on the shores of northwest Greenland, they declared, was a preposterous idea. The captain replied that he would take orders only from Peary or his wife. From now on, Jo not only was responsible for the care of her injured husband, but would also make crucial decisions he would entrust to no one else.

On July 26, the *Kite* arrived at McCormick Bay, which would serve as the expedition's base for the forthcoming winter journeys. Peary's objective was to make a crossing of the northern Greenland ice cap, determining whether Greenland was an island or the immense peninsula of a great Arctic continent. If Greenland was an island, he would chart the extent of its northern shores; that would be essential for any further expeditions to the North Pole, which was as yet unclaimed. Suffering some indignity, he was taken ashore the following day strapped to a plank, to see for himself the site that Jo had selected for their expedition headquarters. With the ice threatening to press in on the *Kite,* the small team of seven were left among their piles of equipment on the beach. No sooner was the ship out of sight than a furious gale swept up the fjord.

Jo's first experiences of the High Arctic were challenging on many levels. Peary's decision to bring her on the expedition had caused consternation among his team. The other five team members were all under thirty years of age, fit, healthy and enthusiastic, and none of them wanted to "babysit" a woman with no Arctic experience. Furthermore, they were envious of the close company their leader could enjoy while they had left their sweethearts behind. Within days of leaving the United States, they were already discussing the disadvantages of having a woman on board. Among the men were the energetic young surgeon Frederick A. Cook and Peary's "body servant," Matthew Henson. The names of both men would forever be linked with Peary's.

Before long, Jo found the male company grating. "Bert is absorbed in his plans for future work & I hate the people who surround me more & more every day," she confessed to her journal on November 15. Matt Henson was the only man among them that she felt she could trust. Dr. Cook, she recorded, although good-hearted, was "an exceedingly coarse man with not an idea of gentlemanly behaviour... Altogether he is a dirty specimen of manhood." John Verhoeff drew criticism for being an "uncanny & very homely dwarf," and she thought Langdon Gibson "lazy, shiftless, a flatterer & a thoroughly deceitful fellow, besides being a coward." Altogether, she saw her companions' every action as being ugly and coarse. "I am afraid I am too much of an aristocrat to ever get used to such people as these. It is very evident to me that [Bert] does not share this feeling & rather resents it in me." Peary would have his fair share of disagreements during his expeditions, but he could not condone his wife's negative opinion of the others. She could not expect men to be the same in the field as they were in a drawing room in Washington. "Bert thinks I ought to treat them as my equals & see only their good points & feels hurt that I do not do this; he has no idea what it costs me to even treat them with ordinary politeness. I would much rather ignore them."

Out of her depth and regarded as a burden, Jo tried at first to become one of the team by joining in with the men's crude banter. Her attempt to fit in backfired. Verhoeff, a cocky twenty-five-year-old who had paid for the privilege of joining the expedition, declared that a "refined lady" would never say such things. He encouraged the others to share his grievances. They began to refer to Jo as "the woman" and delighted in provoking her. It was not his fault if her modesty was shocked, crowed Verhoeff, when Jo looked uncomfortable that Verhoeff appeared in his underwear in her company: it was up to her if she looked or not.

It was not until the following spring that Jo's companions began to regard her more favourably. By then she had realized that a little laughter and a few home comforts went a long way. The building of their expedition headquarters had been completed by the men just ten days after the sailing of the *Kite*, and Jo did her best to make Redcliffe House a sanctuary. She prepared special meals as best she could for birthdays and other celebrations. Recipes had to be inventive, given the provisions she had to hand: little auk stew with green peas; broiled breasts of eider duck; and plum duff from preserved fruit. The New Year celebrations were a particular success. She made invitation cards by hand, then formally greeted her companions dressed in a canary yellow and black silk tea gown trimmed with lace. She offered the men freshly made chocolate ice cream and cake, along with "Redcliffe cocktails."

These high points in the calendar were rare, and Jo found the isolation harder to bear than any of the physical discomforts of living so far from home. The only other people in the vicinity were Inuit, and Jo, typical of a woman of her class and time, found the differences in culture insurmountable. "These Eskimos were the queerest, dirtiest-looking individuals I had ever seen," she wrote after her first meeting with a local family. "Clad entirely in furs, they reminded me more of monkeys than of human beings." The husband, "round as a dumpling," had long, coarse black hair and was dressed in bird and seal skins. The wife looked almost identical, Jo continued, and she had difficulty telling one from the other. Having never before seen white people, the remote tribe of Inuit were equally puzzled by the Pearys.

One old woman examined Jo carefully before saying slowly, "I have lived a great many suns, but have never seen anything like you."

Jo was well aware that the success of her husband's expedition was dependent on the support of the local Inuit community. The assistance of the women was imperative to ensure that fur clothing was made and maintained properly, but above all else, the expedition members needed experienced hunters to help them fill caches for the forthcoming sledging season. Nevertheless, the dietary habits and lack of hygiene of the Inuit continued to appall Jo. Moreover, she wrote, they were "alive with parasites, of which I am in deadly fear, much to the amusement of our party." On some occasions she allowed the women to sew in her room, although she would make sure that they never went near the bed. After they left she would sweep the room carefully and sprinkle it with a solution of corrosive sublimate. Every night she would rub herself and her husband down with alcohol before retiring as a further protection against lice.

On one occasion, the Pearys were caught in a violent blizzard while travelling. The only shelter was an igloo. After crawling through a passage for about six feet on her hands and knees, Jo entered the domed interior, with its platform covered in reindeer skins, "which almost crawled away, they were so very much alive."

On the edge of the platform sat the host, with his feet resting on a chunk of frozen raw walrus from which some of the other hunters were hacking pieces to eat:

> I sat down, not without a shiver, on the edge beside Mr. Peary, self-ishly keeping him between the half-naked women and myself... [Then] to my dismay the Eskimo ladies belonging to the house took off all their clothing except their necklaces of sinishaw, just as unconcernedly as though no one were present... The odor of the place was indescribable... and leaning on my elbow, I sat from ten at night until ten in the morning, dressed just as I was on the sledge. But I made the best of the situation, and pretended to Mr. Peary that it was quite a lark.

Occasionally Jo joined the men on their hunting excursions, always keeping her own .38-calibre Colt and ammunition close at hand. Peary recalled his wife on one occasion sitting beside him in the stern of a small boat, calmly reloading the men's empty firearms while a herd of infuriated walruses surrounded them, attempting to get their tusks over the gunwale and capsize the boat. Their "savage heads," he recalled, were so close that his wife could have touched them. "I may perhaps be pardoned for saying," he wrote, "that I never think of [this] experience without a thrill of pride and admiration for her pluck." Later, Jo commented that she had thought it an even chance that she would be shot or drowned. "I cannot describe my feelings when these monsters surrounded us, their great tusks almost touching the boat, and the bullets whistling about my ears in every direction."

With the onset of winter, ice began to form on the fjord, and preparations for the forthcoming journeys intensified. Jo worked hard making protective canvas bags for the expedition's scientific and navigational instruments; nevertheless, the oncoming darkness seemed at times infinitely depressing, especially with the thought that she would soon be left at Redcliffe House while her husband forced his way north. Peary's surprising vulnerability also worried her. His fractured leg was stronger, but an attack of the grippe had renewed his fear of failure. "He has lost confidence in himself," she wrote in her journal, "and is harder to nurse than after his accident on board of the 'Kite.'" By the first week of May, preparations for the major expedition were complete, and Jo watched as her husband and Henson left to join the other men who were breaking trail. As they faded from sight, she turned back to Redcliffe, where she and Verhoeff would remain until the party's return.

Resenting being tasked with looking after Jo, Verhoeff was an argumentative and sour companion. Jo tried to keep herself busy, but her thoughts were continually of her husband. On her birthday she routinely put out some wine, but could not eat or drink. She took her gun and walked to nearby Quarter-Mile Valley, sat by a stream on beds of purple saxifrage, watched the cheerful flight of a small flock of snow buntings and "indulged in a fit of homesickness. Never in my life have I felt so utterly alone and forsaken."

The return of Cook, Henson and Gibson, Peary's supporting party, on June 3 had been a small comfort, but it would be some time before she could expect Peary's return. As time went on she grew in confidence, and she would often walk out to escape the strained atmosphere at camp and to hunt. None of the hunters had been successful at finding deer, and she craved venison. Seal meat, she wrote, "is all but nauseating to me." Carrying provisions of tea, potted turkey and biscuits, with her shotgun over her shoulder, she would walk for hours alone across the tundra to check or lay fox traps. Uneventful though most of these lone excursions were, there were times when she was knocked to the ground by the wind or disoriented by sudden blizzards; once, she was almost thrown over a cliff as she slipped on loose shale and ice.

At 5 AM on July 24, she woke to a sharp, shrill whistle—the *Kite* had returned. The next few days were filled with news from home and long conversations with Professor Angelo Heilprin, who had been assigned by Jo's family the task of bringing her home. Jo refused his entreaties, declaring that she could never leave while there was the faintest chance of her husband being alive. In any case, she noted crossly, she was perfectly capable of looking after herself.

> As for cold, hardship, and hunger, that is nonsense. Of course, if I feel so inclined, I can go out and sit on an iceberg until I freeze to it, and let the wind and snow beat upon me, even starve myself; but my tastes do not run in that direction.

The Inuit cheerfully informed Jo that her husband must be dead. To offset their dark forebodings, she reread a note that Peary had left for her on his departure, assuring her that he would return by August 1. If there should be a delay, he insisted, it would be a delay only. She must remember, he added, that he had provisions for one hundred days. Ninety-three days after her husband had left, she wrote:

Saturday, August 6. From a half-sleep I was roused early this morning by the plash of oars and loud talking, and before I had fully grasped the idea that the professor's party had returned, someone jumped over the rail on the deck just over my head, and a familiar footstep made its way hurriedly toward the companion-way. I knew it was Mr. Peary, but was unable to move or make a sound. He came rushing down the stairs and rattled at my door, calling me to open it; but I seemed to be paralysed, and he forced it open and stood before me, well and hearty, safe at last.

Peary returned triumphant, having made the extraordinary journey across the ice cap to the far northeast corner of Greenland. All the men were safe except for Verhoeff, who had disappeared following a small excursion to the head of Bowdoin Bay. Although search parties were sent out to try to find him, he was never seen again.

Five days after Peary's return, in a secluded valley carpeted with alpine flowers, the Pearys celebrated their fourth wedding anniversary with warm milk and fried liver from the two deer that Jo had just shot. Later that evening, she impressed everyone by bringing in a narwhal with a single bullet to its head. Her prize was "a gleaming ivory horn, straight as an arrow, and almost as sharp as a stiletto."

FEELING CONFIDENT THAT she could handle herself and a gun in the North, Jo returned to the High Arctic the following year, this time pregnant with her first child. On September 12, 1893, under the supervision of a Mrs. Cross—a stout, middle-aged Irish maternity nurse and recovering alcoholic—Jo gave birth to Marie Ahnighito Peary. In his published writings, Peary appeared delighted by his daughter's arrival:

This little blue-eyed snowflake, born at the close of the Arctic summer day, deep in the heart of the White North, far beyond the farthest limits of civilized people or inhabitants, saw the cold, gray light of the Arctic autumn once only before the great night settled upon us. Then she was bundled deep in soft, warm arctic furs, and wrapped in the Stars and Stripes.

Throughout the winter she was the source of the liveliest interest to the natives. Entire families journeyed from far-away Cape York to the south, and from Etah to the north, to satisfy themselves by actual touch that she was really a creature of warm flesh and blood, and not of snow, as they at first believed.

From that moment on, Marie was nicknamed the "Snow Baby."

Although Peary's writings indicated he was smitten with his daughter, in truth his mind was set on the task ahead of him. As far as he was concerned, there was no time for sentimentality. One of his men, Eivind Astrup, who had been tasked with establishing depots of supplies as far into the inland ice as possible, had been taken seriously ill with gastric fever, and three sledges had been blown away in high winds. Back at the new headquarters they called Anniversary Lodge, Jo could not fathom why her husband had not even touched their daughter. A week after Marie's birth, Jo wrote simply in her diary: "Baby doing well, but Bert takes no stock of her at all." In the weeks to come, Peary's avoidance of his daughter became all the more obvious. He looked gaunt and troubled, and for the first time since their marriage, Jo felt truly vulnerable. As a precaution against her own death, she began feeding Marie a small amount of condensed milk every day to get her used to the bottle.

On October 31, a huge wave swamped the shore; it destroyed a boat, then carried off vital supplies and several husky pups. "The fates and all hell are against me," Peary exploded, "but I'll conquer yet." Within eight days of setting out from the expedition base, members of Peary's party were "reduced by sickness and frostbite." Then came the storms. It was a disastrous year for the expedition.

In the summer of 1894, their transport ship, the *Falcon*, returned unexpectedly. The ship was one year ahead of schedule, because of concerns from home for the welfare of Jo and the Snow Baby.

The ship's arrival, and the enthusiasm of many of Peary's team for leaving early, severely disrupted plans. Peary refused to cut short his expedition but insisted that Jo return home, despite her vehement protestations. She had endured privations, had shown bravery and commitment, and believed she had proved that she and the baby were capable of remaining at the expedition base without being a burden. Peary's uncompromising attitude to her entreaties to stay wounded her deeply. Jo boarded the *Falcon* with her baby, broken-hearted.

Peary regretted his decision as soon as the ship had sailed. He threw himself across their bed, he wrote, "too weary of myself and all the world for words." The bedroom they had shared, once their haven, now reminded him of a tomb. By January 6, 1895, he had reached a crisis point.

Cold and more cheerless yet seems the room tonight, and I stretch yearning across to you from a sad heart. Never have I felt more lonely than tonight, never if God grants me to take you in my arms again will I leave you for so long again. The past runs black, the future blacker... I feel at times that I am going mad. I have lost my sanguine hope, my elan, I am an old man; I think at times I have lost you.

Peary was heartsick. By the time they started their "attack" of the ice cap in the spring, one of his team remarked that Peary took so little care when crossing crevasses that it seemed he did not wish to survive.

As for Jo, returning to the United States without her husband filled her with emptiness. The exquisite bond she had felt while with him in the Arctic was broken. She was now, as her daughter later described, "entering a new phase of her life as the wife of an explorer: the *waiting* time."

2

Eva Nansen

THE SINGER IN THE SNOWDRIFT

You remember always that I
will be coming with you to the North Pole?
Otherwise, it'll be all up with me.

EVA NANSEN

THE DAY AFTER Robert Peary and Jo left for the Arctic on their second expedition, a new rival began heading north. Fridtjof Nansen's plan was audacious—some said suicidal—but it was unquestionably inspired. The Norwegian explorer-scientist intended to take advantage of the currents of the Arctic Ocean and, in a ship specially designed to withstand the pressure of ice, drift right across the North Pole.

On June 24, 1893, in a "dismal parting atmosphere," Nansen said goodbye to his wife, Eva, in their bedroom, walked across the garden and boarded the *Fram*'s motor launch. A crowd of several thousand had gathered on the Christiania (now Oslo) waterfront to see the ship depart. By 10 AM, the *Fram*'s engines were fired and ready for departure, but the expedition leader, barely able to tear himself away from Eva, had still not appeared. Eventually losing patience, the crowds began to disperse. By the time Nansen arrived in the launch, the waterfront was almost deserted. Grim-faced, he boarded his ship and steamed away. The English journalist Herbert Dickinson Ward was on board the *Fram* that day and observed Nansen on the bridge, straining to catch a final glimpse of his wife as the ship rounded the headland:

> The sun, struggling through the rain clouds, cast a faint beam upon the shore, a mile distant. Upon the rocks stood Mrs. Nansen, clad in a conspicuous white dress. The view lasted only a few moments, the brief sunshine vanished, and the distant shore became once more but a blurred shadow without outline... I shall never forget the pathos of it all... Nansen was very brave, but one could see he was suffering terribly, struggling with himself.

"I thought everything was black," Nansen later confessed. "Within me I was torn apart, as if something would break, and at that moment if someone had given me the choice of going or not, I could not have trusted myself." Such was his misery that he feared that he would return to find his beloved wife dead. Eva was equally distressed. The moment he left she took to her bed and wept.

As the *Fram* worked her way up the coast, Nansen sent streams of letters back to Eva. "What does it matter if distance separates our bodies... Whether it be a long or short time, and even if we don't come after 2 years; even after 3 years, you will wait with undaunted courage." He could not bring himself to tell her that it could be a full five years before he returned. Instead, as he and his men prepared to head into the unknown, Nansen wrote a letter reminiscent of those that Ernest Shackleton would write to his own wife, Emily, in the years to come:

> The hour of parting strikes. Let my last word to you be: don't worry about me, whether I am away for a long or a short time. You

must know that I will not expose myself to any danger, *there is no danger,* absolutely none at all, and I will come back to you safe and strong.

With the letter Nansen enclosed pressed flowers from the Siberian plains, a place through which he imagined they might one day travel.

Up to the time of the launching of the *Fram,* Eva had been adamant that she would be a part of the expedition. But the protestations of Captain Otto Sverdrup, coupled with the fact that she was pregnant, had put paid to her ambitions. The enforced separation from the man she believed was her twin soul was a hardship she faced daily, but one she knew she must accept. Exploring, she declared to a journalist, was "his life's work, and without an attempt at it he could never have been happy. Since he was so unfortunate as to have such a desire, it was my duty to assist him in satisfying it." When the journalist picked up on the word "unfortunate," Eva shot back, "I cannot say I call it fortunate to have him up near the North Pole while I am sitting here."

THE FIRST GLIMPSE the aspiring explorer had of his future wife was of Eva's legs kicking wildly from a snowdrift. An adventurous skier, she had floundered during a bold manoeuvre near Frognersetersko-gen in Norway in early February 1888 and plunged headfirst off the piste. With Nansen's help, she emerged laughing from the snow, introducing herself as Eva Sars. He recognized her name immediately. She was a rising star in Norway, an acclaimed mezzo soprano, well known for her bewitching performances of lieder—poetic, romantic songs composed by the likes of Schumann. Furthermore, she was the daughter of a man for whom Nansen had had the utmost respect.

Eva's father, Michael Sars, was both a clergyman and an internationally respected pioneering marine biologist whose groundbreaking studies inspired generations of deepwater scientists. He was a gentle and brilliant man, devoted to his parish on Manger, an outlying island off the west coast of Norway. His wife, Maren Welhaven, a woman of intellect and taste, gave birth to nineteen children over twenty years on the island without a doctor or midwife, though she saw only seven survive infancy. Eva Helene was her last, born on December 7, 1858, in Christiania, after Michael had taken up a zoology chair at the university there.

Eva grew up in an atmosphere filled with creativity and political discussion. Her mother was remarkably well connected and ran a popular salon in Christiania. Far from wealthy, the Sars family were expertly self-sufficient. As servants and nannies were a luxury they could not afford, the older children looked after the youngest, and Maren unashamedly ruled both kitchen and parlour. The only sadness in an otherwise happy childhood was the death of Eva's father when she was eleven. Although Maren struggled financially as a widow, she ensured that their home was a welcoming and lively place. Eva was the darling of the family. The youngest by far, she was creative, boisterous and sunny. She had, commented one guest, a "heathen innocence" and thrived in the company of the writers, musicians and intellectuals who were drawn to the family's liberal home.

Eva excelled in music and art, and under the guidance of her brother-in-law Thorvald Lammers, one of Norway's foremost singers and composers, she quickly became an accomplished performer. At twenty-three, she made her debut in Oslo, and by twenty-eight she had moved to Berlin, where she immersed herself in the world of music, theatre and student parties—daringly drinking beer with unattached men and staying out until three in the morning. When she returned to Oslo, a little more worldly-wise, she gave her first solo recital. Her soulful performance was an immediate success, a pianist friend recalled:

> Most singers know how to sing light-hearted songs—very few completely manage the dark and the gloomy, those that paint the innermost seriousness and horror of... the soul. But was it not here that Eva... was strange and unforgettable.

"Strange and unforgettable" she may have been to some, but Nansen was yet to fall under Eva's spell. At the time of their initial encounter, the young curator of zoology was in the final throes of planning his first polar adventure—a daring crossing of the unexplored Greenland ice cap from east to west. It was a journey that would require athleticism, skill and courage: qualities, he believed, that were in his blood.

Fridtjof Wedel-Jarlsberg Nansen, a descendant of the polar explorer and statesman Hans Nansen, was born on October 10, 1861, at Store Frøen near Christiania. He was in character very like his mother, Adelaide, who as a young woman scandalized her family, the aristocratic Wedel-Jarlsbergs, by taking up skiing—regarded as a male-only sport at the time—and then eloping with the son of a baker, with whom she had five sons. When her husband died of cholera, Adelaide was devastated but went on to marry her lawyer for the security of her children. Two and a half years into this arrangement, Fridtjof was born and then, a year later, came his brother Alexander.

Although relatively successful, Fridtjof's father, Baldur Nansen, kept a simple household. At his insistence, porridge was served morning and evening. Attendance at church was strictly observed, and the family said prayers together every evening. At all other times the boys were encouraged to play outdoors by their mother. Summer and autumn days were spent fishing, swimming or shooting in the Nordmarka forest; in the winter they would skate and ski over the nearby Oslo Fjord. Adelaide did her best to instill a love of nature in her children, until her unexpected death when Fridtjof was just fifteen.

As he grew older, Nansen became increasingly adventurous and pushed himself to excel at skating and skiing. With a gift for science and a passion for being in nature, he decided to major in zoology at the University of Christiania. Engaging and ambitious, he impressed the lecturers to such a degree that in 1882 he was sent to the Arctic for almost five months to collect specimens of marine life. No sooner had he returned than he was offered the position of curator of zoology at the Bergen Museum. Within months he was working on groundbreaking research into neuroanatomy—the structure of the nervous system—with a particular focus on lower marine creatures. Inspired by Darwin's theory of evolution, Nansen believed that his research could contribute to the understanding of the human nervous system and the workings of the mind.

Although passionate about his research, Nansen felt restless. His brief sojourn in the Arctic had planted the seed of an idea for a polar journey that would perfectly suit his skills—the first crossing of the interior of Greenland on skis. In this he had a competitor: Peary had attempted the crossing in 1886, only to turn back after travelling a hundred miles. There was just a small window of opportunity for Nansen before Peary returned to make good his attempt.

With barely six months to prepare, the twenty-six-year-old cajoled potential sponsors, consulted veteran explorers on survival and travel techniques, and tested all manner of polar equipment. Finding much of it too heavy or unsophisticated, he designed replacements, including a lightweight sledge and stove, and clothing and tents made in separate pieces so they could also be used as sails on the sledges. Tall and athletic with arresting blue eyes, Nansen used his charisma to convince potential supporters to back his plans. His manner of presentation was not always a perfect success. Sven Hedin, a Swedish explorer, commented that he found Nansen "really a thoroughly unusual apparition." Nansen was fiercely anti-fashion, choosing to wear tight-fitting Jaeger sports suits with open-necked shirts and a cap tipped jauntily to one side, a relaxed style very different from the starched shirts, cravats and long-tailed coats favoured at the time. Even his brother, Alexander, had written urging him to try to dress more fashionably to avoid the ridicule he was attracting in the city. Characteristically, Nansen replied: "What concern is it of mine, what other people say or do?"

However questionable his sense of dress may have been, many women found Nansen irresistible. Eva, in her own words, had instantly become "hopelessly infatuated," although she suspected she had little chance of winning his interest. Small, with dark curly hair, brown eyes and homely features, she was plain in contrast to the elegant, beautiful women who usually piqued his interest. By the time Nansen left, Eva was just one among many who had been promised letters during his forthcoming journey across "the great ice."

ON AUGUST 15, 1888, Nansen, Otto Sverdrup, Kristian Kristiansen, Oluf Dietrichson and two Lapps, Ole Nielsen Ravna and Samuel Johannesen Balto, finally set foot on the Greenland ice cap. Since leaving the comfort of the sealing ship *Jason,* it had taken them almost a month to find a suitable place at which to climb onto the inland ice, and already Nansen's companions felt exhausted, hungry and despondent. Between them and the west coast lay some six hundred unexplored kilometres of crevasse fields, mountains and ice as "rough as waves on the sea."

Time and again the men plunged through snow bridges straddling wide chasms, managing to save themselves only by gripping their ski sticks horizontally to stop the fall. The surface of the ice cap was unpredictable; one moment they skidded across burnished ice on which it was almost impossible to gain purchase, the next they were plunged into deep, abrasive snow that made hauling the sledges a monstrous task. Nansen's careful planning of the expedition also had its weak points. His newly invented stove was not as efficient as he had hoped, and there was barely enough food to keep starvation at bay. In addition, his order of pemmican had been made with hardly any essential fat—a fact he discovered too late, and one which would have a significant impact on their energy levels. After a particularly challenging day, the usually quiet Kristiansen exclaimed, "My God, how can people wish so much suffering on themselves that they do this."

After nineteen days on the ice cap, Nansen was feeling the cold. His nose was frozen, and his throat was beginning to seize and freeze around his larynx. Acting quickly, he massaged his face until the blood flow was restored and wrapped wolfskin mittens and a hood around his neck. He tied a felt hat over his crotch to prevent the worst possible case of frostbite. But the farther they penetrated into the interior, the colder it became. Then came the blizzards. By September 6, they were stumbling blindly into a swirling, stinging whiteout. With difficulty they made camp, crawled into their sleeping bags—three men to a bag—ate cold liver and biscuits and tried to sleep as the storm raged. The following morning, Balto crept out of the tent to begin preparing the sledges, only to return almost immediately, his face and clothes so caked in snow he was unable to breathe. The storm, he reported once he could speak again, was "as strong and thick as running water." Reinforcing the tent from the inside with skis and sticks, the men were forced to wait, "caught like rats in a trap," as the wind and snow buried them.

When finally the storm abated the men dug themselves out of the drifts and continued their march. The going was no easier: "To say that it was like dragging [the sledges and ourselves] through potter's clay is not saying enough," Nansen complained. But by September 17, a month after they had set foot on the ice cap, they had cause for celebration. For the first time, they had a sense of going downhill. The glimpse of a snow bunting near their camp confirmed their hopes—it was a sign that they were nearing ice-free land. With the wind in their favour, Nansen persuaded his companions to lash the sledges together and raise the sails. The speed of the catamaran-style structure was astonishing; it went so fast, in fact, that the men were unable to keep pace with it. Then came the cry they had been longing for: "Land ahead!" A few days later, after negotiating some of the most perilous terrain they had yet faced, the men were finally off the ice cap. Nansen was elated:

> Words cannot describe what it meant just to feel earth and rock underfoot, the sense of wellbeing that rippled through us when we felt the heather give under our soles, and to smell the wonderful scent of grass and moss.

They still had at least another hundred kilometres of hard travel between them and Godthåb, where they hoped they would find a ship willing to take them home. Leaving the others in charge of the sledges and equipment, Nansen and Sverdrup dragged, then paddled, their makeshift raft toward succour. Four days later the two men arrived at the Moravian Brotherhood mission of New Hernhut, to be greeted by a large party of Inuit and Gustav Baumann, the acting governor of Godthåb. According to Nansen, Baumann began:

"Are you Englishmen?" To which I could safely reply in good Norwegian: "No, we are Norwegian." "May I ask your name?" "My name is Nansen, and we come from the ice cap." "Ah, I thought as much. May I congratulate you on your doctor's degree."

Nansen and Sverdrup's arrival at Godthåb was celebrated with great fanfare. The entire community of the small capital of South Greenland turned out to greet them. The women in particular looked "splendid" in their traditional clothing, noted Nansen, adding how peculiar it was to see the colony's four Danish ladies in petticoats "amongst all these fur and trouser clad beauties." The relief at reaching some sort of civilization, however, was tempered. There was only one ship left in the district, and a hurried exchange of letters sent by kayak confirmed that, with ice building, the captain of the *Fox* could not risk waiting for Nansen to rescue the rest of his men. They would have to spend the winter in Greenland.

Over the next six months, Nansen was fully absorbed into the community. He adopted traditional dress and became "more and more completely Eskimo." He mastered the techniques of the kayak and learned how to handle the harpoon. "I live their life, eat their food, learn to appreciate their delicacies," he wrote in his diary, "like... rancid blubber etc. I talk to them as best I may, work with them... shoot [and] fish... with them." According to two hunters from Godthåb, Nansen was intent on learning their language and was soon able to communicate quite easily. "He understood most things... he would be down on the shore to greet the homecoming kayaks... we always... thought of [him] almost like our own kind."

While he was learning all he could about the Inuit and their hunting and survival techniques, Nansen's reputation elsewhere soared. His hurried letters sent home on the *Fox* had prompted news wires to flash his achievement across Europe. As a result of his "perilous undertaking," the *Times* in London reported, the young Norwegian had "acquired world-wide fame." The life of simple pleasures Nansen enjoyed in Greenland had come to an abrupt end. With the return of the sun came the first ship of the new season, bearing mailbags groaning with news and fan mail. "That you got across Greenland wasn't bad," wrote his brother-in-law Axel Huitfeldt. "But if you can survive with equal health the deluge of letters . . . newspapers, honours, etc., etc., which is now pouring over you, you will have done even better." Huitfeldt's letter was a friendly warning of the blizzard of publicity Nansen was about to face. Since the news of the expedition had been broadcast, the world seemed gripped with "Nansen fever":

> Nansen here and Nansen there, Nansen, Nansen, nothing else but Nansen, Nansen caps, Nansen cakes, Nansen cigars, Nansen pens, a Nansen March, and so on *ad infinitum* . . .

Nansen's half-sister Ida also wrote with a touch of concern: "Please don't be ruined by all the adulation which will be yours when you arrive home."

As Nansen and his companions drew near to Christiania, hundreds of sailing boats crowded the harbour to greet them. The quayside and castle walls were thick with people, the excitement so tremendous that the police feared many would be pushed into the water. One witness estimated that the cheering, exultant crowds numbered some fifty thousand. Nansen had become a national hero, elevating his neglected country onto the world stage.

Nansen's new-found fame naturally increased the longings of the women he had left behind. Eva was among them, although she tried desperately hard to conceal her feelings. While Nansen was gone she had accepted one social invitation after another and flirted conspicuously. Nansen's friendships with a number of beautiful women were no secret, and she doubted it would be her company he chose once the press and the public had released their grip on him. Yet the image of Eva had haunted Nansen's dreams during the winter in Greenland. The full force of attraction had finally struck him. He confessed that "the first time I saw you, on skis, so bewitchingly fresh and forthright, you acted on me like a fresh wind from a new world I did not yet know."

Skiing to Eva was as natural as it was to Nansen, and as a young woman she had created quite a stir when she and her friend Cecilie Thoresen Krog became the first women to participate in the ski jumping event Husebyrennet. In later years Eva reminisced: "When I look back on the years since . . . I began skiing, the many brisk tours out in the Norwegian winter are the happiest and most precious memories that life has given me." It was not just the sport that was attractive, but the freedom it afforded.

> When, as I often do, I think about this, I am always glad to see how much better off the girls of our age are in that respect. [I remember] how a few years ago . . . young girls . . . often pale and miserable, dragged themselves from one dance hall to the other—it was about the only way young people of both sexes could meet. [But now] young girls . . . can move freely through the forest, unhindered by the many prejudices we had to defy.

Eva's adventurousness impressed Nansen. She was, he proudly insisted, "the best woman skier in Norway." In the years to come they would embark on ski tours across mountain plateaus and other territory where no woman on skis had dared to go. Eva, to the horror of some gentlemen onlookers, sported her revolutionary ski suit, swapping the traditional long, cumbersome skirts for a shorter style that fell just below her knees, worn over trousers. The outfit attracted considerable attention and confusion; she was often mistaken for a boy. Nansen, with his own curious sense of fashion, simply thought she looked magnificent. It was their shared passion for the sport and for being in nature, above all, that convinced him they were meant for one another. Despite his well-known hostility to marriage, Nansen had fallen in love. "What have you done to me?" he wrote to Eva during their early courtship. "I don't understand it; everything which had attraction, the beauty of Nature, the sea, work, reading, everything is equally uninteresting . . . I am thrashing about like an impatient child."

Eva, for her part, feared that the attraction of other women would prove too much and that their romance would end in heartbreak. The attentions of a famous beauty of Christiania with whom Nansen was supposed to have enjoyed an affair before his Greenland expedition made her particularly uneasy. The woman's name was Dagmar Engelhart, but she was more popularly known as Klenodiet, or "the Treasure." Even though Nansen insisted the relationship was over, Eva was consumed with jealousy whenever her rival's name was mentioned, declaring, "That my own, beautiful property should ever have thought of anyone except poor little Eva is so disgusting." But Nansen had no doubt that Eva was his soulmate. On August 11, 1889, he proposed at a mountain farm outside Christiania. His proposal accepted, he skied in the darkness to wake his half-sister and her husband to jubilantly share the news.

The news of their engagement surprised many. Eva's family also had reservations. Her mother was wary of Nansen's ambition and unshakable self-belief. Knowing that exploration would always be his priority, she warned her daughter that she would be marrying only half of the man. In years to come, people would continue to comment on the unlikely couple. In *A Winter's Jaunt to Norway*, Mrs. Alec Tweedie reported: "What a strange contrast the Nansens are! He is a great, big, tall, fair Norwegian, with all the strength of the Viking race in his manly bearing and earnest face. His very name, Fridtjof, means a Viking, or more properly speaking, a 'thief of peace'... She is a jolly, bright little woman, with dark hair, and all the merriment and warm colouring of a more southern people, although she, too, is pure Norwegian."

Ignoring the misgivings of friends and family, Eva married Nansen on September 6, less than a month into their engagement. Work commitments prevented the newlyweds from enjoying a honeymoon. Instead, the day after their wedding they left for England for Nansen's lecture tour, where he—the "great Viking"—was celebrated as the "hero of the year." Eva Nansen intended to share her husband's future adventures. For a time, he appeared to agree.

IN FEBRUARY 1892, Eva wrote a note to Nansen that was remarkably similar to a letter Jo Peary had sent to her husband just three years earlier. "You remember always," Eva declared, "that I will be coming with you to the North Pole? Otherwise, it'll be all up with me." Eva was at a low ebb. Four months earlier she had delivered a stillborn child, and before that she had endured a miscarriage. Still grieving himself, Nansen was forced to leave again for England and another lecture tour. Although they both knew the tour was essential, Eva felt desolate. "Why must I be punished so hard?" she cried in one of their many anguished exchanges.

> Write to me a little and comfort me ... Tell me if you think we will ever have little living children we can go skiing with ... We *must* have children, otherwise it will all be meaningless.

Nansen was just as miserable. Without Eva, he felt like "half a human being," and the tour took its toll. Like other explorers, he was expected to work hard to gain support, and he did, delivering twenty-one lectures in twenty-nine days. He received much critical acclaim, but his heart was not in England. "You toil and moil just for my sake," Eva wailed. "For if you hadn't married me, you would have had no financial worries ... Now ... you have a wife who wants to go with you to the North Pole, and who you are mortally afraid will die up there."

For some time Nansen had been planning another expedition—one far more challenging than his last. His goal would be not only to reach the North Pole but also to prove his philosophy that success would come from working *with* the forces of nature, rather than against them. He would set his ship into the ice near the New Siberian Islands, with the intention of using the transpolar drift to carry him across the North Pole. To support his plans, Nansen cited the research of the meteorologist Henrik Mohn, who had discovered that ship relics, including those from the wrecked American vessel *Jeannette,* had been carried by ocean currents from Siberia to the shores of Svalbard and Greenland.

Although there was some skepticism about the viability of his plan, the force of Nansen's personality, together with tremendous support from the press and public, persuaded the Norwegian government to pledge two-thirds of the financing needed. It was a matter of national pride. Nansen was provided with funds, a crew, provisions and the best in polar equipment, including the *Fram*, which was built to his specifications. This time around, he also had the security—and the pressure—of his fellow citizens' expectations. But the hardest thing he had to face was the thought of leaving Eva behind. She was pregnant for the third time, and accompanying her husband to the Arctic was simply out of the question.

3

Eleanor Anne Franklin

THE FORGOTTEN BRIDE

Spread thy canvas once more, keep the Pole Star before thee,
'Tis Constancy's type and thy Beacon of Glory,
By the Lake, by the Mountain, the Forest, the River,
In the wilds of the North, I am thine, and for ever.

ELEANOR ANNE FRANKLIN

ALMOST SEVENTY YEARS to the day before Jo Peary set out on her first Arctic voyage, Eleanor Anne Porden sat at her writing desk in her elegant family home in London and began to compose a letter, not knowing when or if it would ever be read. At the top of the page she wrote the date, May 23, 1821, aware that the letter's recipient would recognize it as the anniversary of his departure from England two years earlier. The letter was to Captain John Franklin, who, Eleanor imagined, was at that moment engaged in some daring pursuit in the wilds of the Canadian Arctic. For Eleanor, Gothic poet and ardent fan of heroic endeavour, nothing was more romantic than the thought that her letter might eventually be read in a wilderness that as yet lay undiscovered.

Eleanor was among a handful of ladies who could boast—had she felt so inclined—that she had an intimate correspondence with a famous polar explorer, although such privileges had their drawbacks.

Like the sweethearts of sailors and soldiers, she had to make do with a courtship conducted almost entirely through letters, some of which would not reach the hands of their intended for many months, even years, after they had been written. The previous year she had been mortified to discover that, having just missed the sailing of the fleet carrying news to the expedition, it would be a further twelve months before her letters would leave British soil. This time, she made sure that she delivered her news on time.

Witty, spirited and clever, Eleanor Anne Porden was a popular member of the London literati. She had been a frequent attendee at Royal Institution lectures since the age of nine, had her first book of poetry published at the age of nineteen, had been elected to the prestigious Institut de Paris—a rare honour, particularly given that the shadow of the Napoleonic Wars was still hanging over Britain and France—ran a respected literary salon called the Attic Chest with her father and counted writers, artists and leading lights in science and exploration among her friends. Her ambitious poems, often tens of thousands of words long, had attracted praise from journals such as *Quarterly Review* and the *London Literary Review* and also the attention of countless admirers, including Franklin.

As Eleanor wrote her letter, Franklin was conducting tense negotiations with a chief of the Copper Indians, whose support was vital for the success of his forthcoming summer journeys. The chief, Akaitcho, insisted that if Franklin and his men were fools enough to attempt a journey along the coast of the polar sea, they would all be certain to perish. Franklin, however, remained positive. The discomforts of the hard, dark winter were easing as the sun returned. A few days earlier robins and geese had appeared at their camp; blueberries, crowberries and cranberries could be gathered in handfuls, and reindeer were advancing northward. These were the infallible precursors of warmer weather, and Franklin would allow no doubt about his expedition's success.

By the time of his first meeting with Eleanor, Franklin was already a national figure. He was a respected veteran of the battles of Trafalgar and Copenhagen and had beaten out hundreds of officers to take on the role of second-in-command of a groundbreaking Arctic expedition in 1818. He was by no means a maverick, nor was he fit or particularly good-looking, but he was courageous, straightforward and dependable. Although in later years Franklin would be portrayed as a dullard, a slow yet amiable fool, in his own time he was seen in a very different light. By the time he returned from his second Arctic expedition he was regarded as a lion. He had encountered the sublime horrors of the polar wilderness and survived to tell the tale.

The ninth of twelve children, John Franklin was born on April 15, 1786, in a room above a shop in the small Lincolnshire town of Spilsby. His father, Willingham Franklin, was a local merchant and banker who clearly inspired a sense of adventure in his offspring. By the time John was at school, two of his older brothers were already carving out impressive careers for themselves: Willingham Jr. would become chief justice at Madras and James Franklin a military engineer in India. John preferred to follow the lead of his brother-in-law Matthew Flinders, a brilliant navigator and explorer. Once the young John Franklin was seaward-bound, he never looked back. After a spell on a merchant ship, he joined the Royal Navy. Aged fourteen, he boarded the sixty-four-gun vessel HMS *Polyphemus* and went to war.

In early 1801, just two weeks before his fifteenth birthday, Franklin found himself in the throes of a brutal battle. Britain was floundering against Napoleon, and the League of Armed Neutrality formed by Russia, Denmark, Norway and Prussia had begun to challenge Britain's right to intercept and seize the cargo of any merchant ships believed to be trading with France. With orders from the Admiralty to frustrate the league, the Royal Navy, under the command of Admiral Sir Hyde Parker with Vice Admiral Lord Nelson as second-in-command, set out for Copenhagen to a battle that would later be considered one of the navy's hardest-won victories.

In the chill of dawn on April 2, Franklin watched as the surgeon below decks laid out his instruments in preparation for the inevitable gruesome activity to come. Earlier that morning the hammocks of the midshipmen and mates had swung lazily in the gloom; it was likely to be a hell-like place by the afternoon. The surgeon and his assistants had no antiseptic or anaesthetic. "When a man's limb was smashed," a chronicle of the times described simply, "they laid him on the midshipman's mess table and amputated." It was no wonder that many injured men refused to be carried downstairs. Ships were not easily sunk, and battles would commonly last for many hours as ship pounded ship with cannonball, grapeshot and chain shot—all designed to cut through masts, rigging, timber hulls and flesh. Franklin's first experience of battle would always remain with him, and many years later he would still vividly recall the hundreds of corpses floating in the clear waters of Copenhagen harbour.

A spell exploring the coast of Australia on Matthew Flinders's *Investigator* was a welcome change for Franklin from being on a man-of-war. But he once again saw battle at Trafalgar under the command of Nelson. As signals officer on the *Bellerophon* Franklin carried the message signalled by Nelson's *Victory*—"England expects that every man will do his duty"—on a signal slate to his captain, joined the crew in three cheers and prayed along with them that success would be theirs. Little more than a quarter of an hour later the *Bellerophon* was hit mercilessly and could neither sail nor move. A sharpshooter clinging to the rigging of the French ship *L'Aigle* picked off officers and men, including Franklin's best friend, who died at his feet. In just fifteen minutes, fifty-four men of the crew of fifty-eight on the quarter-deck were killed or injured; on the poop, out of forty men, only eight remained unwounded, including Franklin. Captain John Cooke of the *Bellerophon* died, like Nelson, on board ship in the arms of his crew.

Those who survived remembered a terrifying ordeal: the lurching of the ship as the cannons fired; the screams and the mutilated bodies; the surgeon and his assistants working like butchers in the bowels of the ship, up to their calves in blood and vomit and gore; the fury of sound and the stench of fire, gunshot, singed hair and flesh. Franklin, remarkably, was virtually unharmed, suffering only partial deafness. He went on to earn a medal and a mention in dispatches at the battle of New Orleans. But after fourteen years of drama at sea, Franklin, like many of his fellow naval officers, found himself becalmed. It was three years before he was offered a suitable post by the Admiralty; he saw it only as a "filler" while he waited for a long-term appointment. Yet his command of the *Trent*, as part of a prestigious polar expedition, ensured that he was quickly regarded as quite a catch.

AS THE 1820S approached, London society was coming around to the idea of polar exploration as a noble pursuit. With the Napoleonic Wars recently over, Britain had been left with a surplus of ships, officers and crew that was rapidly draining Admiralty resources. Inspired by news in 1817 from the respected whaling captain William Scoresby that large swaths of the Greenland coast were unusually ice-free, John Barrow, second secretary of the Admiralty, and Sir Joseph Banks, president of the Royal Society, began a campaign to convince the government that this was the ideal opportunity for their best naval men. The Admiralty should turn its attention to polar exploration and the collection of valuable data concerning magnetism, which was essential for safe and accurate navigation. Realizing that high-profile expeditions could provide a welcome distraction from its floundering popularity in the postwar years, the government decided there should be an assault on the North for the glory of Britain. The *Isabella* and the *Alexander*, under the command of Captain John Ross and William Edward Parry, would search for the Northwest Passage—the fabled shortcut to the Orient—while Franklin in the *Trent* and Captain David Buchan of the *Dorothea* would attempt to discover the North Pole.

Eleanor Porden visited the Royal Docks at Deptford in 1818 shortly before the ships' departure. She was so taken with the endeavour that she penned the two-hundred-line poem "The Arctic Expeditions," in which she envisioned Franklin, Buchan and their crews pitting themselves against the sublime magnitude of nature in the quest for knowledge.

Sail, sail, adventurous Barks! Go fearless forth,
Storm on his glacier-seat the misty North,

Give to mankind the inhospitable zone,
And Britain's trident plant in seas unknown.

Although the expedition failed to penetrate the pack ice north of Svalbard and spent only one summer in the Arctic, Eleanor had created through her poem a stage upon which the expedition could never fail:

Then on! Undaunted heroes, bravely roam,
Your toils, your perils, shall endear your home,
And furnish tales for many a winter night,
While wondering Britons list with strange delight.

The heart-felt welcome to your native land,
The dear embrace, the gratulating hand,
When joyful thousands throng the white-cliff'd shore
To greet as brothers men unseen before:
On each strong limb, each storm-worn feature dwell,
Yourselves more wondrous than the tales you tell.

It was these glory-filled lines that inspired Franklin to beg for an introduction to her. According to Eleanor, although neither would openly admit it, it was love at first sight.

There are few descriptions of Eleanor's character except, surprisingly, those written by the woman who would become John Franklin's second wife, Jane Griffin. Jane heard of the explorer's interest in the young poet through Sarah Disraeli, sister of the future prime minister, who regularly attended a book society that Eleanor had initiated. Jane was intrigued, and Eleanor soon came under her critical eye:

She is a plain, stout, short young woman, having a rather vulgar though a very good-natured countenance & I saw nothing of pedantry and pretension in her manner, but rather some embarrassment & timidity... She has dark hair and eyes, and a reddish, coarse face, and appears about or near thirty years of age, tho' she is said not to be more than twenty-three.

It is possible Jane's unflattering description was tinged with envy that Eleanor had secured the affections of Franklin. If the portrait of Eleanor painted by Mary Ann Flaxman at the time is accurate, she was in fact a petite, pretty woman, with cupid lips and warm, smiling eyes. Certainly she had a good number of suitors. Fundamentally, however, Jane felt that the poet was not in her league, nor quite of her class.

Eleanor Anne Porden was born on July 14, 1795, at home in London to the architect and intellectual William Porden and his frail wife, Mary Plowman. Like many women of her time, Mary suffered time and again from the premature deaths of her children. Out of ten, only Eleanor and her older sister, Sarah Henrietta, survived adolescence. Unlike noble-born Jane Griffin, who grew up surrounded by easy wealth, Eleanor had a childhood overshadowed by the constant care required by her paralyzed mother. By the time she was fourteen, she was responsible for running the household. The family as a whole had a modest blood line. Eleanor's grandfather, Thomas Porden, had been a labourer from Kingston-upon-Hull, and even though his son William completed several high-profile assignments, including the design of the spectacular stables, riding house and tennis court—now known as the Corn Exchange—at the Brighton Pavilion for George iv, he was nevertheless a self-made man. It was only because Eleanor was so charming on their second meeting in 1819 that Jane felt duty bound to see her again. Even then, she observed Eleanor's lifestyle as being sufficiently unusual to warrant comment.

On our return to the Drawing room, we talked & joked with Miss Porden on her universal talents—she makes all her own clothes, preserves, pickles, dances quadrilles *con amore*, belongs to a poetical bookclub, pays morning visits, sees all the sights, never denies herself to anybody at any hour, and lies in bed or is not dressed till nine o'clock in the morning.

Eleanor's mischievous wit and fascination with science gave her a far broader outlook than many of her contemporaries. She disliked small talk and was no shrinking violet. While she was attending, as usual, a lecture at the Royal Society, a man behind her commented loudly that rather than take up valuable space at a scientific lecture, young women should instead remain at home and make a pudding. "Oh," Eleanor responded gamely, "we did that before we came out." Such unusual qualities in a woman piqued Franklin's interest, and within days of their first introduction, he became a regular visitor to the Porden family home.

Eleanor saw explorers such as Franklin as the modern knights of progress. In reality, Franklin was not naturally drawn to such matters and confessed to his sister that he felt hopelessly out of his depth in the company of scientists; his interest lay in the adventure itself. Thankfully, he added, "the bare circumstance of going to the North Pole is a sufficient passport anywhere." Nonetheless, Eleanor believed that he was a man of great consequence, and when his second polar expedition was announced, she had discovered her own polar hero.

IN MAY 1819, Franklin, along with two midshipmen, George Back and Robert Hood, and the surgeon John Richardson, left Gravesend in Kent for Canada, via Hudson Bay. Their objective was to follow the Coppermine River to the Arctic coast, creating accurate charts of the area and recording crucial scientific data.

The first winter passed without incident. They successfully collected a body of botanical and zoological specimens and surveyed hundreds of miles of virgin coastline. Their return, however—far too late in the season—proved a cautionary tale of ill planning and ferocious bad luck. The dozen Canadian voyageurs who had been assigned to assist them struggled with the heavy scientific equipment, and as provisions ran low the group suffered greatly. Franklin's journal and astronomical readings were lost in violent storms, and soon starvation and exhaustion set in. As winter approached, their situation became critical. The men were reduced to eating rock lichen and, eventually, their own boots.

Franklin decided to split the men into two teams. The weaker men, including Hood, Richardson and Seaman John Hepburn, would follow Franklin's team, who would press on ahead in search of food and help. Together with Back and the strongest voyageurs, Franklin set off to reach a camp where there seemed the certainty of supplies and warmth. They arrived to find that the larder was bare. Back continued on, but by now Franklin and the voyageurs were too weak to follow.

In time, their companions from the first team joined them. Half-dead from starvation, exposure and fright, these men relayed the horrific tale of their struggle to reach safety. One of the voyageurs had gone insane and had savagely murdered a comrade, then feasted on him. Hood was his next victim. Fearing that he and Hepburn were next to be killed, Richardson unceremoniously executed their tormentor. Back's fortunate return with supplies brought Franklin and the other survivors back from the brink. In all, ten men had died a gruesome death from starvation, hypothermia or cannibalistic murder.

While such horror stories were unfolding in the North, Eleanor Porden had her own trials to deal with. Within the space of a year, both her parents had died. The last months of her father's life had been particularly fraught. With his alarming decline in health, William Porden pressed Eleanor to consider a proposal from one of her suitors, but she refused to rush into any commitment. Nine of her admirers were politely but firmly turned away. There was only one man she could contemplate marrying, and he was in the polar wilderness.

IN OCTOBER 1822, Franklin wrote to Eleanor from the Hudson's Bay Company ship *Prince of Wales*, offering her his heartfelt congratulations on the publication of her epic historical poem *Cœur de Leon, or The Third Crusade*, which she had written in his absence. He was finally on his way home, and he intended to make the poet his wife.

After three and a half years apart, Eleanor and Franklin were reunited. Eleanor's joyful character infused the reserved captain, and within weeks, Franklin confessed that he was "desperately in love." She felt the same way, writing playful love letters to him while he was visiting his family:

After sitting whole days with my arms folded, my legs crossed
and my feet on the fender, devising excuses for your absence; after
building castles in the air; and discovering them to be but frost
work; drawing your portrait in the fire, and demolishing it with the
poker; or cutting it out in paper, and blowing it away with my sighs,
I arrive but at one conclusion—that I am utterly forsaken.

Before long, rumours were circulating that the poet and the
explorer were secretly engaged. Eleanor wrote to her friends,
defending her choice of husband-to-be:

I sometimes feel as though I have made an *odd* choice and at this
moment I have naturally all the dangers and perils of such a change
arrayed in all their force before me, but on the other hand, I have
the strongest reliance on the worth of his character, and his regard
for me... After writing so long about *Cœur de Leon*, I have con-
trived to catch hold of a Lion's heart have I not?

A lion she may have caught, but she was concerned that Franklin
was too different from her flamboyant literary companions to be fully
understood. He had confessed to her that he had a "horror of new
faces," and Eleanor worried that his shyness could be misconstrued:
"Neither his late journey of three years and a half, estranged from all
civilised society, nor the being made a lion of, has contributed to wear
off a natural crust of reserve. It will, however, I trust dissolve before
your smiles. If not, you must be content to suppose, as others perhaps
have done, that 'I love him for the dangers he has passed.'"

WRITING FOR Eleanor Porden was second nature; nothing would
prevent her from it, even if her quill was damaged and there was no
ink at hand. "I have been forced to make the best of what has been
every body's hack for these three days," she once wrote to Franklin,
"and as to the ink, the heat of the sun had dried it up, and I was compelled to liquefy it with port wine, so that I know not what colour it

may assume ere it reaches you! My letter is certainly therefore written under the influence of the grape." Remarkably, this precious letter still survives, with the port wine ink perfectly readable.

Eleanor's love for her betrothed invigorated her writing. For Valentine's Day, she composed a poem called "The Esquimaux Girl's Lament," imagining she was a lovestruck Inuit woman who was calling her explorer lover back to the Coppermine River. One of the verses read:

Return! and the tempest shall pause in his wrath;
I will breathe out my spells on the land and the sea.
Return! and the Ice shall be swept from thy path,
Nor the winds nor the waves dare be rebel to thee.

Spread thy canvas once more, keep the Pole Star before thee,
'Tis Constancy's type and thy Beacon of Glory,
By the Lake, by the Mountain, the Forest, the River,
In the wilds of the North, I am thine, and for ever.

Unlike Eleanor, Franklin found writing to be irksome, and he confessed that he wished he possessed her talent. Unaccountably, however, his voluminous praise of her work changed to concern that it was improper for his future wife to indulge such a tawdry pursuit as writing for publication. Eleanor was confused: "That you had an objection almost amounting to horror to anything like publication in any one connected with you ... I have seldom received so severe a shock." Her harmless poems, she pointed out, would give him a small fraction of the emotional strain that his expeditions cost her. Naturally, she would not for a moment ask him to abandon his dreams. In return, she hoped that he not deprive her of the only employment that could interest her in his absence.

Franklin's declaration that desire for literary fame was vanity highlighted the double standards of their time, which Eleanor felt an intelligent couple should be able to rise above. His objections seemed so unlike the man she loved that she was prompted to ask hotly, "Which is the counterfeit, and which the true man?" The argument, she concluded, lay in a nutshell: the poems that were already printed bore her name, so he had to accept, whether she continued to write or not, that he was proposing to marry an author. Chastened, Franklin responded that she was right. They would put such things behind them and make plans for their wedding.

ELEANOR MARRIED John Franklin on August 6, 1823, in Marylebone, wearing a luxurious silver brocade gown. Franklin wrote in delight to his friend Richardson that the wedding dress had been embroidered with three plants they had discovered on their expedition: "The *Eutoca* is placed in the centre surrounded by the *Richardsonii* and *Hoodii* . . . This chit-chat will excite your smile, and I fancy you saying aside to Mrs. Richardson 'he is falling into the invariable custom of a new-married man and can fill his letter with no other subject than what relates to his wife.'"

Franklin hoped that his new bride would agree to give up her London home to become a part of his close-knit family network. However, it soon became apparent that Franklin's beloved Lincolnshire could never be a contender for their marital base. Almost immediately the damp air of the Fens affected Eleanor's lungs, and Franklin was so alarmed by her fits of breathlessness that he quickly delivered her to the home of his sister, where the air was more congenial to her health. Remarkably, he then returned alone to Lincolnshire to enjoy the festivities arranged in celebration of their marriage. "A pretty story, you will say for him to be running off so soon," Eleanor wrote sadly to her sister, "but it is all my fault, and so I have no right to complain."

Eleanor's frailty brought with it unforeseen challenges. Frequently she was troubled by chest infections, and her health deteriorated rapidly with the onset of bad weather. After a day trip to Mill Hill, she was so affected by the damp that she took to bed without dinner. "Indeed, had I not kept sipping lemonade and eating strawberries all the evening and night, I believe I should have been in a high fever next morning." Leaving the Fens behind, the couple moved into 55 Devonshire Street, London. It was the house in which Eleanor had been born, the place where she too would give birth and then would see out the last of her days.

ALTHOUGH FRANKLIN had a fervent dislike for London with its "fog, greed and interminable parties," through Eleanor he developed a new interest in the city. Soon the once humble seaman was keeping company with leading figures in exploration, literature, art and science, some of whom would help shape his future. Surprisingly, he appeared to have found a taste for society. "Such a flirt as he is!" Eleanor wrote playfully to Franklin's sister Betsey. "The like was never known."

Among the ladies for whom her husband had developed a fondness was Eleanor's new friend Jane Griffin. During the springtime of 1824, with Eleanor heavily pregnant and confined to her bed, Franklin and Jane saw each other several times at parties hosted by mutual friends or at the Griffin family home. The explorer, Jane noted to her satisfaction, was always extremely attentive. When he invited Jane and her sister for a jaunt across the Thames in a small collapsible craft he had named the "walnut shell," they joyfully accepted. As they laughed and rowed in a brisk breeze across the river, Eleanor was going into labour. The next day, on June 3, 1824, she gave birth to a daughter, Eleanor Isabella Franklin. According to their friend Captain George Lyon, the baby was the spitting image of her father: "like looking at Captain Franklin through the wrong end of a telescope." Yet fatherhood did little to encourage Franklin to stay at home.

Eleanor indulged her husband's social exuberance but privately felt abandoned. On one occasion, she heard that he had been the gallant escort to sixteen young ladies of society who on impulse stormed a nearby estate, then danced and sang in the gentleman's gardens. It was reported that Franklin's singing was particularly admired during a tender Italian duet with a young Miss Laws. Typically lighthearted, Eleanor responded: "He has had a good deal of practice lately in singing to Baby, and were it not for the approaching Expedition, I should expect to see him come out as a successor to Braham," an opera singer of the day.

The expedition would be Franklin's third to the Arctic, with the aim of exploring the country west from the Coppermine River to Icy Cape in Alaska. Eleanor fully supported the endeavour. "Her mind is so thoroughly English," Franklin wrote proudly to his sister, "that she would cheerfully make any sacrifice to promote our national character and more particularly where my professional fame may be concerned."

Friends and relatives worried that his polar journey could bring only difficulty and physical hardship, yet Eleanor remained Franklin's most faithful advocate. Meanwhile, rumours circulated that she had consumption. She was so weak that she often needed assistance to lift a hand or a foot. She was seen less and less in public, Franklin more so. After a ball hosted by Captain Parry in Franklin's honour, she heard through the newspapers how at the ball "the ladies pulled [her husband] to pieces ... He was in such request that I wonder they left a bit of him for me. I do not quite know what to say of his flirting in such a manner with half the Belles of London." Jane Griffin, on the other hand, relished being one of his belles, on one occasion writing, "As soon as Captain Franklin saw Fanny and me, he gave us each an arm, and seemed to have us under his protection the greater part of the evening, which surely must have made us the objects of envy." It is certain that the attention Franklin was showing Jane while his wife was confined to her bed did not go unnoticed.

Though Eleanor's health deteriorated, her baby thrived, particularly in the brief, precious times her father was at home. The baby was, Eleanor observed proudly, "luxuriantly well ... and very fond of riding on her papa's shoulders. I am not sure whether the horse or the rider is best pleased." When the home was filled with such pleasures, talk of the expedition caused her excitement rather than dread. In October 1824 Eleanor wrote to her sister that the boats, men and abundant supplies were in place for the expedition: "As far as human prudence can foresee or provide, all seems most auspicious."

Two days later she fell desperately ill. Her doctor ordered she be bled with leeches. By December, it was clear that her condition was serious. A friend saw the illness as being far more advanced than the Franklins wanted to acknowledge: "I saw, what at that time her own sister had not suspected, that she was dying."

In January 1825 the well-known physician Sir Henry Halford diagnosed Eleanor with chronic tuberculosis. Franklin was devastated. His expedition was due to depart the following month, but he could not conceive of leaving his wife and their eight-month-old under such circumstances. Eleanor would not hear a word of it. Franklin's duty was to further the course of science and endeavour, and that should take precedence. Her remaining strength was spent in keeping up the appearance, as best she could, of her health and support for her husband.

On Friday, February 11, Franklin wrote to his brother-in-law Henry Sellwood that Eleanor was "nearly at her last extremity—we have indeed been every hour this night expecting her last sigh." He was scheduled to leave his wife's side in just two days to make his way to Liverpool for the expedition's departure. He confessed to Sellwood that, since the sacrament had already been performed, he hoped God might choose to take Eleanor before he left so that he could be with her at that moment and also arrange for the care of their daughter. "I hope my dear friend," he concluded, "you will not suppose from my devoting so much of this letter to business that I am unmindful of the awful scene around me." The following day Eleanor rallied and, like many other polar wives, lovingly presented her husband with a flag she had spent weeks embroidering for his expedition. For her sake, she insisted weakly, he should look forward and head north. Franklin's sister noticed that although Eleanor was extraordinarily brave, she could barely disguise her grief. She knew it was the last time they would see each other.

On February 16, Franklin departed from Liverpool. Six days later, just before midnight, Eleanor Anne Franklin died.

In April, Franklin wrote to his sister from Lake Huron, ignorant of the events at home. Soon he would be paddling a canoe toward the Mackenzie River. His days were brightened, he confessed, by the hope of his wife's recovery. To Eleanor he wrote:

> I daily remember you and our dear little one in my prayers . . . with what heartfelt pleasure shall I embrace you both on my return! Your flag is yet snug in the box, and will not be displayed until we get to a more northern region. Mr. Back and his men have arrived—

That evening he noted in his journal: "The distressing intelligence of my dearest wife's death has just reached me."

When he felt it appropriate, Franklin finally unfurled Eleanor's silk flag and planted it on a remote island. "I will not attempt to describe my emotions," he wrote in his journal, as the flag expanded in the breeze.

Eleanor Anne Franklin was carried from St John's Wood Chapel by the explorers Francis Beaufort, George Lyon, Frederick William Beechey and David Buchan, men whose names were indelibly imprinted on the shores, islands, peninsulas and mountains of the Arctic. Standing nearby, handkerchief in hand, was Jane Griffin, John Franklin's future bride. In years to come, Jane would call upon these polar men—whom she had met through Eleanor—to mount one of the most impressive rescue missions the world had ever seen.

4

Jane Franklin

THIS ERRANT LADY

I hope I shall never be talked of as one of your bold,
clever, energetic women, fit for anything.

JANE FRANKLIN

O N A MILD summer's day in 1846, Jane Franklin reached the summit of Mount Washington in New Hampshire and marvelled at the clouds drifting over the White Mountain Forest far below. Climbing well-known peaks was the highlight of her often dangerous tours through wild country. Her conquest of this 6,288-foot peak, at the age of fifty-four in a boned corset and many-layered petticoats, was made all the more thrilling by her certainty that, at that moment, her husband, Sir John Franklin, was carving his way through the ice-chocked waters of the Northwest Passage. It was largely due to her that Franklin had been chosen again for the command of such an impressive expedition. Soon, she hoped, he would emerge triumphant into the Pacific, in the culmination of a quest that had claimed the lives of many brave men before him.

At the height of her celebrity, Jane, Lady Franklin was as much a household name as her contemporary Florence Nightingale.

Formidably well-connected and determined, she was the mistress of persuasion. Captains of industry, the British prime minister and even the president of the United States found their will bent inexplicably to hers. Her activities were discussed all over the land, from parlour rooms to Parliament; over polished tables at the Admiralty and creaking trestles in dockside inns. Dickens lent his pen in her support. Folk ballads were sung about her. Psychics carried messages to her from other realms. So influential was this petite, indomitable woman that innumerable expeditions were sent to the Arctic in her name.

ON EASTER MONDAY 1818, Jane Griffin first entered her future husband's name into her daily journal. Like Eleanor Anne Porden, Jane had spent the day at the Royal Docks at Deptford. The place was unusually busy with elegantly dressed day trippers who had gathered to catch a glimpse of the four expedition ships about to sail to the Far North.

Carpenters, crew and stevedores streamed back and forth between the ships and the rigging house, the sail loft and the victualling yard—a nineteen-acre site of supply houses that included a brewery, a cooperage, a bakery and a butchery complete with pens of sheep, cattle and hogs and two slaughterhouses. With just a month to go before the ships' departure, the excitement in the air was palpable.

Amid the cacophony of hollered orders, the loading of supplies and the clatter of tackle and rope was Lieutenant John Franklin, a rotund, kindly-faced naval officer who, while keen to prove his worth as a leader, nevertheless remained wonderstruck at his appointment as second-in-command of such an ambitious expedition. "It would be impossible for me to convey to you the amazing interest our little squadron has excited," he wrote to his sister two weeks after Jane's visit, on April 6, 1818. "Deptford has been covered with carriages and the ships with visitors every day... Indeed their coming in such shoals has greatly retarded our equipment."

A novice traveller herself, Jane had procured from a friend a letter of introduction that secured her and her sister a tour of the *Isabella*.

They examined harpoons, ice saws and the sealskin canoe "belonging to the Esquimaux who is to accompany the expedition on board the *Isabella,* as interpreter." Jane and her future husband did not meet on this occasion. Even if they had, Jane's attentions were focussed elsewhere.

Dark-haired, blue-eyed and well versed in parlour etiquette, Jane Griffin was only ordinarily pretty, but rarely short of suitors. Described as "piquante" by an admirer, she was a curious character: a flighty, sharp-eyed adventurer who quailed at the thought of these revolutionary qualities of hers being discovered. By the age of twenty-seven she had extricated herself from a turbulent five-year on-again, off-again romance with the son of a celebrated physician to the European nobility. She was infatuated instead with Peter Mark Roget, an enigmatic doctor and scientist thirteen years her senior who would become the creator of *Roget's Thesaurus.* Her feelings for Roget, however, were not reciprocated. Taking the advice of her aunt that perhaps she needed to find a man possessed of less genius, romance and "ardent sensibility," Jane withdrew from husband hunting and found solace in her studies.

The Griffin family was highly regarded in London. Jane's ancestors were among the cream of Huguenot society, originally French Protestants who fled religious persecution in the 1600s. Her father, John Griffin, was a wealthy man of influence and taste who owned a concern in Spitalfields that produced exquisite silks and velvets. Her mother, Mary Guillemard, also from Huguenot stock, had been born to a wealthy family of "silk men" who originated in Normandy.

Jane, born on December 4, 1791, barely remembered her mother. She was just three years old when her mother died, shortly after giving birth to Jane's sister Mary. Jane was a naturally inquisitive and intelligent child, and her thirst for knowledge was something that her father actively encouraged. With no university accepting female students at the time, Jane was first introduced to scholars at Oxford and Cambridge and then drilled in algebra, grammar, history, literature and philosophy by her maternal uncle, the intellectual John Guillemard. In addition, Jane and her sisters were taken on extended tours of England and the near Continent. Each journey, however small, was treated by Jane as a great undertaking, meriting records of eye-watering detail. In the end, her 157 journals, chronicling over sixty years of travel, would cover everything from weather statistics to the local management of silkworms. That these whimsical observations survive is due not to Jane's own lasting fame but to that of the explorer she would eventually marry.

JOHN FRANKLIN had learned of Eleanor's death in April 1825. The news was devastating. But by the onset of the polar winter, Franklin was in a state of grace. From Great Bear Lake in the Canadian Arctic he wrote to his sister describing his neatly ordered quarters, ornamented with books and instruments and a well-stuffed leather bed. Far from "the often too fascinating allurements of pleasure," he assured her that he was more calm and cheerful than he had been for some time.

By the time he returned to Britain, his grief and guilt over Eleanor's lonely death had passed. Franklin's priority was to find a new wife and mother for his daughter. Jane Griffin—healthy, intelligent and wealthy—was an obvious choice. Franklin had already named a piece of virgin territory in the Arctic for her, just as he had done for his first wife, and he began courting Jane as soon as he set foot back in England. His regular visits and gifts such as reindeer tongues and shoes "made by native Indian women" made the explorer's intentions perfectly clear.

Jane, by now aged thirty-five, was perfectly willing to remain single. She had given up the idea of marrying purely for love, and she did not need to marry for money. Any potential husband would have to offer her something worthwhile. John Franklin, standing just five foot six and weighing a wholesome fifteen stone (210 pounds), had neither the looks nor the charisma of her two previous love interests, nor was he wealthy. But he was a widower of solid character with an attractive level of celebrity. Furthermore, it was understood that Franklin would soon be awarded a knighthood. If she became his wife, she would be accepted in the highest social circles as Jane, Lady Franklin.

Intrigued by the prospects of aligning herself with the doughty explorer, Jane arranged to meet one of his sisters and discovered Griffin Point among the places named after polar and naval luminaries and politicians on a recently drawn map. In her notebook, she confessed she felt very nervous. At the home of Franklin's sister she also met Franklin's little girl, Eleanor Isabella, or Ella: "Daughter pretty and fair, but rather sickly." Jane considered herself beyond child-bearing age, and a child did not fit into the adventurous life plan she had for herself. Even so, when in July 1828 John Franklin asked John Griffin for his daughter's hand in marriage, Jane was delighted.

Jane married the soon-to-be polar knight in the village of Stanford on November 5, 1828, just a month short of her thirty-seventh birthday. Franklin's daughter was not present at the wedding. Writing to her new sister-in-law Isabella Cracroft, who had been charged with the child's care, Jane confided: "I am afraid I must appear to her rather a supernumerary and obtrusive mama, and I do not expect to hear that she can feel reconciled to admit me all at once to so high an honour. This will come however in good time."

In truth, the role of stepmother would never sit easily with Jane. The Franklins' honeymoon tour in France gave her a taste of her new-found status; the newlyweds were welcomed at the court of King Louis Philippe, and Franklin was presented with the gold medal of the French Geographical Society. To Jane's undoubted discomfiture, on their return they immediately moved into the home of Franklin's first wife, where Ella soon joined them.

Franklin received his knighthood in April 1829. He continued to receive praise for his polar work, but with no further expeditions on the horizon, Jane became anxious. This time of idleness filled her with "feelings very akin to shame and remorse." Relief of sorts came in the summer of 1830, in the form of a posting for her husband aboard the twenty-eight-gun frigate HMS *Rainbow*. Tensions were running high in the Mediterranean. The Greeks were pushing for independence from Turkish Ottoman rule, which had stimulated a powerful alliance between the Ottoman Empire and Egypt and fierce opposition from Greece, Russia, France and Britain. The *Rainbow* would be strategically situated in Malta to ensure that a British presence was felt in the region.

While Sir John settled into his new post, Jane tried to make the best of being the homebound wife. Her new title had its benefits, and she relished the recognition her association with Franklin afforded her. "Do you know who she is?" she reported one gentleman had exclaimed loudly to another at a ball. "She's the wife of no common person—look at her—she is the wife of that great Captain Sir John Franklin." She took Ella to Brighton and was introduced to King William IV, she wrote to her husband, wearing "white crepe over satin... the train emerald green satin, and trimmed with blonde and silver cord; head dress, ostrich plume, and a diamond wreath and lappets, necklace, pearls and diamonds... You need not be surprised therefore to hear that I was said to look extremely well." Ella, however, Jane reported, was like her mother, with a tendency for coughing fits. Above all, Jane despaired to her husband of her stepdaughter's energy:

> Her spirits are unbounded, and her activity excessive, and all that subdued and meek manner which made strangers suppose she was as gentle as a lamb, is flown. I think she is as *little* like you in disposition as a child can well be, and when people talk of her likeness to you, which is very evident, it is the likeness of feature, and not of expression.

> Your countenance is open and mild, full of benignity and candour; hers is full of the acutest vivacity, of no common share of self satisfaction, and of intellectual sharpness. This is not to my mind the *beau ideal* of the female countenance or mind, but we must work upon the materials we find and strive to mould them to our purpose.

Franklin himself was thoroughly content. His new wife's wealth had made life considerably easier. Jane was so robust that he didn't feel the same responsibility he had for the frail, creative Eleanor. His daughter was safely cared for. And although HMS *Rainbow* was a man-of-war, the only battles to be fought were diplomatic. Such was life on ship that those living under his command nicknamed the *Rainbow* "Franklin's Paradise" and "Celestial Rainbow." According to his nephew Frank Simpkinson, Franklin was completely relaxed on board. Almost too much so:

> He was somewhat absent, occasionally negligent of his person. I remember once his coming on deck with one half of his face shaved, the other still lathered, much to the entertainment of the midshipmen. I never saw him the least out of temper or heard him speak harshly to any of his officers.

Jane would have been horrified to see her new husband so unkempt. Already she was frustrated with his eager-to-please attitude, which she believed made him appear ineffectual. "You describe everybody alike as being so amiable and agreeable, that I cannot tell one from the other, and by that means don't care for any of them," she complained.

A year and a half of domesticity in London, with its incumbent maternal responsibilities, had been enough for Jane. She moved back to her own family home in Bedford Place, leaving the ghost of her predecessor firmly behind, but still she felt unsettled. By the spring of 1831 she was making plans to meet her husband in the Mediterranean. With war looming, Franklin tried to persuade her otherwise, but she countered: "Should there be war it will make no difference. I had much rather be in the midst of it, than sit at home brooding over disaster and bloodshed at home... Nothing but absolute impossibilities or what you consider as such, will prevent me from coming out sooner or later. On the contrary... in the company of brave men I should be courageous also... Don't think things *impossible* for me which are only a little *difficult*." Ella would not accompany her. She could not feel justified in putting the child in such danger, she declared.

In August 1831, having returned Ella to the care of her aunt, Jane journeyed toward Spain with her father, her maid and a manservant, hauling innumerable trunks and her four-poster iron bedstead. Soon after their departure, her father returned to England, and Jane found herself in charge of her own destiny.

EN ROUTE to the Holy Land and "within the sight and sound of actual war," Jane was in her element. In her handbag, which she always clutched tightly to her, was a letter to ensure safe passage through a land still gripped by conflict, written by the controversial dictator the Pasha of Egypt, Muhammad Ali. It was seven months since she had set out from England with the excuse of being close to her husband. She intended to travel for many more.

Jane had been introduced to the pasha in April 1832 on board the American corvette *Concord* in Alexandria. "The Pasha never receives ladies unless they disguise themselves in a man's dress," she wrote in excitement to Sir John. But as a special guest, Jane was spared the embarrassment of such theatrics. The pasha, she reported, was "a little and rather vulgar faced man about 62 years old, with an extremely quick little eye in perpetual motion, and a mouth expressive of humour and satire—some people think they see in it the cunning, and ferocity which mark the sagacious, and bloody murderer of the Mamelukes [*sic*], and I am rather of this opinion." Despite his fearsome reputation, it was the pasha who appeared intimidated, turning tail when he first saw Jane before "thinking better of himself" and asking to be introduced. Weeks later, enjoying the protection of the pasha's letter and the free passage offered by almost every ship of war in the Mediterranean, Jane discovered that there were considerable benefits to being the wife of a British polar hero and naval officer.

Jane had been advised not to travel to Spain, as "Ferdinand was enraged against the English," nor to go to Corfu, on account of malaria. Instead, she had taken the advice of her family friend

Captain Beaufort and had steamed along the coast of North Africa to the "snow-white city of Tetuan," one hundred miles east of Tangier. Being plagued by bugs and mosquitoes only added colour to what was the "amazing tonic power of great excitement... the comparative absence of *mental* anxieties, and petty perhaps but to me wearing and importunate household cares... which ruin my health."

Her only obligation was to occasionally meet her husband, though such rendezvous were not always satisfying. A meeting they had planned in Malta was not as romantic as they had expected; they had been apart for a year, but strict quarantine regulations prevented them from physically touching. The plague had swept through Malta in 1675, leaving eleven thousand dead. It had returned in 1813, carrying off a further five thousand. With such a catastrophe in recent memory, visitors were required to "do time" at the quarantine station on Manoel Island. Tantalizingly close, Jane and Sir John could only holler to one another. The ordeal of shouting for two hours in the heat at her partially deaf husband forced Jane to her bed immediately on returning to her ship.

With Sir John's return to the *Rainbow,* Jane felt duty bound to make the most of her freedom, even if those at home were anxious about her plans. Their concerns were understandable given the threat of encounters with "marauding Arabs" that she described in her letters. Just as serious to Jane was the loss of her precious handbag through the rudder hole of a decrepit vessel she had been forced to travel on. No matter that she was choked with sickness from the intolerable stench on board, nor that the only accommodation forced its inhabitants to sleep in a heap "like pigs"; her deepest regret was that she had lost her opera glass, "through which I see better than through any telescope and without which I feel like a blind person." Such an item would have been invaluable when travelling to Greece, she wrote darkly, "the archipelago being now infested with Pirates, and really to be dreaded."

Despite her father's written protestations, she continued on to ride a donkey into Nazareth, as Jesus had done. Unlike Jesus, she rode with a guide, an Egyptian servant, five janissaries of an elite military outfit and a dozen Bedouin. "You should have seen our mounted guard, as we crossed the desert plain of Jericho toward the [River] Jordan," she enthused to her sister Mary. "Exciting one another by wild screams; letting off their muskets and pistols, balancing and thrusting their lances at full gallop, wheeling, pursuing, receding, sweeping across our path, yet always with the nicest care avoiding being actually in our way." Afterwards she bathed in a sacred stream and was carried into the waters of the Dead Sea before travelling toward Constantinople.

From Constantinople Jane crossed the Sea of Marmara to the ancient city of Bursa, once the Ottoman capital, and onward to the 8,300-foot peak of nearby Mount Uludag, believed by some to be the original Mount Olympus. Jane returned to Constantinople to find the streets almost deserted: the bubonic plague had broken out. Walking quickly to her rooms, Jane covered her face with a vinegar-filled hand-kerchief and held a parasol fiercely at her waist while following hard on the heels of her servant, who used a staff to keep others at bay. Making a quick escape, Jane and her small retinue continued on toward Troy.

By now Jane had realized that appearing elegantly vulnerable brought her far more respect and assistance than if she had struck out manfully on her own. Obtaining letters of introduction and safe passage on warships and finding travelling companions of intelligence and status was so much easier when one was the respectable wife of a naval officer. But Sir John was beginning to show concern at his wife's constant adventuring. Through the network of ships in the area, he sent messages to her suggesting that she take a rest from her travels and await his return in Malta. Jane ignored his request. She promised that she would return to Malta once he was there, but in the meantime she joined a touring group of raucous French antiquarians. Jane roundly disapproved of their foul language and heavy drinking, but she had to confess that "the coarse way in which we lived . . . agreed with me astonishingly."

By the 1830s there were a few adventurous middle-class women striding across Europe—some travelling even farther afield— but the notoriety that went hand in hand with such spirited travels was something to be avoided, particularly for someone so socially conscious. God forbid that Jane would be grouped with such social outcasts as the eccentric and sexually liberated Lady Hester Stanhope, who had been consumed by her passion for the East, or the curious Miss Hamilton, whose path Jane had crossed during her travels: an elderly Scotswoman who dared to travel entirely alone, without even a servant.

For all her adventurousness, Jane claimed that she was crippled by intense shyness and "an excessive susceptibility of ridicule." She lived in fear "of being thought a *strong-bodied,* as well as strong-minded person, bold, masculine, independent, almost everything in short that I most dislike." Like Sir John, Jane believed it was vanity for a married woman to have her writing published. Even though she wrote exhaustively in her journals and enjoyed reading the travel accounts of other women, she would not, like Eleanor Franklin, dare to be seen as a published author. Her travels were motivated and justified, Jane insisted, by her sense of duty to be near her husband—a notion she made a mockery of by continually avoiding meetings with Franklin at predesignated places.

Privately, there was no concealing Sir John's admiration for Jane's pluck and adventurous spirit. "You have completely eclipsed me," he declared, "and almost every other traveller—females certainly." Equally, he was aware of the criticism his wife's determined adventuring was attracting at home. The thought that she could be associating with unsavoury characters was one concern; others commented on her unwillingness to embrace the role of stepmother. Although the offspring of wealthy women were generally tended to by nurses, to abandon one's stepchild in order to gallivant around the Mediterranean rather hinted at conceit. But Franklin, who had once been so sensitive to appearances, had clearly mellowed. It would be wrong to assume, he insisted, that his wife travelled out of vulgar curiosity. Instead, her constant travelling indicated a desire to "inform herself and broaden her mind so that she can be more interesting to others."

Jane's hardened adventuring and tendency to plunge into "fits of hysterics" eventually caused an irreparable rift between her and her servants. When, in spring 1833, Franklin turned up unannounced in

Nauplia hoping to surprise Jane, he found to his dismay that his wife had left two days earlier and that her young maid had resigned from service and was planning to make her own way back to England. Her manservant had also decided to quit.

In Athens Jane found two new servants. Their arrival saved her from a "desolate condition." But her new manservant, with whom she attempted to climb 3,366-foot Mount Hymettus, did not have the intuition or the climbing skills of his predecessor. Dusk found them on the edge of a precipitous cliff, beyond which appeared to be a chasm of darkness. Realizing that they must find a quick way off the mountain, they slid down the steep slope on stones, grabbing whatever they could to support themselves. "I was much impeded by the strong bushes of prickles and briars which generally caught my petticoats behind," Jane wrote, "and I left a very considerable portion behind me. My shoes were actually in tatters, and my limbs were so weak, that when it was necessary to stand upright again, I could only proceed by placing my two hands on the shoulders of [my manservant], who went a step before me." The news of her failed climbing expedition and her dishevelled reappearance in Athens by moonlight soon spread. To Jane's discomfort, Admiral Sir Pulteney Malcolm exclaimed upon meeting her, "Oh, all of Athens is talking about you." It was not the last time that Jane's adventures would become a talking point.

By the close of 1833, Sir John Franklin's four-year posting on the *Rainbow* was at an end. During his absence, Jane had also been away from home for over two years; she had spent just three months of that time with her husband. Franklin was beginning to experience what it was like to have an itinerant partner. Understandably, he expected Jane to accompany him back to England. She resolutely refused. After all, she wrote to her husband, was it not her inquiring nature that had made her so "very irresistible in your eyes?"

During her travels Jane had tolerated, as she described them, "horrors unequalled." She had endured leaking, stinking cabins in old boats, encountered limbless beggars, avoided robbers and— worst of all—suffered companions who shrivelled her patience and numbed the intellect. Yet the thought of returning to England was far worse. Asserting that she must uphold her promise of travelling with friends up the Nile, she turned from the prospect of "dear, yet dreaded England," with all its obligations, and journeyed instead to Alexandria.

WITH FRANKLIN'S DEPARTURE from the Mediterranean, Jane no longer enjoyed the protection that his presence there had accorded her status and reputation. So far, she had been welcomed into the hierarchy of well-to-do travelling gentlefolk. Now alone, except for her servants, she was in danger of being regarded as a liability and a curiosity, and her drop in status was immediately apparent.

Jane had been invited to accompany the British consular agent and merchant Robert Thurburn and his family to Thebes. It was an opportunity she could not resist, but she soon realized that she was now considered the least important member of their party. Of the four vessels that would travel up the Nile, she was assigned to the smallest and least comfortable. As the cruise continued, she suspected that she was becoming an object of ridicule. She missed several excursions due to the slowness of her boat, and with the only kitchen being on one of the faster boats, she frequently missed meals. Heavy rain drenched her cabin; lice overran the stays of her corsets, and rats crept into her hair at night, prompting howls of indignation. Her discomfort came to a head on the final evening when she watched enviously as the Thurburns' boat overtook her, lit like a beautiful ballroom.

By the time they arrived in Cairo, Jane was finding her companions utterly uncongenial. In a dramatic climax to their shared travels, she joined them on a visit to the Great Pyramid of Giza, only to be abandoned in the dark. Swooning in terror, she had to be dragged into the sunlight. Had she not managed to cry out *"Burra, burra"* (Out, out), she wrote later to Franklin, "I should probably have fallen as dead as I find Dr. Hogg did in the great Chamber there."

In Cairo, a more appropriate companion appeared in the form of Rudolph Theophilus Lieder, a Swiss-born missionary who was planning a journey to visit Coptic churches in upper Egypt. Lieder agreed to accompany Jane up the Nile as far as Waddy Halfa and the Second Cataract, postponing his own business until their journey was complete. Jane made it known that Lieder would have his own boat, which would travel alongside hers, so that propriety would be observed. She also emphasized the size of their retinue: her maid, an Arab guide and interpreter, twelve men for military protection, the *reis* (captain) who was in charge of the boat and ten boatmen. Even so, from this moment on, Jane's travels would be of an entirely different nature.

Jane could not have imagined a more heroic guardian. Educated, courageous yet gentle, Lieder was fluent in several languages, including Arabic, and was a homeopathic physician. He was also strikingly good-looking. Tall and lean with fine features, he was a terribly charismatic Christian. On their departure, Jane scarcely recognized him as he swept on board with his sword buckled around his great coat and his penetrating light grey eyes flashing beneath his turban.

Such freedom, however, made Jane uncomfortable. With Franklin in England, each step of her journey began to feel like an indiscretion. When she met former travelling companions she was coldly received. Every delay reminded her of the expectations of her husband, friends and society at large. The only alleviation of these troublesome thoughts was her growing fondness for her attendant missionary.

Within just a few days of leaving Cairo, Jane privately noted that Lieder "seemed to live only to serve me." After an exhausting journey across the desert to Fayoum, they discovered it was too late to return to their camp by nightfall. Lieder sought out the only available accommodation, and had the best room swept and prepared with fresh mats. He then laid out his own Persian carpet "& lay down on it with me to take tea." Understanding that the intimacy of the situation could be misconstrued, Jane noted in her journal that Lieder did not stay long, as she was not well. The following day they visited an archaeological dig. Since her frightening experience with the Thurburns, she had avoided any similar situation. Gaining confidence from her companion, she went into many dark chambers and stifling passages. Together they saw mummified bodies that in the flickering torchlight appeared to be almost alive. "But my health and nerves were better, and the conviction I felt that no serious harm could happen to me if Mr. Lieder were near, saved me from even the apprehension of it."

Egypt had now become the exquisite backdrop for romance. Jane blushed happily when she was mistaken for Lieder's wife in a letter of introduction to a resident European, and she assured the abashed missionary that there was no need to correct the error. In the days that followed, the two became ever closer. Lieder presented Jane with some branches of sweet-smelling flowers from which he had carefully stripped the thorns, wishing "that he could even with bloody fingers pull off all the thorns in my path thro' life." She replied it was better she should meet with some, then put the flowers in her bonnet. In the evenings while embanked on the shore of the Nile, they often talked until the early hours of the morning. At other times, Jane would lie in her bed listening in wonder to "his full, mellow voice singing sacred songs to his guitar" as the sound drifted over the water.

The two boats swung north, following the river's course above Philae. No sooner had they changed direction than they were greeted by hurricane-force winds. Lieder urged the crew of Jane's boat to drag their vessel to a sheltered position farther along the rocky coast. "Mr. Lieder himself dragged rope, ran along rocks, threatened, insisted, almost swore, while men throwing off their clothes or retaining only one [garment], plunged into water... and dragged and pushed." In the gathering darkness, the men struggled to haul the boat to safety. Without warning, a rope snapped, and Jane's boat keeled over into a muddy bank. Lieder plunged through the mud and fast-running water to reach the boat, where Jane was struggling to keep herself steady atop a divan above the surging waters. Dropping to his knees, Lieder firmly grasped her waist to steady her and asked if she was alarmed. "No," she replied, "not as long as you are here."

As night fell, with her boat no longer in grave danger, Jane begged the reluctant Lieder to return to his own vessel half an hour upriver.

"My head and feelings told me of great change," she confessed to her journal, "and [I] went to bed unwell." Then followed a night of self-pity and misery. Rain poured into her cabin until everything was sodden. Crippled with sickness and headache, she ordered her servant to use plates to catch the leaks. Lieder was not mentioned again in her journal for some time.

A month later, in May 1834, Jane was back in Cairo. After travelling together to Thebes, she and Lieder had parted company, with Jane taking his faster vessel downstream. He remained behind to visit the missions that had been the original object of his trip. Now Jane found herself living in his home, "using everything of his, as if it were my own." But without his company, she felt lost and vulnerable. She wrote asking Lieder to once again cut short his assignment to join her. He never received her letter, as he had already speedily made his way to Cairo to be by her side. Lieder, "who to the meekness & prudence of a Christian Minister, joins the courage and energy of a soldier," put aside his own mission to conduct Jane safely to Greece. There is no record of when they parted. Nor do any letters between Jane and Lieder survive.

Jane would have far preferred to stay in Greece, but she knew any further delay was impossible. A year before she had confessed to her sister: "I cannot tell you how much I dread a return from these hot climates . . . I feel it would be fatal to all the improvement I have made . . . My drawbacks have been moral rather than physical ones."

When she arrived back in England on October 19, 1834, Jane had been travelling for over three years. Her return demanded more of her resolve than she was willing to admit. The parting from Rudolph Lieder, for whom she clearly had a deep regard and affection, must have been very painful. Complaining of fever, she retreated to her room in Falmouth and refused to leave her bed for two weeks. But by the time she resurfaced and returned to London, her sights were once again firmly set. She would find Sir John a suitable project, and would once again spread her wings.

5

Emily Shackleton

AN EAGLE IN THE BACKYARD

I cannot flatter myself that it was only for me—it was his
own spirit "a soul whipped on by the wanderfire."

EMILY SHACKLETON

On OCTOBER 21, 1907, Emily Shackleton stood on Dover Pier and watched as her husband slipped from view. On board the Channel steamer, Ernest Shackleton was disconsolate.

Later that day, on the train to Paris before going on to meet his ship the *Nimrod* in New Zealand, bound for the Antarctic, Shackleton wrote his "splendid glorious woman" a love letter:

Your dear brave face is before me now and I can see you just as you stand on the wharf and are smiling at me as my heart was too full to speak and I felt that I wanted just to come ashore and clasp you in my arms and love and care for you: Child honestly and truly, parting from you was the worst heart-aching moment of my life. If

I failed to get to the Pole and was within 10 miles and had to turn
back it would or will not mean so much sadness as was compressed
into those few minutes.

Shackleton hadn't realized until that moment how much he relied
on his wife's judgment and support. One look in her "Sweeteyes"
and he felt invincible. "You are a thousand times too good for me
darling," he wrote, "and I see and know it in a hundred ways, but I
can say no more than this that I will try and be worthy of the glory
that is you. From early days you have been my light and my pride."
As he travelled farther toward New Zealand, he became increasingly
homesick. He constantly showed his fellow passengers photographs
of Emily and their two children and was filled with longing when
he heard people singing songs that reminded him of home. Sleepless
nights prompted letters to Emily filled with poetry and promises of
his determination to be worthy of her pride in him.

Although he and his men would be facing implausibly tough
conditions, Shackleton would not, he assured her, run any
unnecessary risks for fame. "You will be with me wherever I go in
storm or calm and if inclined to do anything rash I will think of my
promise to you and not do it." Thoughts of his homecoming were a
driving force to overcome every hardship he was about to face. "*Never
never again*," he insisted, would there be a journey so important as
to cause them to be separated. Such heartfelt pledges would become
familiar to Emily, as were similar promises made to other polar wives
by their husbands on each new departure.

Emily Dorman had first met the young merchant seaman at "the
height of the rose-season" in July 1897 when visiting one of his sisters. Six years Shackleton's senior, Emily was polite but unmoved by
their meeting. In contrast, according to his friend Hugh Robert Mill,
the discovery of this elegant blue-eyed woman "drove the thought of
ships from [Shackleton's] mind." The aura of "inexhaustible animal
spirits, of exuberant vitality, of explosive energy" that one contemporary portrayed Shackleton as having did not seem to impress Emily.

She regarded him instead as an adventure-prone dreamer, dislocated from his loving family and seeking a launch pad for a future he could not yet foresee.

Born in 1868 in Kent, Emily Mary Dorman, like Shackleton, was from a large family. She was graceful, slim and confident, with a talent for singing, and had attracted several admirers. Her father, Charles Dorman, a wealthy and well-liked solicitor with a passion for orchids, raised his six children to have an appreciation of literature and nature. By the time of their first meeting, Shackleton had already spent seven years at sea, gathering a collection of outrageous tales with which to entertain and impress. Understandably, Emily believed his attentions to be nothing more than the flighty crush of a restless seaman.

Born in County Kildare before his family's move to Sydenham, Ernest Henry Shackleton was by turns a dreamer and a fighter, earning the nickname "Mick" from childhood friends. He was, as a shipmate described, "several types bound in one volume." In the years to come, Shackleton would be regarded as a visionary and a great leader of men, yet also as a financial liability and a failure. He was a romantic who adored the company of women, especially his eight sisters; he joked they embodied his "harem." As his sister Kathleen later recalled:

> "Come all my wives," he would shout when he entered the house after a voyage. He would lie down and call out: "You must entertain me. Zuleika, you may fan me, Fatima, tickle my toes. Come, oh favoured one and scratch my back." Of course we all loved it.

Their father, Henry Shackleton, who became a doctor after abandoning life as a farmer during the potato famine in Ireland, was devoted to his family. Known as a kind and gentle man, he instilled in his brood a love of poetry and open-handedness. Henry wore a spectacular beard, was an advocate of homeopathy and was unafraid to embrace new ideas. When Ernest declared that he wished to go to sea,

Henry arranged for a secure, if not glamorous, berth with the Mercantile Marine.

Ernest Shackleton quickly became known on board for his cheery manner and his love of literature. "Old Shack's busy with his books," one of his contemporaries, Thomas Peers, remembered other lads on board commenting. His love of letters might have made him a target for bullying, but Shackleton was too likeable, quick-witted and tough to attract that sort of trouble.

Although she appreciated Shackleton's poetical letters from far and wide, Emily Dorman was swayed by the opinion of friends who thought the relationship could not last. Her polite refusal of Shackleton's advances, on the pretext that their difference in age was insurmountable, made him all the more keen. He was relentless in his pursuit. When he was not with her, his head and heart boiled with emotions:

> It is because of my unhappy nature to stick to the truth, to be true to others as to myself; that things seem so hard! I walk on Hells Paving stones burning my feet, yes twisting my hearts roots in the pain of it. Down in the dark with no ray of light . . . I think, curse it all, think again and hope; that is all, truly a happy life . . .

Driven by his desire for Emily, Shackleton grew focussed on the need to make more of his prospects. James Dunsmore, one of his shipmates, recalled a conversation he and Shackleton had on the deck of the Welsh Shire Line ship the *Flintshire* in 1898. To Dunsmore's question "What do you think of this old tub? You'll be skipper of her one day," Shackleton replied:

> "You see, old man," he said, "as long as I remain with this company, I'll never be more than a skipper. But I think I can do something better. In fact, really, I would like to make a name for myself (he paused for a moment or two) and her." He was looking pensively over the sea at the moment, and I noticed his face light up at the mention of "her."

After a year and a half of his ceaseless attentions, Emily began to take notice of Shackleton. In December 1898, the *Flintshire* ran aground during a winter storm. After ensuring the safety of the ship and those on board, Shackleton requested leave in order to see his father on his birthday. He immediately hastened to find Emily at her parents' house. In years to come, she would fondly remember the incident:

> We spent the evening in the billiard room at the Firs. He told me how he loved me, & was deeply moved. I remember so well, because he put his cigarette on a ledge in the big oak chimney piece, & it burnt a deep dent, which we tried to rub out, and we often looked at it in after days, but no one else noticed it! ... I can see it all now. I let him out through the conservatory about 10.30, I think, and he kissed my hand. He went home then to wish his father "many happy returns."

As summer approached, Shackleton became a regular visitor to the Dorman family home. On one occasion he discovered that his companions on the train were antique dealers also heading to the Firs to attend an auction. One man turned to Shackleton and asked, "What are you going to get out of the old man?" Shackleton replied, "His daughter, I hope."

By the winter of 1900, Shackleton was caught in a whirl of ideas, longing and crushing uncertainty about his future. His disquiet worsened when he learned that another suitor was lurking in the background. "I know that I was the interloper," Shackleton wrote in distress to Emily in the spring of 1901:

> I suppose it is [a] mans way to want a woman altogether to himself: I said it in the old days "Love me only a little, just a little" and now it seems as I grow older I am saying "Love me altogether and only me" ... I have nothing to offer you: I am poor: I am not clever, it is as wicked of me to want you to keep caring for me ... When like today you spoke about him: something catches at my heart and I

feel lost, out in the cold ... Why did I not know you first? Why did
you not tremble to my touch first of all the men in this world. Of all
tales of love and sorrow I feel ours stands out for there was no hope
in the beginning and there is none now.

The signal change in Shackleton's fortunes came when his
application to join the British National Antarctic Expedition—later
known as the *Discovery* expedition—was accepted. Although he had
no particular pull toward the polar regions, he recognized that the
project, under the command of the young naval lieutenant Robert
Falcon Scott, would guarantee him the experience of a lifetime and
might also impress Emily. It did. With Emily won over, Shackleton
wrote to Charles Dorman asking for his daughter's hand in marriage.

Being so close to achieving what his heart desired most, it was
with mixed emotions that Shackleton approached the day when he
would embark on the dangerous southern journey with Captain Scott
and Dr. Edward Wilson. On November 1, 1902, Shackleton wrote a
letter to be given to his fiancée in the event that he did not return.

Beloved I hope you may never have to read this, but darling, loved
one if it comes to you, you will know that your lover left this world
with all his heart yours. My last thoughts will be of you my own
dear Heart... I cannot say more my heart is so full of love and
longing for you and words will not avail. They are so poor in such
a case... Know once more that I love you truly and purely and as
dearly as a woman can be loved. And now my true love goodnight.

THE FOLLOWING MORNING the three men of the southern party left
the comfort of the *Discovery*, at anchor in McMurdo Sound, and set
off for the South Pole. Cheered on by the ship's company gathered on
the floe, the men were in excellent spirits. But after seven weeks on
the trail the condition of the men was poor. Wilson advised Scott that
Shackleton had angry-looking gums—a sure sign that he was suffering from scurvy. By Christmas, Scott and Wilson were also suffering;

Wilson's left eye was so painful that he was dosing himself with morphine and drops of cocaine solution in his eye in order to sleep.

As their journey continued, the effects of scurvy intensified. Increasingly weakened from physical exhaustion, exposure and inadequate provisions, the three men battled forward. Tension was beginning to surface, but Scott seemed determined to reach the Pole at any cost. On December 30, 1902, Scott and Wilson left Shackleton to guard the camp at 82°15' S while they reconnoitred a nearby inlet. The weather was so thick that they were compelled to return after just one or two miles, but Scott noted their new farthest-south point as 82°17' S. Shackleton, having been left behind, was denied the opportunity of sharing the new record. By then it was clear: to have any chance of survival, they had to turn back.

The return to the ship was unmitigated agony. By mid-January, all of the dogs they had brought with them had died or been shot, now more of a hindrance than a help. As starvation set in, their conditions worsened. Shackleton started to cough up blood. On January 15, Wilson confided to his journal that Shackleton was worryingly sick. Wilson ordered him to stop walking in harness. As Shackleton reluctantly took his place behind the sledges, Wilson confronted Scott. The more their companion's health had deteriorated, the thinner Scott's patience had worn. He cuttingly referred to Shackleton as the "lame duck" and "our invalid"—which only added to Shackleton's crushing sense of shame. A "volley of home truths" from Wilson seemed to ease the tension, but from that moment Scott and Shackleton would forever nurse their differences.

Ten days later Shackleton once more began to share the load. But with each blizzard he suffered violent attacks of asthma, occasionally causing him to be livid and speechless. On January 29, he was fighting unconsciousness as he heard Wilson say to Scott that he did not expect Shackleton to last the night. Mustering all his strength Shackleton carried on until finally, on February 3, they were intercepted by Reginald Skelton and Louis Bernacchi from the *Discovery*, who barely recognized the three broken men.

After a short period of recuperation, Scott ordered Shackleton to be invalided home on the relief ship the *Morning*. Matters were complicated by the opinion of Dr. Reginald Koettlitz, who claimed that both Wilson and Scott were in even worse medical condition. Now fully recovered, Shackleton appealed to his leader for a change of heart, but Scott was adamant.

Shackleton's return to Britain ahead of the rest of the *Discovery* expedition could have crushed a lesser man. His reunion with Emily cheered him, however, and he was developing a flair for turning disastrous situations to his advantage. Quickly he discovered that, though he had been invalided home, there was an audience hungry for stories of polar adventure. He was an exhilarating speaker, a genial, racy raconteur. As one listener recorded: "I can hear the deep, husky voice rising and falling with the movement of his story, and sometimes raised, by way of illustrating his point, to a rafter-shaking roar." But instead of saving his lecture and editorial fees for his life together with Emily, Shackleton gave the proceeds to the *Discovery* relief fund. It was apparent that if he wanted to marry, he would have to find a position that brought in a regular income.

Shackleton swung from one glorious idea to another before putting himself forward as secretary to the Royal Scottish Geographical Society in Edinburgh. With the position secured, he was finally on the path to respectability. The Antarctic was forgotten, and his letters brimmed with enthusiasm and love. With their wedding imminent, he wrote to Emily:

> I am coming my own sweet to you and all I can say to you is small and feeble to the great love that I feel which is welling up to over-flowing dearest heart. The best of me is miserably poor to give you my Queen and yet my love is so strong that it will redeem the poverty of the rest of me. Money I have none but Child o'mine all my heart cries out for you. In the spring we are to be married and it will be spring always in our lives... for our love will be always spring and so we will go on and on till the twilight... We have

long, long years before us of joy and love . . . and you will ever feel my arm there to protect and keep to guide your feet and smooth the path for you the fairest and dearest of women.

On Saturday, April 9, 1904, at Christ Church, Westminster, Ernest Henry Shackleton married his Emily. The following day, the new bride wrote an emotional letter to her sisters: "4 large sploshing tears, 3 have gone on the blotting paper—I mustn't cry darlings must I—for really I *am* happy . . . I love feeling married." Her only disappointment was Shackleton's insistence that they should forgo their honeymoon so he could work. She, like other polar wives, would soon discover that however much she was loved by her husband, birthdays, anniversaries and even honeymoons would always take second place to the quest for adventure and fame.

Marriage did little to calm Shackleton's energetic temperament. The position of secretary was far from fulfilling, and Shackleton soon felt he had outgrown the geographical society. There were some joyful distractions. In February 1905 Emily gave birth to their first child, Raymond. "Good fists for fighting!" Shackleton exclaimed proudly. But he was increasingly restless. He wanted not only to return to the Antarctic but to command an expedition himself.

By Christmas Day 1906, Shackleton had convinced himself that for Emily's sake, and now with two children—their daughter, Cecily, had been born two days earlier—he should win the South Pole. Remarkably, given that he did not tell her of his plans until the expedition was already decided, Emily fully supported him. After all, she mused, "How could you keep an eagle tied in a backyard?" Her encouragement prompted an outpouring of love:

I am afraid that when I got your wire so full of feeling and sweet-
ness that I broke down. My own dear Heart you are a thousand
times too good for me and I am feeling it very much now but it
will only be one year and I shall come back with honour and with
money and never, never part from you again . . . Darling I am full

of distress mingled with great desire to do a great thing and you have risen like the real woman and real friend that you are and I am just longing to hold you and tell you that you will be a part of history.

Emily was not well known in her own right as were Eva Nansen, Eleanor Franklin and, in later years, Kathleen Scott. She was not an adventurer like Jane Franklin; nor was she a courageous companion, as Jo Peary and Marie Herbert would be on their husbands' polar travels. But she was, without doubt, a source of strength and stability for the ever-restless Shackleton. Emily herself in later years commented:

I never wittingly hampered his ardent spirit, or tried to chain it to the domestic life which meant so much to me. He used to say he went on the *Discovery* "to get out of the ruck" [get beyond the struggle] for me!—it was dear of him to say it because I cannot flatter myself that it was only for me—it was his own spirit "a soul whipped on by the wanderfire."

On February 11, 1907, Shackleton officially announced that the arrangements for his British Antarctic Expedition were under way. The expedition would leave later that year, with the aim of reaching both the South Magnetic Pole and—the ultimate prize— the geographical South Pole. Shackleton was fully focussed on his mission: "I am representing 400 million British subjects," he declared enthusiastically to Emily. Royal patronage only intensified his feeling. On August 5, 1907, a farewell dinner was held on the *Nimrod*. In the place of honour was Emily, with Shackleton on her right hand. Behind them hung a Union Jack that had been presented to Shackleton by Queen Alexandra.

Although there had been innumerable challenges in pulling together an expedition in so short a time, there was one issue that for a time overshadowed all the rest. Shackleton had envisioned basing the expedition at the old *Discovery* headquarters of McMurdo Sound.

From there he would launch several journeys and a comprehensive scientific program. There was one obstacle to his plan: Captain Scott. When Shackleton announced his plans for the expedition, Scott had written to him strongly objecting to the possibility of Shackleton using "his" base:

> I don't want to be selfish at anyone's expense and least of all at that of one of my own people but still I think anyone who has had to do with exploration will regard this region primarily as mine... It must be clear to you now that you have placed yourself directly in the way of my life's work—a thing for which I have sacrificed much and worked with steady purpose... If you go to McMurdo Sound you go to winter quarters which are clearly mine... I do not like to remind you that it was I who took you to the South or of the loyalty with which we all stuck to one another or of incidents of our voyage or of my readiness to do you justice on our return.

Shackleton's attempts to win Scott over failed miserably. His old commander had some powerful advocates, including Sir Clements Markham, Sir George Goldie, president of the Royal Geographical Society, and J. Scott Keltie, the society's secretary. Even Edward Wilson, whom Shackleton had counted among his friends, clearly stated his allegiance to Scott. "Now Shackles," Wilson wrote, "I think that if you go to McMurdo Sound & even reach the Pole— the gilt will be off the gingerbread because of the insinuation which will almost certainly appear in the minds of a good many, that you forestalled Scott who had a prior claim to the use of that base." Wilson advised Shackleton to avoid McMurdo at all costs, even if it cost him the Pole. After much deliberation, Shackleton acquiesced. He signed an agreement that, in the eyes of all parties privy to it, would give him only a marginal chance of success.

COMPARED WITH HIS intensely private farewell to Emily at Dover, the scenes in New Zealand ten weeks later, on New Year's Day 1908, were thunderous. By the time Shackleton left aboard the *Nimrod,* he had charmed and inspired the country to such an extent that fifty thousand people flooded the streets of the small harbour town of Lyttelton to catch a last glimpse of the adventurers before they headed toward the Pole. Their cheers and chatter drowned out the rousing tunes of the brass bands that were in danger of being pushed into the water. The harbour was choked with a flotilla of waterborne supporters on ships and private yachts. Such was the enthusiasm for Shackleton's venture that Raymond Priestley, one of the scientists on board, commented that several vessels were listing dangerously as their passengers rushed across the decks to cheer *Nimrod*'s passing.

Shackleton and his men sailed toward Antarctica, brimming with excitement and confidence. But their hope of establishing a base at King Edward VII Land was soon thwarted. Barred by ice and battered by heavy seas and storms, Shackleton had no choice but to turn the *Nimrod* toward the "prohibited" McMurdo Sound. He was in an impossible situation, and it tormented him. Only to Emily could he confess how deeply it distressed him to go back on his word to Scott. On January 26, 1908, he wrote:

> Child o' mine I have been through a sort of Hell since the 23rd and I cannot even now realize that I am on my way back to McMurdo Sound . . . that all my plans and ideas have now to be changed and changed by the overwhelming forces of Nature . . . All the anxiety that I have been feeling coupled with the desire to really do the right thing has made me older than I can ever say. Child I must now write my heart out and it is to you alone that I can do for I never, never knew what it was to make such a decision as the one I was forced to make last night . . . I know you can read between the lines and realize what it has been to me to stand up on the bridge in those snow squalls and decide whether to go on or turn back my whole heart crying out for me to go on and the feeling against of the lives and families of the 40 odd men on board.

Although each mile they travelled to the west felt like a betrayal, Shackleton had no choice but to continue. As Captain Rupert

England of the *Nimrod* frankly informed him, wintering on any other part or inlet of the Ice Barrier (today called the Ross Ice Shelf) would be suicidal. Further, "my duty to the country and King since I was given the flag for the Pole and lastly but not least my duty to all who entrusted themselves to my keeping" required it. Having agonized over the decision, Shackleton simply had to press on. "My conscience is clear," he wrote miserably, "but my heart is sore... I have one comfort that I did my best... I know you know that I have done all that any man could have done under the circumstances."

A YEAR LATER, in January 1909, Shackleton and his companions Frank Wild, Dr. Eric Marshall and Jameson Boyd Adams broke through a mental, physical and geographical barrier in one of the most inhospitable places in the world. They were closer to the ends of the earth than any human being in history. On January 9 Shackleton recorded: "We have shot our bolt and the tale is 88.23 S. 162 E." Unfurling the Union Jack that had been presented to the expedition by Queen Alexandra, the men quietly congratulated one another. It was not elation they felt, however, but crushing exhaustion, disappointment and hunger.

The thought of Emily, his own children and the families of the men with him precipitated Shackleton's decision to return. They were within ninety-seven miles of the South Pole but could go no farther with any certainty that they would make it home alive. Later Adams would comment, "If we'd gone on one more hour, we shouldn't have got back." Shackleton's decision to turn away from the South Pole— so tantalizingly close—to ensure the safe return of his men was one of the greatest moments of courage and foresight recorded in polar history. Now they had to face the seven hundred gruelling miles back to their ship.

There was no guarantee that they would make it back safely. Provisions had run alarmingly low, and Shackleton was acutely aware that exposure, fatigue and exhaustion could have the most dire effect on the strongest-willed men. Nevertheless, he pressed forward without thought for his own physical distress. "I don't know how

S. stands it," wrote Wild as they staggered homeward. "Both his heels are split in four or five places, his legs are bruised and chafed, and today he has had a violent headache through falls, and yet he gets along as well as anyone." Adams also admired their leader's persistence. "The worse he felt, the harder he pulled," he noted.

Two weeks after reaching their farthest-south point, the men were at their lowest ebb. When they ran out of food short of their expected depot, Marshall produced a cocaine preparation he called "Forced March" tablets to give them the energy to push a little farther. Constantly winded and bruised as they fell into crevasses, they dragged themselves along at a funereal pace to the next depot. After resting and gorging, they made it to the Ice Barrier, but again food rations ran low. Wild was unable to eat the sparse leftovers of pemmican and horsemeat and was surviving on biscuit alone. Dangerously weak, he began to collapse in his harness. It was Shackleton who revived him with his own rations, Wild recorded:

> S. privately forced upon me his one breakfast biscuit, and would have given me another tonight had I allowed him. I do not suppose that anyone else in the world can thoroughly realise how much generosity and sympathy was shown by this; I DO and BY GOD I shall never forget. Thousands of pounds would not have bought that one biscuit.

On Shackleton's birthday his three companions pooled the few strands of tobacco they had left to make a thin cigarette as a gift.

At home in England, Emily attempted to distract herself from the anxiety that gnawed away at her during any quiet moment. There would be no peace, no relief, until news came from New Zealand. Finally, on March 23, 1909, Emily was inundated with telegrams, including one in code that had been sent via her brother Herbert:

> Cable from K. Hunter reached Rome. All well Daisy silent
> Say nothing.

The *Nimrod* (Hunter) had reached New Zealand (Rome) safely and the *Daily Mail* (Daisy) had the scoop. Until the news had been printed, Emily must tell no one. Shortly after, a cable arrived from her husband—"Absolutely fit ... Home June"—and another from Shackleton's companions Bernard Day, Ernest Joyce, Raymond Priestley, George Marston and Frank Wild, offering "our heartiest congratulations on the success of your heroic husband and our brave Commander." Emily was elated.

By the smallest of margins, Shackleton and all of his men were safe. Although they had not made it to the South Pole, their expedition had logged a new farthest-south record, had discovered the location of the South Magnetic Pole and had made the first ascent of Mount Erebus. Given that the expedition had no governmental or institutional support, their achievements were all the more commendable. Shackleton was swept into a tour of honour in New Zealand and Australia, giving lectures in Christchurch, Sydney, Melbourne, Adelaide and Perth. He donated his lecture fees to local hospitals. It wasn't until June 12 that he ran down the pier at Dover to be reunited with Emily. It wasn't quite the private moment they both wished for, shared as it was by the mayor, select press and some expedition members. Emily accepted that, from now on, the public would also demand part of her husband.

The following day they drove to a favourite hideaway at Tidebrook, where the couple had forty-eight hours to privately share stories of the last twenty months. According to later recollections by Emily, Shackleton typically made light of the worst parts of the journey, in particular the awful moment when he realized that they must turn back from the Pole. "A live donkey is better than a dead lion, isn't it?" she recalled her husband saying. She remembered responding gently, "Yes, darling, as far as I am concerned."

On the afternoon of June 14, the gates of Charing Cross were closed to prevent the ten-thousand-strong crowd of well-wishers from surging through the station. Waiting on the platform along with Shackleton's father, his sisters, countless relatives and close friends

were little Ray and Cecily, the Shackleton children. Farther down
the platform other people of note had gathered, a handful of whom
had little regard for Shackleton but could not be seen to snub the
man of the hour. Such men included the latest president of the Royal
Geographical Society, Major Leonard Darwin, as well as Sir George
Goldie, J. Scott Keltie and Sir Clements Markham, all of whom had
backed Scott's claim to the base at McMurdo. Prominent among the
crowd was Scott himself, who had gloomily agreed to make a show
of celebrating his former subordinate's achievement; in truth, he saw
Shackleton as the usurper of the accolades Scott believed should have
been his.

"No one who was present," Shackleton's close friend and
biographer Hugh Robert Mill would write, "is ever likely to forget
the roar of cheering from the crowd which filled the Strand and
Trafalgar Square as the open carriage, with Shackleton, his wife and
children, made its way slowly along the streets where no attempt
had been made to keep a passage open, for the police had failed to
foresee this burst of enthusiasm." According to popular reports of
the day, the horses were taken out of their shafts and the carriage
hauled by teams of men through the streets into the city. A hero was
born; Shackleton was at last satisfied. "The loved ones at home were
well, the world was pleased with our work, and it seemed as though
nothing but happiness could ever enter life again."

6

Kathleen Scott

A FATHER FOR MY SON

They were an enchanting crowd,
but I kept my goal, my star, firmly fixed.
None of these was the right,
the perfect father for my son.

KATHLEEN SCOTT

E VEN AS A CHILD Kathleen Bruce had known what she wanted. Her single most important goal in life was to bear a hero son: a boy who would become a great leader and have an extraordinary impact on the world. It naturally followed that, to guarantee such an outcome, she needed to find a man who was up to the task.

It was at a "party of lions" hosted in London by the socialite Mabel Beardsley early in 1907 that Kathleen first met Captain Robert Falcon Scott. Scott had "just returned from a very heroic though rather sensational exploit," Kathleen recorded in her journal, but that was not enough to impress her. Instead, she reported, he was "not very young, perhaps forty, nor very good-looking." His only plus points, it seemed, were that he looked healthy and alert. He, on the other hand, was fascinated by Kathleen. But they had barely exchanged a few words before she made polite excuses and strolled off alone into the night.

Kathleen Bruce was a restless twenty-nine-year-old artist with flashing blue eyes, a Greek-Scottish temperament and an insatiable appetite for vagabonding that compelled her to sleep outdoors whenever possible, even when she was living in a city—a balcony was a prerequisite to any apartment she lived in, whether it be Paris, London or Florence. She lived life robustly. Her charm, gaiety and vigour intoxicated innumerable men and women. She was unlike anyone that Scott had ever encountered.

After the relative success of his *Discovery* expedition, the thirty-six-year-old naval captain turned explorer was embraced by the cultural elite of London. Although he had not attained the South Pole, Scott had achieved a new farthest-south record, and he had returned with a good body of scientific data and some heroic polar stories to boot.

After the relief ship the *Morning* left Antarctica in early 1903, carrying the dejected Shackleton, Scott galvanized his men to undertake an ascent of the Western Mountains and an exploration of the interior of Victoria Land and beyond, with the hope of discovering the South Magnetic Pole. Their journeys started brilliantly. They covered fifty miles in just two and a half days and were in good spirits. But before long, high winds had carried off vital equipment. They rescued their sleeping bags and clothing, but their navigation tables had been swept over the precipitous falls of a glacier. "Now we shall never know where we are," noted Reginald Skelton in his journal. Battling stinging ice storms, the team pressed on. They were forced to dig down into snowdrifts to shelter their tent from the brutal force of the wind. All were suffering from frostbite. For a week they were pinned to the same spot, lying in their sleeping bags for twenty-two hours out of every twenty-four. They called this spot Desolation Camp. They escaped only to encounter treacherous ice and more furious winds. "The wind is the plague of our lives," Scott complained. "It has cut us to pieces. We all have deep cracks in our nostrils and cheeks, and our lips are broken and raw; our fingers are also getting in a shocking state ... There is a good deal of pain also in the tent at night, and we try to keep our faces as still as possible; laughing is a really painful process, and from this point of view jokes are not to be encouraged." As they turned back, Scott wrote:

> Here, then, tonight we have reached the end of our tether, and all we have done is to show the immensity of this vast plain. The scene about us is the same as we have seen for many a day, and shall see for many a day to come—a scene so wildly and awfully desolate that it cannot fail to impress one with gloomy thoughts ...

> We, little human insects, have started to crawl over this awful desert, and are now bent on crawling back again. Could anything be more terrible than this silent, wind-swept immensity when one thinks such thoughts.

Eventually, to the men's untold relief, they made it back to McMurdo. They had almost been entombed by driving snow and had survived both a high-speed descent down a three-hundred-foot drop and a terrifying fall into a crevasse. It was dramatic stories such as these, Kathleen Bruce noted in her journal, that made Scott "subject to the torture of intrusive popularity" on his return to London.

BY THE TIME of her first encounter with Robert Scott, Kathleen Bruce was already an accomplished sculptor. She had studied at the Slade School of Art in London, then moved to Paris to join one of the best salons in Europe. She had a coterie of close friends who, to modern eyes, read like a creative who's who: the renowned sculptor Auguste Rodin; the pioneer of modern dance, Isadora Duncan; J.M. Barrie, the Scottish author who would later write *Peter Pan;* and the playwright George Bernard Shaw, to name but a few. Kathleen was a highly creative, passionate woman, prone to disappearing at a moment's notice: in pursuit of adventure or to escape from boredom or overzealous admirers. Even at a young age she impressed those around her. One of her contemporaries at school remembered Kathleen as being a sturdy, indomitable little figure with bright blue eyes, a mane of thick brown hair and a clear-cut classical profile. There is no doubt that she was attractive, for behind her stretched a wasteland of broken hearts. Yet she was no society beauty. J.M. Barrie was to say of her later that she was half man, half woman, adding that her female half was more of a woman than any other he had met.

Kathleen loved others universally, but modestly, which only increased the longing of those she refused. Frequently she received tear-stained letters from frustrated would-be lovers. On one occasion in Italy she awoke to find that a smitten young English artist had clambered over the Florentine rooftops just to watch her sleeping in the moonlight on the balcony of her small studio. One admirer spent endless nights on a vigil in the street below her window, then pushed ardent poetry under her door. Others simply begged her outright to marry them. "There is no end to your young men," commented a friend. Kathleen agreed, writing later that they all made up "a large and exceedingly varied assortment. They were an enchanting crowd, but I kept my goal, my star, firmly fixed. None of these was the right, the perfect father for my son. None, I feared, could even be trained for the role."

This dream of bearing the perfect son was a constant theme throughout Kathleen's writings. On looking back over her life years later, she painted a nostalgic picture of her fate—a God-given destiny coloured by the devout atmosphere of the convent in which she spent her early years. Some of the girls there worked themselves into such a state of religious overexcitement that they saw visions. Kathleen was no exception:

> To me, a full-hearted child, the little, fat baby once came down from the Madonna's lap and snuggled warmly into my yearning, immature arms. That day I was deified. How could I explain what made me late for the cold, dreary supper? I accepted my rebuke

with a queer, suppressed smile. My little breasts were still warm where the babe had lain. I could still feel his little fingers on my lips.

By the time she experienced this vision, Kathleen had lost her mother, her father, her grandfather, her uncle (the archbishop of York) and the great-uncle who had been her guardian. Out of such profound loss, she grew into a vibrant and joyful woman. Rather than withdrawing into herself, she instead demanded love from all those she met.

Kathleen's family history was colourful and impressive. Her family tree included the fourteenth-century king of Scotland Robert the Bruce and an emperor of Constantinople who ruled in 800 AD and whose son married the illegitimate daughter of the emperor Charlemagne. Her grandmother was the daughter of the last grand Postelnik of Wallachia. Her grandfather, James Henry Skene, was the son of the brilliant watercolourist James Skene of Rubislaw, described by Sir Walter Scott as "the best draughtsman in Scotland."

Kathleen's mother, Janie, was by all accounts a vivacious, artistic and beautiful woman. Janie had at one time been asked by the painter Dante Gabriel Rossetti if she would pose for him. Yet she made what seemed an unsuitable match in the "dull" Reverend Lloyd Bruce in Oxford in 1863. Janie cared little what her family thought, however, and she threw herself wholeheartedly into starting a family of her own, giving birth to six children—including two sets of twins—within just three and a half years. Understandably exhausted, she then had a complete collapse. The diet for her recovery alternated champagne (six times daily) with turtle soup, chicken broth, beef tea, and arrowroot with milk. The doctor advised that she was suffering from hysteria, and that the remedy was for her to have more babies, which she promptly did. Edith Agnes Kathleen Bruce, born on March 27, 1878, was her eleventh child. Janie was blind by the time of Kathleen's birth, and on October 1, 1880, aged forty-two, she died of chronic nephritis. By the time Kathleen was seven, her father too was dead. For the remainder of her childhood and adolescence, she was passed from one aging relative to another.

IT WAS 1901, and Queen Victoria had just passed away. Yet according to Kathleen Bruce, the late queen's "parasol of propriety still shaded the eyes of most well-bred young ladies from the too strong rays of the sunshine of life." Like many of her artistic contemporaries, twenty-three-year-old Kathleen longed to wrap herself in the warmth of creativity and adventure, and she saw Paris as sunshine itself. The French capital was a hub of bohemianism. "The life of the young artist here," wrote the satirist William Makepeace Thackeray, "is the easiest, merriest, dirtiest existence possible."

Those who met Kathleen were immediately impressed by her quirks of character and open nature. Auguste Rodin became her friend and mentor. "The main thing," he told her, "is to be moved, to love, to hope, to tremble, to live." Kathleen valued Rodin's compliments about her work and treasured his letters to her. The master sculptor had a long history of love affairs with his students, but Kathleen valued her new-found independence and was fixated on being a virgin bride to the man who would eventually father her son.

The only time Kathleen was in danger of falling in love was when she met the enigmatic American photographer Edward Steichen, whom Rodin would later call the "greatest photographer of the time." Their "relationship" was conducted in silence in a cheap Parisian café where they both ate regularly. Always sitting two tables apart, Kathleen and Steichen mirrored each other perfectly: two talented, charismatic artists living and studying in unfamiliar territory, neither daring to engage with the other. It was deliciously agonizing. The longings of five months climaxed in nothing more than a kiss the night before Steichen returned to the United States. According to Kathleen, it was "the first event of my prudent little life." She was twenty-four. "The odd thing is that it was all I wanted," she wrote. "I was glad, exhilarated, with the knowledge that he was going away... For four stormy years I was faithful to that hour."

ROBERT FALCON SCOTT, or Con, as friends and family called him, was a very different animal from the creative, experimental Steichen.

Since the age of thirteen, when he was sent by his father to join the naval training ship *Britannia* in Dartmouth, Scott's life had been fully bound up with the navy. His schooling consisted of lessons in navigation, astronomy, geometry, trigonometry and discipline. Order and obeisance to his superiors were his guiding principles. Holidays spent at the family home of Oatlands in Devon came as happy pauses in an otherwise austere regime. As a boy, Scott showed few outward signs of ambition. He was conscientious and wanted to do well, but heroics were not a natural part of his character. A financial crisis at home was the catalyst that drove him forward.

Although Scott's grandfather and uncles had all served in the forces, his father, John, had escaped a military career, and instead had inherited the task of running a brewery in Plymouth. In 1894, when Robert Scott was twenty-six, his mother, Hannah, announced to the family that they were on the verge of bankruptcy. Three years later Scott's father died, leaving them penniless. By the age of twenty-nine, with both his father and his only brother dead, Scott was the sole financial and emotional anchor for his mother and sisters. It was vital that he find a project that would both secure a financial reward and increase his sense of self-worth.

The perfect assignment seemed to find him. While home on leave in June 1899, Scott bumped into Sir Clements Markham, then president of the Royal Geographical Society, whom Scott had met some time before in the West Indies while on naval duty. Markham was impressed with Scott's intelligence and charm, and on meeting him again he told Scott about a prospective Antarctic expedition. Not long after, Scott was awarded the position of commander.

As noted, the *Discovery* expedition was heralded as a great success. The Ross Sea was explored; land to the east was sighted for the first time and claimed for King Edward VII; the Polar Plateau was discovered; and a new farthest-south record was achieved when Scott and Wilson reached 82°17' S.

While Scott was on the second phase of the *Discovery* expedition, Kathleen Bruce was engaged in her own adventures. It was 1903, and she had spent two years in Paris. Her work had been accepted by the Salon; she had experienced opium dens and overcome her queasiness at the sight of male nude models. Playful and headstrong, Kathleen felt as though her life was positively bursting with experience. Then Noel Edward Buxton, a young English politician and friend of her brother Rosslyn, turned her world upon its head. Kathleen, he told her bluntly, was wasting her time.

Buxton had visited Kathleen at her small studio and, during their conversation, begun talking passionately about the troubles in the Balkans. Earlier that year, Macedonia, and the town of Kruševo in particular, had become the site of an intense rebellion against the Ottoman Empire. On the night of August 2, 1903, at the signal of the Internal Macedonian Odrin Revolutionary Organization, the people had taken up arms. With assistance from thirty thousand armed rebels, the whole territory divided into rebel regions, and by the end of August the rebel offensive had liberated several hundred villages and small towns.

Kruševo, liberated on August 3, became the first socialist republic in the Balkans. It lasted just nine days. Quickly under siege by a vast army of Turkish soldiers and Bashi Bazouks, the town could not withstand the artillery bombardment, and the rebels surrendered. Within three months the uprising had been suppressed, and the people of Macedonia were plunged into a period of terror, slaughter and starvation. Kathleen listened wide-eyed to it all. "The plight of the people there is unspeakable," said the young politician. "Babies are being born quite untended, that nobody wants, and quite unprovided for; terrible cases." The next day she locked her studio door and rushed to England to volunteer.

Not long after, Kathleen was on her way to Salonika under the guidance of the austere and aging widow Lady Thompson. At Monastir they were met by the charismatic agent of the Macedonia Relief Fund, Henry Brailsford, and his wife, Jane. Together they headed out into the worst-stricken areas.

To begin with, Kathleen regarded their journey as a jolly adventure. The party passed a burned-out village where refugees held up their babies to be carried to safety: "All swaddled, they felt like brown paper parcels when one took them." At night the group lit cigarettes to frighten away any packs of wolves.

Eventually the travellers found themselves in the mountain village of Kastoria. Here, on a hillside overlooking a picturesque lake, they set up a small and simple hospital with the help of some French Sisters of Mercy from Salonika. The spectacular scenery gave Kathleen little indication of the horrors they would soon face. On December 21, she treated a woman with a bleeding cancer on her breast and tried to calm a girl who had been locked in a cellar by her grandmother to hide her from the soldiers and had gone mad alone in the darkness. Another girl sat inconsolable at the window, crying for the Turk who had raped her.

Rape was widespread, and madness brought on by the horror of conflict commonplace. Villages had been razed, and lawlessness and disease were rife. Peasants who had fled into the mountains to escape the skirmishes were forced back down the hills by hard weather and arrived at the camp with livid, gangrenous wounds. Ghastly operations were done without anaesthetic. Kathleen's self-appointed job was to sit by those whose death was unavoidable and imminent:

> Here I learnt calmness and lack of dread of death... In very few cases was the fearful death rattle I had heard of... Only once did I falter. The dying patient was a boy of about fourteen, with large brown eyes like a racoon, and tousled black hair. He clung to my hand with a strength that made me hope that they were wrong in abandoning him, and that he might not be dying... And then, very suddenly, with his eyes still open, he stopped breathing.

Kathleen's faith, which had been waning, "went out with a spirt." On Christmas Day she walked past fifteen corpses shrivelled and unburied on a hillside. Five days later she wrote, "Even the children's faces seem wrinkled with a chronic shiver. Women tell one their horrible tales, but one has heard them before. Little boys look starved, but one knows they are starved. Old, old priests tell how they have

been beaten, but others have been beaten. Our whole being is pity."
Leaving the French Sisters in charge of the hospital, Kathleen and
Lady Thompson began a tour of the most distressed areas, along
with a group of mounted soldiers. Travelling through wild and
mountainous country, they were confronted with more horrors and
anguish.

There was no escape from the dirt and sickness, and Kathleen's
way of coping with it was to work even harder, never sparing herself.
One day as she walked by the lake, she discovered a leg and two arms
that had been severed from a body and lay "stretched like the three
fingers of a great starfish." The country was not only gripped with
the horror of endless fighting; it was fiercely cold. Kathleen wore
five layers of wool and at night slept in a sleeping bag covered by two
blankets, a fur coat, two golf capes and a fur throw, with hot-water
bottles alongside. Still she found no warmth.

After months of this new gruelling life, Kathleen visited a distant
village which had been struck with a particularly virulent form of
typhoid fever. Shortly after, she noticed an alarming rash on her body.
She wrote: "I don't want to die out here . . . I say 'die' because I could
not be ill out here and not die, of that I am convinced." A few days
later, on yet another journey, the party was struck by a ferocious
storm: "Snow! It was rather great slabs of frozen horror that hit you
in the face and cut. It blinded and choked me and made me so numbed
I was incapable of resisting the infuriated gallop of my little animal,
who sought to extricate himself from the horror that surrounded
him. This lasted for miles, over horrid ridges, streams, boulders,
everything." The following day she fell desperately ill. She ran a
fever and started hemorrhaging.

For what seemed like an eternity, Kathleen lay in a squalid
garret, desperately lonely and frightened, unable to speak or move,
often delirious, with rats scurrying across the foot of her bed.
Occasionally she was clear-headed enough to hear the Greek doctor
from the hospital or the Turkish district doctor murmuring that she
would surely die. Lady Thompson had no time to care for her ailing

companion, and so Kathleen was left in the gentle care of Nico, a middle-aged Greek carpenter who understood no English and just a smattering of French.

Just when it seemed as though all hope for Kathleen's recovery was lost, Jane Brailsford reappeared and immediately took charge. She procured clean bed linen, gently washed her patient and slept in the same room when the delirium was bad. Kathleen was suffering from a malignant form of influenza with symptoms like typhoid's; without proper care, the disease often resulted in death.

One of the French Sisters of Mercy was also very sick, and she was to be transported to Salonika. Although Kathleen was not really well enough to travel, she half sat, half lay in an "antidiluvian cacique" as it battled through a snowstorm, trying to ignore the constant moans of her companion. Eventually she made it to Naples and found solace and health in Capri before touring Italy.

Italy—in particular Florence—was a godsend after Kathleen's tough experiences in Macedonia. She rented a small apartment on the Via dei Bardi and discovered new friends who reignited her passion for art. It was an intoxicating time: "I found bathing parties, dances, revels and copious sunshine. Health came back by leaps and bounds. There were queer and ugly things in Paris. There were ugly and terrifying things in Macedonia. Here, to me at any rate, all seemed as spontaneous as a Botticelli picture." By the time she returned to Paris, she looked more like a sun-gilded Amazon than a typhoid convalescent.

While Kathleen was regaining her strength in the sun, Scott was being feted in London. He received medals from numerous geographical societies around the world, was given an honorary doctorate of science from Cambridge and was made a member of the French Legion of Honour. He took an extended leave from the navy, during which time he planned to write a book and give a lecture tour. As polar explorer of the moment he was welcomed into the elite salons of London, to balls, dinners and parties, and he relished his new-found celebrity so much that he was caricatured unflatteringly as a dandy by "Spy" in *Vanity Fair*. Scott's social horizons opened to a vibrant arena filled with artists, writers and politicians. Unwittingly, he had entered Kathleen's world.

AT THE TIME she met Scott, Kathleen was happily enjoying her freedom. She had admirers of all nationalities, but she was yet to find the man she was looking for. "It was odd," she wrote later, "my son didn't seem to mean anything at all to any of them . . . 'Vraiment, ma petite,' they said, 'tu es difficile.'" (Truly, my little one, you are difficult.) Her response was to become absorbed in a whirl of social engagements in both Paris and London. Among her regular haunts was the drawing room of Mabel Beardsley, who had been a friend since Kathleen's days at the Slade and was the sister of the celebrated artist Aubrey Beardsley. Scandalously, Mabel was said to have given birth to her brother's love child as a result of a prolonged incestuous relationship. Kathleen did not balk at such infamy but rather enjoyed the way it coloured her own life by proxy. It was Mabel who brought Kathleen and Scott together for a second time at another of her soirees in 1907. Kathleen, confessing to her diary that "the like of [Scott] should not go to tea parties," nevertheless reviewed her scant wardrobe and, sitting barefoot on her bed in her nightgown, created a new hat for the occasion by cutting up two old ones with a pair of nail scissors and sticking them back together with pins.

Like all of Mabel's parties, the gathering consisted largely of well-known artists, dramatists and actors, several of whom Kathleen already knew. Scott was sitting in the back drawing-room in conversation with an elderly lady. "What an unexpected setting for a simple, austere naval officer!" Kathleen later wrote. Yet this time something about him intrigued her. After the gathering had been entertained "by the gay comedy of Ernest Thesiger and the heavy disdain of Henry James," Scott appeared at her side. Years later, she remembered the moment:

> Then all of a sudden, and I did not know how, I was sitting in a
> stiff, uncomfortable chair with an ill-balanced cup of tea, and

being trivially chaffed by this very well-dressed, rather ugly and celebrated explorer. He was standing over me. He was of medium height, with broad shoulders, very small waist, and dull hair beginning to thin, but with a rare smile, and with eyes of quite unusually dark blue, almost purple. I had noticed those eyes ten months before. I noticed them again now, although by electric light. I had never seen their like. He suggested taking me home.

Kathleen threw over another dinner engagement she had planned in Soho and strode home with Scott, "laughing and talking and jostling each other, as we lunged along the river-side in hilarious high spirits." For the next ten days they spent almost every waking moment together. When they were apart Scott would try to telephone her, and then send love notes to ask her out again: "Dinner and the play, dinner and no play, anything you like but do let me come and carry you off." In response she wrote: "To know only the joy of going forward, only the joy of going forward. It's madness, and I cling to my madness and revel in it . . . Pick up the joy. I have such faith, joy and life and love."

When Scott was called back to his naval duties, Kathleen sat as a model for the Royal Academy artist Charles Shannon. The hours of enforced silence gave her the chance to turn things over in her mind. She wondered whether she could wrench herself from her "tumultuous friends and take this innocent rock as the father of my son for whom I had been searching." The artist, unused to Kathleen being so preoccupied, complained at last: "You don't love me at all today." Kathleen responded that she had just decided she would marry Captain Scott. Shannon promptly left the studio and walked under a bus—not intentionally, nor fatally, but it confirmed Kathleen's fears that there would be "a lot of upheavals and severing . . . looming ahead." However, it was quite clear to her that "this healthy, fresh, decent, honest, rock-like naval officer was just exactly what I had been setting up in my mind as a contrast to my artist friends, as the thing I had been looking for." Kathleen, at last, had found her star.

7

Marie Herbert

ON TOP OF THE WORLD

Every day with Wally felt like holiday.

MARIE HERBERT

"I CAN STILL REMEMBER the future picture I had of myself on Christmas Eve 1969—the day I married a polar explorer," Marie Herbert wrote in her journal inside a small hunter's hut in northwest Greenland: "A devoted wife vicariously following her husband's hazardous journeys through his dispatches, which would arrive smudged and battered, having travelled perhaps for thousands of miles in a sledge bag before they could be posted at some remote settlement in the frozen North." Marie smiled as she looked out through the small window across the barren icescape bristling with arthritic-looking meat racks. It was ninety miles across a frozen fjord and a wind-whipped glacier to the nearest postbox, a journey not to be taken lightly. Any letters home to family and friends would take a while to arrive.

Marie McGaughey had first heard of Wally Herbert when she saw an article about him in the *Sunday Times* on July 9, 1967, entitled "The Longest, Loneliest Walk in the World." The paper reported: "Four men and four teams of huskies will set out this winter on the last great polar trek—3,800 miles on foot across the frozen Arctic Ocean from the north Alaskan coast to the Norwegian island of Spitsbergen." Marie barely read the first paragraph before putting the newspaper aside, wondering why anyone would be interested in snow and ice.

MARIE, THE YOUNGEST of five children, was born in Dublin on May 25, 1941, to Tom Walpole and his wife, Alice. Tom, twenty-one years older than his wife, was from a well-to-do Catholic family and owned a thriving painting and decorating business. Marie's family lived in a large, elegantly furnished house and wished for nothing. Then everything changed. With war threatening Europe, no new business was coming in. Before long, Tom had to let all his men go. Shortly after, he was bankrupt. With no work in Ireland, he was forced to take a labouring job in Liverpool. It was a heartbreaking drop in status, and the work was brutally hard given his age, but there was no choice.

Within a year, the family was in dire straits. Tom had been injured falling off scaffolding and was unable to send money home. Alice could barely afford to feed her children, and they were forced to move to a basement flat on the outskirts of Dublin. Plaster peeled from the walls. One room was so damp and covered in mould that it was unusable. The whole family slept in one room.

It was not just Alice and Tom who were suffering from the effects of the war. All over Ireland families were in dire predicaments. Alice, even though she had barely anything to offer, opened her home and her heart to those worst affected. Her children were increasingly undernourished. Marie, by now aged three, was still being breastfed.

As their situation worsened, a relative heard that the family was in a desperate state and called the authorities. Alice was accused by extended family members of being "criminally generous." A few days later her children were told to present themselves to the children's hospital and orphanage. If they refused to do so, their mother would be put in prison. While Alice desperately tried to overturn the judgment of the authorities, the barefoot children slowly made their way to the gates of the hospital. It was the last time that Marie saw or heard of her family for many years. Unlike her siblings, who stayed in Ireland, Marie was adopted by a cousin who had married a widower with six sons. She joined her new family in Cambridge before being taken to Ceylon (now Sri Lanka) where her new father, Charles McGaughey, was to inaugurate the chair of veterinary science at the University of Peradeniya.

Marie's childhood, scarred by grief at the loss of her family and the often cruel authority of her adopted mother, found a happier balance when, at the age of twelve, she was sent to a convent school in the wild, verdant hills of Tamil Nadu in India. The next few years were on the whole joy-filled. Most of Marie's friends were from a privileged background. Several were princesses. Marie made up for any deficiency in status by carving a niche for herself as an all-round entertainer. If she wasn't spontaneously performing music hall songs, she was terrifying her school friends with ghost stories in the dormitory as hyenas cackled in the distance.

Marie's natural exuberance and theatricality found a more focussed outlet when she was accepted at the Central School of Speech and Drama in London in 1958. But although she completed the course, the singing and stage career she had hoped for did not materialize. She escaped to Copenhagen for six months, working as an English correspondent for an advertising firm. There, friends showed her a pair of polar-bear breeches, explaining they were used by hunters when dog-sledging. "You know, Marie," one friend said prophetically, "you love nature so much, you should go to Greenland. You would adore it." Marie laughed and replied, "I can assure you that is the last place in the world that I will ever get to."

Like many young actresses and singers, Marie endured a run of temporary jobs, including a position at the Prince Galitzine public relations company in London. The morning after reading about

Wally's proposed expedition, Marie arrived at work to be greeted by the prince. Smiling, he told her that if she would like to accept it, the company had a permanent post for her. Furthermore, for the next six months, the agency was to become the headquarters of an innovative Arctic expedition. The leader of the expedition, Wally Herbert, would be arriving the next day.

After reading the *Times* article properly, Marie was intrigued. The expedition intended to make a crossing of the Arctic Ocean along its longest axis, via the North Pole and the Pole of Inaccessibility—the point farthest from land in any direction. For a year and a half, Wally Herbert, Allan Gill, Dr. Roy "Fritz" Koerner, Dr. Ken Hedges and their teams of huskies would live on and travel across the world's most unstable terrain. The Arctic Ocean, Marie read, was a constantly moving, fracturing surface. At times it could split silently, leaving dark welts of open water, leads that were impossible to cross; at other times, the ice was forced up into chaotic, mountainous pressure ridges. Not only would the team have to endure continuous temperatures of well below -50°C, but for several months they would also have to cope with the twenty-four-hour darkness of the long polar night. Marie wondered what kind of man could possibly conceive of such a dangerous mission.

Good-looking, with intense, compact energy, Wally Herbert was like no other man Marie had ever met. "You could almost see the far horizon in his beautiful hazel eyes," she later recalled. For the next few weeks she made every excuse to see the explorer. Her role as researcher for the firm gave her a head start. Her first priority was to learn more about the leader of the expedition.

Like Marie, Wally Herbert had an itinerant childhood. Born in York on October 24, 1934, to a soldier and a country girl, he had been taken to live in Egypt at age three. Shortly after the outbreak of the Second World War, Wally, his baby sister, Kath, and his mother, Helen, were evacuated, put ashore in South Africa and told to fend for themselves until the war was over. For the next few years, they lived a strangely dislocated existence. Wally and Kath did not meet their father again until after the war had ended.

Almost every male member of Wally's family over the past four hundred years had served in the forces. Naturally he was expected to follow suit. At seventeen, Wally joined the army. It was, his family convinced him, the only way that he could ever fulfill his dream of becoming an explorer. Escorted to the recruitment office by his father and two uncles, Wally was signed up for twenty-two years. But army life did not suit him. After discovering a loophole in his contract, Wally left. He had been in the army for three years, had been posted to Egypt and Kenya and had had the very best training as a military surveyor. Aged twenty, he hitchhiked back to England from Egypt via Cyprus, drawing portraits for his board and lodging and, as often as not, sleeping rough under the stars. Just a year later he was making his way to the Antarctic as a surveyor for the Falkland Islands Dependencies Survey.

With the exploits of Shackleton, Scott and Roald Amundsen still in living memory, Wally felt a powerful connection with the past. The bases and huts built by his childhood heroes were still intact. Over the next two and a half years, he travelled over three thousand miles using dog teams: breaking trail for his companions, pioneering new routes and creating maps of many thousands of square miles of virgin territory. Completely at ease in the polar environment, he became known for his unbounded enthusiasm for life and work. On one occasion he learned that two colleagues were going to travel to a far-distant hut to make observations. It was, they told him gravely, a hazardous journey that would test the mettle of any who attempted it. Wally commiserated with them, shook their hands and wished them a safe journey. A couple of days later, as the two men closed in on their destination, they were certain that they could see a figure through the blizzard, waving outside the hut. Exhausted from the challenging terrain and treacherous conditions, they thought they must be hallucinating. As they arrived Wally opened the door, beaming. "Thought you might be hungry," he shouted over the wind, "so I have put some hot food on for you."

When his initiation into the Antarctic was over, Wally hitchhiked home. His route took him through Argentina and Bolivia to Peru,

Ecuador and Colombia, then on through the United States and
Canada. Arriving in England 13,500 miles of adventures later, he
embarked on an exhaustive lecture tour, joined an expedition to
Spitsbergen, then again returned to the Antarctic. In total, he spent
five summers and three winters there, mapping over 44,000 square
miles of new territory. He was the first to summit Mount Nansen;
he ascended the Beardmore Glacier and descended the route taken
by Amundsen on the fiftieth anniversary of his dash to the South
Pole. Denied a request to proceed to the Pole by the American
base commander there, Wally turned his attention next to the
Arctic, spending nine months with the most northerly tribe of Inuit
in Greenland. He retraced the routes of Cook and Sverdrup on
Ellesmere Island in preparation for his new goal, to cross the Arctic
Ocean via the North Pole. "This man," Marie noted with admiration,
"had lived several lifetimes before he was even thirty."

After orchestrating several "chance" encounters with the explorer,
Marie was finally asked out for a drink. She was enthralled. "I was
awed by his vision, amused by the particular slant of his humour,
captivated by his stories, and moved by his sense of mission. Within
two weeks, I was convinced that he was the only man I could live
with for the rest of my life."

In December 1967, Wally left for Alaska. He and Marie had not
discussed how things might be when he got back. "He was to be
away for a year and a half. It was a long time to keep the threads of a
relationship intact, but I took comfort from the fact that there were no
women on the Arctic Ocean. Our relationship would literally remain
on ice, and I found the idea fresh, exciting, and at times intoxicating."

THE BRITISH TRANS-ARCTIC EXPEDITION got off to a slow start.
The wife of Fritz Koerner, the only married man on the team, was
about to give birth, and Wally naturally would not expect Koerner
to set off before he knew mother and baby were well. Ahead of them
too was a belt of mush ice fifty miles wide. The fast-moving mush
ice, the consistency of porridge, would not hold the weight of a single dog, let alone four men, their teams of dogs and heavily weighted

sledges. There was nothing they could do but wait until the ice conditions improved enough for them to reach the stronger polar pack ice. Finally, Wally made a reconnaissance flight:

> The vast expanse of drifting ice was awesome—limitless... Cracks and open leads caught the sun like molten silver and darted around on the surface of the pack before turning into jet black scars that marked the blue-grey skin of the frozen sea. It was a moment of profound relief—the moment of decision. Tomorrow, the team would set out on a journey from which there could be no turning back.

Their beds, most nights, would be on ice which might split at any time or buckle into vast pressure ridges. Over the next sixteen months they would encounter 21,000 such ridges. There would not be a single day when the floes over which they travelled were not drifting with the currents or driven by the winds: "There would be no end to the movement; no rest, no landfall, no sense of achievement, no peace of mind, until we reached Spitsbergen. Most importantly: there was no possibility whatsoever of rescue."

Their last night at Point Barrow was one Wally would remember for the rest of his life: "It felt like the eve of a battle—still, clear, cold, silent, with no one sleeping; an atmosphere heavy with private thoughts... I was physically sick with fear, and the weight of the trust that my three companions had in me. Which of these two was the greater, I do not know." The following morning, on February 21, 1968, the men headed north.

For the next few weeks they were in constant danger. With only the glow of the northern lights or moonlight to travel by, they hacked their way through pressure ridges and pushed their sledges over creaking pans of ice barely thick enough to support their weight. Then, at the beginning of September, disaster struck. While running beside his sledge, Allan Gill fell and hurt his back. It was diagnosed as a slipped disc. Hedges advised that Gill should be evacuated. It would be an opportunity also for Hedges to leave; with no previous polar experience to speak of, he had found the expedition harder mentally and physically than he could ever have expected, and he was desperate to return home. Gill, for his part, insisted that with rest he would heal perfectly well. This, combined with the extreme danger involved for any pilot who attempted a landing and takeoff in such unpredictable ice conditions, convinced Wally that they should make an early winter camp on a stable ice floe and that Gill would stay.

His decision caused a furor in London. The expedition committee backed the decision of the doctor, rather than the expedition leader. It was a breach of convention, equivalent to overruling the decision of the captain of a ship in favour of one of his officers, and a breach that any experienced polar explorer would contest. Wally was at his wits' end. Thinking that he was on a closed line during his daily radio contact with Squadron Leader Freddie Church—the radio operator and fifth member of the expedition—he privately complained that "the committee don't know what the bloody hell they are talking about." A journalist overheard the conversation and printed his outburst in the *Sunday Times*. The reaction was swift and explosive and made headline news. The committee publicly criticized Wally's decision and threatened to end all practical support for the expedition. From this moment on, Wally would be solely responsible for any action the team would take.

By the time the men saw the first signs of returning light, Gill had recovered. The group had spent the long dark winter camped at latitude 85° north, and during that time they collected vital scientific data. The winter had by no means been uneventful. Vast pressure ridges sometimes seemed to march out of the darkness toward them, toppling gigantic boulders of ice that could swallow man and beast in a heartbeat. On February 24, 1969, the camp was in critical danger. The floe suddenly "cracked up like an eggshell," and the whole area began to gyrate. The nearest fracture in the ice was just three yards from their hut. In the semi-darkness, they abandoned the hut, rescuing provisions, equipment and dogs as they went. Later Wally recalled that they felt like refugees escaping into the darkness.

Navigating by the moon and stars they continued, reaching the North Pole on April 6, 1969. Remarkably, it was the sixtieth anniversary of the day Robert Peary claimed to have reached that same desolate spot. The elation the men should have felt was tempered with exhaustion. Every direction from there was south, but still they had a very long way to go.

Back home in England, Marie had been carefully watching reports of their progress. On May 29, to her delight and relief, she heard that against all odds, and after many more challenges, the expedition had successfully reached Spitsbergen. But the success of the expedition would never be fully recognized. Some members of the expedition committee ensured that publicity for the returning men was kept at a minimum. Even more significant was the unfortunate timing of the moon landing, which coincided with their return. The expedition was in danger of being forgotten even before the men arrived home. Knowing that Wally would need all the support she could muster, Marie telephoned the *Endurance,* the Royal Navy ship which had picked the team up off the ice at the end of the expedition, to speak to Wally and congratulate him. The officers on the ship crowed with disbelief when they heard Marie's plan to meet Wally at the quay. They warned the expedition team that they must not see the girls they had left behind on their first night in port; otherwise, they would find themselves married within three months.

On Christmas Eve 1969 Wally and Marie were married in London. Wally had proposed just two days earlier, but he was not the sort of man to dally once a decision had been made. The press were waiting for them as they walked smiling out of the Chelsea Registry Office. Marie looked stunning in a fur parka Wally had brought back from Canada, worn over the shortest possible duck-egg-blue cashmere minidress and white knee-high boots. Clasped in her hands was a posy of Arctic poppies.

THE FOLLOWING YEAR, just hours after my birth, Wally suggested that our family travel to the Far North to live with a small tribe of

Inuit. For the next two years, he enthused, we could immerse our-selves in the fast-changing culture of this hunting community. Marie was amazed. At no time had she expected to join her husband on his polar expeditions. She was delighted to have been asked, but was understandably nervous now that they had a newborn to look after. Wally reassured her that the Inuit had been rearing children for gen-erations and would surely help.

Over the next ten months, Wally and Marie plowed all their energy into preparing for the expedition. Wally advised Marie on the art of writing sponsorship letters for the supplies they needed. They wanted to avoid being a burden on the community, so everything had to be taken with them. Orders were sent out in quick succession for special clothing, food and camera equipment. Heinz donated one ton of baby food. The British Wool Bureau provided clothing, and the British Sugar Bureau donated tins of treacle. They had cases of tea, a wealth of dried vegetables and meat, boxes of Cadbury's chocolate and, most importantly for Wally, a stockpile of tobacco for his pipe. It was only when they were on the ship heading north that Marie began to feel anxious, and by then it was too late to change her mind.

By the time the three of us arrived at the small settlement of Qeqer-tasuaq, a group of villagers had gathered, curious to get a glimpse of the young white family that was going to live among them. They mur-mured to each other as the boat neared the rocky shoreline, and Marie suddenly felt terribly uncertain about the whole endeavour. Then the group caught sight of the child in her arms. As she later recalled: "A chorus of exclamations and friendly laughs filled the air. As I looked for a footing on the slimy green rocks, a young woman stepped down to steady me. I handed baby Kari to her, and several pairs of hands reached down to take her to safer ground. For a couple of minutes we all stood grinning at each other, rather embarrassed. A little circle had gathered round the woman holding Kari while she gurgled apprecia-tively. The ice was broken and I knew that I would be happy there."

The islanders immediately took us to their hearts. While one of the older women, Savfak, invited us to her home for tea, oth-ers swept our hut, collected coal and ice, and lit the stove. Our fourteen-by-eleven-foot hut was normally used by visiting hunters, but the community had agreed we could rent it for a modest sum for the duration of our stay. It needed attention. The windows were cracked and greasy, dried blood and blubber stained the floor and walls, decaying walrus heads clung to the roof, and a grimy dog skin was pinned to the outhouse. Like most of the other wooden homes in the settlement, the hut had just two rooms: a small, squalid area in which to cook and a slightly larger room with a wooden platform that served as both seat and bed. There was no bathroom or toilet, no electricity or running water. Ice chipped from freshwater icebergs would have to be collected daily for cooking and washing.

We gradually adjusted to the new way of living. While my mother and I stayed mostly within the community, my father would often accompany the hunters on long sledging journeys to find game. Every day I played with our neighbours' children and was soon learning words in Inuktun, the local dialect of Greenlandic. Much to my parents' discomfort I began calling our neighbours Avatak and Maria "Atata" and "Anana"—Mum and Dad in Greenlandic.

In no time Marie had grown accustomed to the daily routine. Along with collecting ice for water, our sealskin boots, or kamiks, had to be taken apart and hung up every evening; tundra grass had to be collected, dried and then stuffed evenly between the inner "sock" and the boot itself for insulation. There was a never-ending stream of visitors to entertain and visits to be made—such social calls were the heartbeat of the community.

As the twilight hours grew longer with each passing day, Marie wondered how she would cope with four months of constant darkness. Collecting ice in the dark could be treacherous, particularly when running a gauntlet of dog teams. One night, after some persuasion, she poured out her worries to Wally. He listened patiently, then presented her with a solution to each fear. That night she found a note from him on her pillow:

For Marie from your loving husband—regarding the coming of winter's darkness:

"Ghaist nor bogle shalt thou fear;
Thou'st to Love and Heaven sae dear,
Nocht of ill may come thee near,
My bonnie dearie."

The winter and early spring were the best time for sledging journeys. The ice was strong, and on moonlit nights it could be surprisingly
bright. Although it was more usual for men to travel long distances
alone, on occasions we would travel as a family. But almost every journey together entailed drama. Our neighbour Maria delighted in telling
my mother stories of near-scrapes she and her children had had with
Avatak. On one journey Maria had been under a cliff when there was a
sudden avalanche. It missed her and the children but formed an enormous wall of snow between them and Avatak. It seemed impossible
that they could have survived. Overcome with grief, Avatak sat on
his sledge and wept. When Maria and the children managed to burrow
their way out and appeared a few yards ahead of him, he was astonished. Perhaps they were apparitions of his lost loved ones. Maria's
teasing soon reassured him, for no angel would speak that way.

In the spring, Marie and Wally prepared to take a trip to the U.S.
air base at Thule to collect their friend Geoff Renner, who planned
to join them for a couple of months. The ninety-mile journey, which
would take them over the 2,500-foot Politiken Glacier, could be
treacherous even for the most experienced polar travellers. I was left
with Avatak and Maria on Herbert Island, where I would be safe and
well looked after.

Once they had reached the base of the glacier, Marie put on a
customary brew of tea while Wally reconnoitred the route. The
glacier was a towering slick of turquoise-dappled ice—recent storms
had scoured the surface and blown away almost all the snow cover.
As they crossed the rubble of the grubby moraine and mounted
the first great tier of the glacier, Marie stepped over a thick coil of
scorched rope left behind by previous travellers. "Whew! Look what
the friction's done to that!" whistled Wally. "What friction?" she

asked. "That's a rope brake," he explained. "You throw them over the runner to slow the sledge down. But that sledge must have been coming down so fast it burned right through the rope!"

In places an ice axe was the only way to gouge clefts in the ice to scramble over. My parents struggled as much as the dogs did to get their heavy sledge to the top, climbing the four mammoth tiers of the glacier with the dogged hope that each one was the last. Dogs and sledge frequently slithered backwards. After reaching the summit, Marie was horrified when she looked down at the way they had just come.

After descending the other side of the glacier, then crossing a frozen river and many miles of sea ice, Wally and Marie were warmly welcomed at the American air base. The extravagance of it all was a world away from life back on the island. That evening, much to Wally's embarrassment and delight, a skimpily dressed young entertainer dedicated a dance to him at the officers' club. Amid the backslapping jollity was an edge of concern: a storm was likely to hit in twenty-four hours. Fearing they could be stuck at the base for several days, Wally decided they should ride ahead of the storm. As soon as Renner arrived, they set off for Herbert Island.

Before long, the party could see dark clouds gathering behind them. Then the blizzard hit. The katabatic winds howled off the rock faces and cut their faces. The snow disoriented and gagged them. "With each breath I felt my lungs choked," my mother later recalled. "All sound was muffled. We slid through the world like phantom figures driving a white hearse. The dogs all looked the same, transformed by the snow." It was impossible to rig a tent, so they had to nail it flat to the ice and crawl in between the layers. Marie took refuge as best she could while the men made the dogs and sledges safe. It was only when the men finally crawled into the shelter that Marie could judge the extent of the danger they were in. Both men wore thick masks of ice. Wally had only one small hole under each nostril through which to breathe. It had been, they confessed, like being slowly buried. Later they discovered that the wind recorded at the nearby air base had been the second-highest recorded on the face of the earth at that time: 207 miles per hour.

Their descent of the glacier was by far the worst part of the journey. The ice had been burnished by the wind, and it was almost impossible to stay upright. Wally took the lead, treading carefully before the dogs. Then there was a sudden shout. "In the thick haze," Marie recalled, "I saw that Wally's feet sank from under him, while his head just missed the sledge runner as it shot past him." In a flash the ground fell away, and Marie, Geoff and the sledge hurtled down the spine of the glacier. Wally hurled himself on the nearest runner, clawing the ground with his feet to break the momentum, risking breaking his back if he let go. "Another rope! Quick!" he shouted. The dogs slithered and fell, and every second the sledge got closer to mowing them down. Eventually the men managed to swerve the sledge sideways into a hollow, where everyone collapsed, badly shaken.

The wind was unrelenting. The whiteout made it impossible to recognize any familiar features, and they were in danger of slipping into a crevasse field. Fearing that they were on the wrong part of the glacier, Wally went on ahead to find a safe route. Unable to keep his footing, he was hurled to the ground and blown across the surface like a rag doll. Marie watched in horror as he scrambled to his knees, then was knocked sideways and blown completely out of sight, his arms and legs flailing as he flew horizontally about a foot above the surface. Marie and Geoff eventually made it to Wally to find him with a dislocated shoulder and a sprained wrist. Amazingly, nothing had been broken.

It was an agonizing few hours. Marie watched as Wally battled wind and ice to get them safely off the glacier. Again and again, he staggered forwards like a punch-drunk boxer, only to be knocked to the ground. By the time they reached the bottom of the glacier, his falls had smashed his shoulder back into its socket.

It was ten days before the party returned to Herbert Island, battered and exhausted—they were supposed to have been back in four. As they neared the village, people streamed out of their huts. "Kari is fine," the women assured Marie as they hugged her and wiped tears from their eyes. "Go and look at her."

> Maria stood outside with my little curly headed girl in her arms. I thought my heart would burst. "Hello, my little darling," I whispered to the puzzled little girl. A wave of sadness hit me then and I sobbed unrestrainedly. Maria stood by, silently, looking calm and grave, before saying, "I am so happy to see you, as we all thought you were dead."

The villagers knew that Wally was experienced in the Arctic, but the storms were like nothing they had seen, and they had lasted so long. The women had urged that a search party be sent out, but the men were hesitant; it was considered an insult to go in search of a man with my father's skill, and besides, they would have risked their own lives going out in such conditions.

AFTER TWO YEARS of living with our friends in Qeqertasuaq, we returned to England. In the months following our return, both Marie and Wally focussed on writing. Marie's book about our experiences, *The Snow People,* was so popular that the publishers asked if she would be interested in writing a second book about living and travelling with reindeer herders in Lapland. She was thrilled by the prospect, but Wally was less enthusiastic. The Lapps (also called the Sami), on the whole, believed travelling writers and photographers were exploitative. He warned the experience would be very different from living among the Inuit. Marie could not be dissuaded, though, and finally he gave in. He would give her six months of his life, he promised, and do anything he could to assist her. In return, he asked her to support him in his attempt to make the first circumnavigation of Greenland.

FACING TOP | Robert Peary, his family and crew celebrate his birthday on May 6, 1901, aboard the *Windward*. The explorer had completed his trek to the ship only the day before. *Herbert Collection*

FACING BOTTOM | Determined to raise enough funds to rescue her husband from the Arctic, Jo Peary conquered her fear of public speaking and in 1895 gave a series of lectures for the National Geographic Society. *Herbert Collection*

ABOVE | Jo Peary's polar adventures with her husband were serialized in the American press, often accompanied by romantic sketches of them in fashionable Arctic garb. *Herbert Collection*

ABOVE | Jo Peary and her daughter, Marie, with Captain Sam Bartlett, were stranded for the winter of 1900–01 on the *Windward* at Payor Harbour in northwest Greenland. Unaware of their predicament, Peary was just 250 miles away. *Herbert Collection*

FACING TOP | Jo and Robert Peary aboard the *Roosevelt* on September 21, 1909. In that tumultuous month, both Peary and his rival Dr. Frederick Cook announced their claims as the conqueror of the North Pole. *Herbert Collection*

FACING BOTTOM | This 1897 illustration depicts the Pearys loading a meteorite from Greenland, draped in the Stars and Stripes, into the hold of the *Hope*. "Mrs. Peary," the caption states, is "at the lever of the jacks." *Herbert Collection*

THE
ILLUSTRATED AMERICAN

VOL. XXII.   New York.   OCTOBER 16, 1897.   Chicago.   No. 401.

GREENLAND'S IRON MOUNTAIN: LIEUTENANT PEARY RUNNING THE GREAT METEORITE FROM THE GREENLAND SHORE INTO THE HOLD OF THE "HOPE"—MRS. PEARY AT THE LEVER OF THE JACKS.

Drawn by E. J. Meeker.   See Page 488.

FACING LEFT | Eva and Fridtjof Nansen were both keen skiers. In this studio portrait c. 1890, she wears her controversial ski wear, which swapped the traditional long skirt for a shorter style worn over trousers. *L. Szacinski, National Library of Norway*

FACING RIGHT TOP | Nansen is shown here at Cape Flora, June 1896. After abandoning the *Fram,* he and his companion Johansen skied seven hundred miles over the polar pack in a desperate bid to reach safety. *F. Jackson, National Library of Norway*

FACING RIGHT BOTTOM | This photo shows Eva and Fridtjof Nansen at their home at Polhøgda in 1902 with their children, Kåre, Irmelin, Liv and Odd. *L. Szacinski, National Library of Norway*

ABOVE | This studio portrait of Eva and her husband was taken in London during Nansen's lecture tour in 1897. He had recently returned from his attempt to sail across the North Pole in the *Fram. Ellit & Fry, National Library of Norway*

Sir John Franklin

EREBUS

TERROR

OPENING THE CAIRN CONTAINING THE RELICS OF FRANKLIN.

FACING | This commemorative engraving of Sir John Franklin depicts the discovery of a cairn containing tantalizing clues to the whereabouts of the explorer and his men after their disappearance on his Northwest Passage expedition in 1845. *Private Collection*

TOP | This carte de visite of Jane Franklin was created from a photograph of an original chalk drawing by Amelie Romilly c. 1816. *W.L. Crowther Library, Tasmanian Archive and Heritage Office*

BOTTOM | This amateur sketch of the poet Eleanor Anne Franklin (née Porden) was done by her sister Sarah Henrietta. *Gell Collection, British National Archives*

— PART TWO —

LOVE

AND LABOUR

8

Jane Franklin
THE PETTICOAT FIASCO

When I look at the vicissitudes of the times…
I am ready to sigh for simplicity and peace and obscurity
in some distant land, a land like Australia.

JANE FRANKLIN

AMBITIOUS, SHREWD AND PROUD, Jane Franklin was a woman who knew what she wanted. She had married a man who was a knight of the realm, a naval hero and a polar explorer. For such a man to be without an occupation was, she thought, shameful.

During her three-year tour of the Mediterranean, John Franklin's time on HMS *Rainbow* had come to a close. Franklin had tried his best to secure another command, and on her return home in October 1834, Jane reinvigorated his efforts. She began by firmly reminding influential contacts of Franklin's achievements. With their support, a door finally opened at the Colonial Office. She advised her husband to decline the first offer of the post of governor of Antigua, and less than two weeks later he was offered the grander position of lieutenant-governor of Van Diemen's Land, now Tasmania.

ON AN UNSEASONABLY cool and blustery January day in 1837 the *Fairlie* drew into the harbour at Hobart, Tasmania. The four-month journey of violent storms, an overboard rescue and three burials at sea on the overcrowded ship had been an ordeal for most of the passengers; for Jane, however, it had been a welcome adventure. It was her new role of governor's wife that she regarded with trepidation. For the sake of her husband, she remained stoic. Leaving the men to their pomp and pageantry, she allowed herself to be led through the midsummer gardens with her stepdaughter, Ella, Franklin's niece Sophy Cracroft and the other ladies to Government House.

The Dutch explorer Abel Tasman had been the first European to explore the mountainous, heart-shaped island, naming it Anthoonij van Diemenslandt after the governor general of the Dutch East Indies who had commissioned the voyage in 1642. In 1803 the island had been colonized by the British as a penal colony. Over a period of thirty years, so many convicts had been landed there that prisoners threatened to outnumber the settlers. Franklin's controversial predecessor, George Arthur, fiercely ambitious and gleefully corrupt, had controlled the colony more like a dictator than like a guardian. The result was a divided community of those who supported Arthur—and were amply rewarded—and those who opposed him. Certainly the atmosphere in the colony was highly charged on Arthur's departure. One newspaper jubilantly voiced the feeling of many of the settlers:

> Tomorrow ought to be a day of general thanksgiving for the deliverance from the iron hand of Governor Arthur. We now have a prospect of breathing. The accursed gang of bloodsuckers will be destroyed ... Perjury will cease to be countenanced ... Rejoice, for the day of retribution has arrived!

Arthur's dream had been to make Tasmania the jail of the British Empire, and by the time he left he was not far from its realization. Scornful of half-measures, Arthur created a new prison at Port

Arthur, decimated the Aboriginal population and relentlessly pursued the bushrangers—gangs of escaped convicts who terrorized the outlying settlements. He tightened the rules on landownership and the cost of convict labour. He was also a firm supporter of assignment, whereby hard-working, non-violent convicts were assigned to settlers to work as servants or labourers in return for food and clothing. Calls for a free press, trial by jury and a representative assembly were all bluntly refused. Arthur had arrived with nothing but his family and a meagre salary, but after over a decade of rotten rule he had left with a significant fortune generated by his colonial properties. His supporters had also grown wealthy. A chaplain of the time remarked: "Many of those who lived in fine houses and drove in their carriages through the streets of Hobart Town and Launceston had amassed money by the most nefarious practices, and had blacker hearts than the trebly convicted felons in the chain gangs."

Such men would hardly allow a newcomer to jeopardize their position. To reassure his supporters, Arthur had left the colony in the hands of three men—of whom two had married into his family—on whom he knew he could depend to sustain his legacy. All three believed they should be running the colony: John Montagu, the "cunning" colonial secretary; Captain Matthew Forster, the chief police magistrate—"a bold fearless character" and an advocate of the death penalty; and John Gregory, the treasurer. The triumvirate, as Jane called them, were convinced that Franklin would become their puppet.

Arthur's retirement from Tasmania was perfectly timed. In the years to follow, the price of wool, which had primarily sustained the colony, would suddenly fall. This, combined with a run of failed wheat harvests and high interest rates on loans that settlers had taken out in the boom time, would cripple the economy. With no experience of colonial administration, a coterie of unscrupulous advisers and a depression looming, Franklin's governorship was never going to be easy. Yet the Franklins saw it as a new beginning. Jane and her husband regarded Tasmania as an "infant Society" that could be moulded and improved. They had dreams of establishing Hobart as a cultural and scientific centre and of promoting education in the colony.

Save for the few occasions in the Mediterranean where he had flexed his diplomatic muscle, Franklin was innocent in the ways of colonial administration. For the next few years, the Franklins would be isolated between two hostile camps. On the one hand were the supporters of the former Arthurite regime; on the other were colonists who looked to Franklin for new direction. Initially the forward-thinking colonists welcomed the new explorer governor and his family. In Hobart every house lit candles in the window in celebration at their arrival; in Launceston Franklin was greeted with an escort of three hundred horsemen and seventy carriages and banquets that included kangaroo soup and joints of wallaby.

On the surface, Hobart was a thriving parochial hub of dinners, balls and tea parties. Free convict labour gave the colonists a sense of superiority and a lifestyle far grander than they could have enjoyed back in Britain. The wide, clean streets were lined with picturesque houses and shops. The wild land had been tamed and cultivated into graceful gardens and meadows. The Derwent River bustled with traffic, and standing majestically over it all was the snow-capped peak of Mount Wellington. It was idyllic, save for one obvious drawback. "Everyone on the first arrival," Jane noted, "almost makes an involuntary shudder at the bare thought of being side by side in the street with convicts. Yet the feeling of security and the knowledge of good order and vigilance soon dissipate this feeling."

Beneath the genteel exterior, however, was a thick seam of debauchery. One contemporary report claimed that the houses of the settlers had become little more than brothels: "Each house containing in the shape of domestic servants its quota of unblushing prostitutes who required neither wooing nor solicitation . . . the most disgraceful scenes were enacted under the roof where the mother and grown daughters dwelt." The daughters of the settlers, being exposed to such licentiousness, were becoming as promiscuous as the prostitutes and were increasingly "in the habit of having intercourse with a road party of men." Gonorrhea and other sexually transmitted diseases were rife.

Many settlers believed the amorality of the women convicts far outstripped that of their male counterparts, but discipline for the women convicts was complicated. Flogging was out of the question, as was assignment to chain gangs. A considerable number of women prisoners were incarcerated in "factories." The most notorious, the Cascades Female Factory—part prison, part workhouse—was described by the newspaper *Murray's Review* as being so overpopulated with "wretched inmates" that the interior resembled the hold of a slave ship. The factories also operated as maternity hospitals for unwed female convicts, and infant mortality in such places was horrifically high. Jane regarded the methods of punishment for female felons as entirely ineffective. Personally, she advocated shaving female prisoners' heads as a punishment.

Disciplining male convicts appeared to weigh less on the authorities' conscience. Felons who had misbehaved were subjected to a flogging at the so-called triangles—tall wooden structures resembling tripods—that had been built throughout the colony on Colonel Arthur's orders.

Such barbarism was abhorrent to the Franklins, and they hoped to make vital changes to the system of punishment. Among the entourage who had joined them from Britain was Captain Alexander Maconochie, an old naval friend of Franklin who had agreed to become his private secretary. Maconochie believed there were opportunities for wide-reaching penal reforms in the colony and agreed to write a report for the Society for the Improvement of Prison Discipline. Jane was thrilled. Maconochie had a fine pedigree: he was a veteran of the Napoleonic Wars and had been both the first secretary of the Royal Geographical Society and the first professor of geography at London University.

Maconochie's views were radical, and some believed them to be potentially damaging to the colony as a whole. Among his critics was John Montagu, the colonial secretary, who saw Maconochie as "a cool-headed, shrewd, ambitious, meddling Scotsman." Franklin's private secretary, Montagu wrote to his father-in-law Colonel Arthur, "will ruin [Franklin] in twelve months and make his government a bed of thorns."

Montagu's summation of Maconochie was startlingly prescient. Within just three months, the private secretary made the astonishing move of surreptitiously sending under the governor's official seal a report to Sir John Russell, the secretary of state at the Home Office, outlining his ideas for reform in Tasmania. The report, a sensational summary of life and punishment in the colony, was sent with the full knowledge of the precarious position in which it would place Franklin, whom Maconochie had known as a friend and colleague for almost twenty-five years.

The first the Franklins knew of the report was when they saw it printed in an English newspaper, along with a statement that it had already been submitted to Parliament. Franklin was furious; Maconochie's report was reckless and incorrect. Jane was amazed by the man's behaviour. Clearly he had ambitions to undermine her husband and become governor in his place. Together, the Franklins composed an official letter requesting the private secretary's resignation. When her husband retired to bed, Jane continued working on it until dawn.

The news of Maconochie's dismissal sent shock waves through Hobart. The colonial secretary and the Arthurite newspapers called it a victory. Those who had hoped that Franklin's arrival heralded a new age for the colony were mortified. The *True Colonist* wrote that Franklin's decision to dismiss Maconochie had "destroyed the last lingering hopes of the colonists that Sir John would ever assume the real authority of his office." There were other unpleasant repercussions. Maconochie's wife, who had been Jane's closest friend in the colony, became "as cold and immovable as a stone, evidently felt wronged and full of disdain and was scarcely moved even by my emotion." It was a significant loss for Jane, who would discover that friends and allies were hard to find.

The letter calling for Maconochie's resignation was not the last official letter Jane would write. Her husband increasingly relied on her when it came to his most important dispatches. The drafts of these, she admitted to her sister, were often submitted to her for correction or alteration. This, she emphasized, was "the *profoundest of secrets.*"

> To you *alone* I tell it. It would be injurious in many ways that it should be known or suspected... To me there is no other gratification in my position than that I am enabled to be of some use to Sir John... You must not suppose that I think myself in very extraordinary position and am a very wonderful person. I think quite the contrary. I suppose every woman whose husband is in public life helps him if she can and if he gives her the opportunity.

In time, Jane also began to decide which letters addressed to her husband he would actually receive, reasoning that any correspondence that criticized him would be hurtful for him to read.

From the start Jane threw herself into promoting a host of worthy causes. She lent her support to the Tasmanian Society of Natural History, encouraged the establishment of new schools and colleges, and planned to create a natural history museum and a botanical garden. A more bizarre pet project was a campaign to rid the island of poisonous snakes. To this end, she offered a reward of one shilling for every snake head that was handed in to the police. Her proposition was met with incredulity from settlers and authorities and glee on the part of the assigned convicts, who promptly jettisoned their duties for this more lucrative pastime. She abandoned her scheme after being constantly lampooned by the press and receiving a decaying snake tail protruding suggestively from a valentine card. It was, she complained, "a loathsome and abominable insult." By the time she called a halt to the extermination, she had given up £600 in rewards—a staggering £26,500 in today's money.

Jane's adventurous spirit attracted even more disdain. Not long after her arrival, she had climbed Mount Wellington, determined that she should be the first European woman to do so. Much to her chagrin, she had been beaten to the prize by a Miss Wandly, who was inspired by Jane's publicly declared ambition. Jane nevertheless claimed priority, informed the newspapers and sent the clippings of her apparent success home. Not everyone thought it worthy of celebration. The *True Colonist* wrote scornfully that she was "in some way accessory to the sticking up of a pair of ladies' boots on a pole of one of the barren rocks of that region of storms."

When it was announced that Jane would undertake an overland expedition from Melbourne to Sydney without her husband, she became the focus of a very public furor. Labelled "this errant lady," she was, the *True Colonist* declared, an eccentric, selfish curiosity whose adventurous tendencies were "a perversion of ordinary female qualities." Her planned six-hundred-mile route would take her through wild country frequented only by poisonous snakes, rabid dogs, bushrangers and Aborigines. The perils and discomfort to which she would be subjected were nothing a "real Lady" would wish to endure. And "who," the *Australian* demanded to know, "is going to pay the expenses of this freak of Lady Franklin?"

Disregarding the vitriolic attacks in the press, Jane continued with her plans. On April 1, 1839, she sailed out of Launceston on the government brig *Tamar* toward the new settlement of Melbourne, along with Franklin's niece Sophy, three gentlemen companions, a retinue of servants and an escort of two mounted policemen. As always, her iron bedstead travelled with her.

On April 6, Jane embarked from Melbourne with her entourage to the cheers of the townsfolk. She recorded events obsessively in a tiny blue notebook. Her miniature, spidery handwriting runs to around 100,000 words, covering everything from the price of butter to the number of sheep or cattle they passed. Her hope was that this information might one day prove useful to her husband, thus justifying her travels.

Covering one hundred miles a week on average, Jane usually rode in a cart that jolted excruciatingly over the hard, pitted terrain. When the bone rattling grew too much she would ride a pony sidesaddle or walk. They dined by the light of a lantern, eating curried black swan, white cockatoos, cranes, a magpie and on one occasion a "large laughing jackass." Most evenings passed without incident, but one night the camp was woken by Jane, who had run through torrential rain to wake the men, insisting she had heard shots. She had heard stories about murderous man-eating Aborigines who preyed on lone white travellers and then disappeared magically. It was a false alarm. Jane offered little complaint when the party encountered treacherous bogs or had to wade past bullocks drowning in mud. Her companions bothered her more than any physical discomfort; they made her feel that they were being dragged along on her account, she recorded, suggesting that she would never satisfy her wanderlust.

By the time they reached Sydney, Jane's party had been on the road for six weeks. The *Sydney Monitor,* in reporting their arrival, claimed Jane was "a fine-looking woman, very intellectual countenance, vivacious and affable. She has a fine colour, with blue expressive eyes." Flattered but painfully aware of the impact such glowing reports would have back in Tasmania, Jane wrote privately: "What a fool [the reporter] has made of himself and me!—and what fine food for the Hobarton newspapers. I am quite amazed at the figure I cut in the papers."

For some time Jane had been regarded by the Arthurite supporters as meddlesome and "poisonous." Montagu was her lead detractor, and he was a dangerous adversary to have. The colonial secretary was a former professional soldier and a veteran of the Battle of Waterloo. He was, as Mrs. Maconochie described, a "snake in the grass, sleek, smooth and slippery... Like so many noxious animals he has the power of soothing and fanning his victims to sleep, never attacking openly."

Montagu had long since taken advantage of his position in the colony, and had always been clever enough to cover his tracks. Everything changed when he was exposed as having abused the system of assignment in collusion with his brother-in-law, the police chief Captain Forster. The affair made headline news. Knowing that the abuse of assignment was being interrogated in England by the Molesworth Committee—set up in 1837 to look into the issue of penal transportation—Franklin had to take a hard line. He eventually suspended the colonial secretary from office.

Montagu was publicly humiliated, and he directed his anger at his fall from power toward Jane. "It is painful beyond description to act under a Governor who has no firmness of character, and is the tool of any rogue who will flatter his wife," he wrote to Colonel Arthur, "for she is in fact the Governor." In the face of Montagu's rage, the disgraced colonial secretary boasted, Franklin "trembled like a leaf—the perspiration ran down his face in a stream. His mouth was filled with saliva—almost to prevent him from speaking—he was as pale as death." Those who knew Franklin intimately would not have been surprised; a friend later wrote: "Chicanery... made him ill, and so paralyzed him that when he had to deal with it he was scarcely himself." Tasmania, Jane confided to her family at home, was a country "where people should have hearts of stone and frames of iron."

It was clear that Jane had become Franklin's primary adviser, and soon even the most innocent conference between husband and wife was misconstrued. Franklin had been partially deaf since the Battle of Trafalgar and leaned on Jane to ensure that he didn't miss vital conversations when attending noisy social gatherings. Many interpreted her intercessions as a sign of her control. Franklin's tendency to defer important decisions until he had consulted his wife only exacerbated the situation.

Life in the colony had become thoroughly miserable. Franklin was blamed by some for the steady disintegration of a prosperous community. Others, including reformers in England, viewed him as a coward for not pressing forward with essential penal reforms. Derided on all sides, by 1839 Franklin was immobilized by exhaustion and stress. Jane wrote to her sister:

All this has hurt Sir John more than you can imagine—one thing comes upon another—he takes little exercise, loses in some respects even his appetite, creates imaginary evils, asks me if I can bear it if he is recalled in disgrace, and in fact is more agitated and depressed than I have ever seen him before, trusting to me for everything, and as I tell him, giving cause to his revilers and mine to say all they do against us. I am sure he is far from well . . . I work like a slave—I cannot tell you what I do not do—and then I have to try to conceal that I do anything.

To Jane's relief, at the summer's end of 1840, Franklin's friends James Clark Ross and Francis Crozier, in the *Erebus* and the *Terror*, sailed into Hobart. The explorers were en route to study magnetism in the southern hemisphere but stayed in Tasmania for a number of weeks to build an observatory. The company of like-minded men was a welcome distraction which, according to Jane and his niece, made Franklin positively "frisky." But too soon the men left Tasman waters for the Antarctic.

YEAR BY YEAR, there were ever more disagreements, misunderstandings and bluster. Jane had become almost universally disliked. She was regarded as opinionated, idealistic and ambitious; furthermore, people resented her influence over the governor. The now deposed Montagu was particularly critical: "A more troublesome, interfering woman I never saw—puffed up with the love of Fame and the desire of acquiring a name by doing what no one else does." Lady Franklin was, he crowed to those who would listen, "a man in petticoats."

In between his bilious attacks, Montagu wrote a controversial letter to the secretary of state for the colonies, Lord Stanley, complaining that his case "turned upon the fact of Lady Franklin's improper interference in the business of the Government, which, because I mentioned it to Sir John Franklin, led to his suspending me from office." His comments ignited a furor. "Woe to that poor woman," Jane wrote later, "if *the man who wishes to rule her husband* suspects she thwarts him in his design." *Murray's Review* claimed it had been proved conclusively that Montagu's dismissal was due to the meddling of Lady Franklin, "in whose hands really is the

administering power, the governing and all directing of the colony."
To seal Jane's unpopularity, the *Colonial Times* declared, "If ladies
will mix in politics they throw from themselves that mantle of
protection which as females they are fully entitled to. Can any person
doubt that Lady Franklin has cast away that shield—can anyone for a
moment believe that she and her clique do not reign paramount here?"

Aware of the growing hostility, Jane wrote her defence to a
confidante:

> With respect to my own conduct, I find myself guilty of being
> devoted to my husband, of trying to be of use to him, of yielding to
> his belief that I can be so, of exerting over him whatever influence
> I possess, not to magnify myself and gratify a love of power or dis-
> tinction, but in furtherance, according to the best of my ability, of
> *his* interests, reputation and character.

Jane was not the only target. Stories ran criticizing Franklin's
"evident incapacity, his demonstrated feebleness" and "deplorable
indolence." One headline—"The Imbecile Reign of the Polar
Hero"—became the de facto opinion of many, even in the highest
circles. To her sister, Jane wrote: "[Montagu's] pride is indomitable...
He lives now for vengeance—in his own elegant and expressive
language he says of Sir John... 'I'll persecute him as long as I live.'"

Back in London, Lord Stanley regarded Franklin's dismissal
of Montagu as misguided. He offered the disgraced civil servant
the position of colonial secretary at the Cape of Good Hope, and
Montagu accepted with alacrity. Franklin was floored. To compound
matters, Franklin's replacement, Sir John Eardley-Wilmot, was
deposited in error on a remote part of the Tasmanian coast on
August 17, 1843. No one at Government House had been officially
informed of Franklin's dismissal, or of the new governor's planned
arrival. Three days later the official dispatch arrived, dated February
10, stating that Franklin's six years of governorship were at a close. It
was an astonishing administrative blunder. Nevertheless, at the final
hour Franklin won at least a few hearts:

Sir John was dressed in full uniform as Captain in the Royal Navy, and wore the stars of the several orders which had been conferred upon him for distinguished services rendered to his country and the cause of scientific discovery. He halted occasionally for an instant to acknowledge the enthusiastic cheers which burst forth from the assembled multitude.

As the guard of honour presented arms and the crowds surged forward to shake the gentleman explorer by the hand, the Franklins must have felt some vindication and an overwhelming sense of relief to be leaving behind so much jealousy and ingratitude. Now it was time, Jane believed, for her husband to regain his popularity as a polar hero.

9

Jo Peary

A METEORIC TASK

I have done things that a year ago
I thought an impossibility, but the consciousness
that I was working for the dearest one, to me,
in all the universe gave me strength and courage.

JO PEARY

O N OCTOBER 7, 1894, the *New York Times* claimed, "Probably the two most interesting persons in Washington to-day are Mrs. Peary, wife of Lieut. Peary, the famous arctic explorer, and her little daughter, Marie Ahnigito Peary. Young Miss Peary is born to greatness she can never escape... She will go down to posterity sung of many tongues, her primary claim to distinction being that she is the first of her kind to begin existence among the glaciers and ice caps of Northern Greenland."

Although the press were enthusiastic at the Snow Baby's arrival, Jo was less than thrilled to be back in Washington. Her return home from the Arctic with her infant daughter a year earlier than planned had placed her in an extraordinarily difficult position. The relief ship *Falcon*, sent by their over-anxious sponsors, had resulted in such a deficit in the expedition kitty that there were no contingency funds to bring back her husband once he had completed his work. Money had to be found from somewhere to fit out another ship to rescue him, and the responsibility of that fell to Jo. Peary's supporters initially refused to contribute any further funds. It had been his choice to remain in Greenland; he would have to find another way of getting back. Peary had reassured his wife that if she was unable to find the support, he would either use a small open boat or attempt to sledge down the west coast of Greenland until he could liaise with a Danish supply vessel which could take him to Copenhagen. His plan left too much to chance, and Jo would not hear of it. But it was hard enough just keeping herself and her child fed and clothed. She had arrived home to discover bills amounting to three times her income. "Oh my dear," she wrote in exasperation to her husband, "I wonder if you knew in what financial circumstances you left me."

Since 1881 Peary had been claiming a naval salary. Remarkably, he had managed time and again to gain long periods of leave to pursue his ambitions in the North. Keeping his superiors in the navy happy was essential, as the family counted on his steady income while he was away. When Peary told Jo that he wished half of his salary to go to his mother, she was deeply hurt but unable to object. "It was," she later confessed, "only another instance where I was put back that another might have ample." It was the child she was most concerned for. On her return from Greenland she had also brought with her a young Inuk woman, Eqariusaq, nicknamed "Miss Bill," to live with them for a year. The situation became so desperate that Jo had no option but to ask Peary's mother to contribute to some of the outstanding bills.

Her return to the United States had been more painful than Jo ever could have imagined. On June 21, 1895, she began a letter to her husband that made her feelings perfectly clear:

Broken in heart & spirit, & wearied in mind & body how can I write you the kind of letter you ought to have... Oh, my life my life there is nothing but disappointment in this world. It is a blessing that we cannot see what is before us for it would require more courage to face it than some of us have.

When you told me your plan a year ago last April as we sat near the shore of Baby Lake, I felt as if you had put a knife into my heart & left it there for the purpose of giving it a turn from time to time.

These turns have been given until now. There is no feeling left except an unspeakable longing, which amounts to the keenest anguish to look upon your dear face once more, to feel your arms about me once again & your lips pressed close to mine & then comes the thought that this may never be & it drives me frantic with pain. Many times the thought has come to me that it would have been far better if instead of bringing another life into this world I had gone taking it with me. My little darling she is all I have now. I have hoped and prayed that you would be successful & that then perhaps you would be content to stay with us awhile.

Deeply wounded by Peary's apparent lack of faith in her, Jo ruminated that the foundations of their marriage might not be as strong as she had hoped. "I have reviewed our married life very carefully, my husband," she continued, "& think I am resigned to the place which you gave me an hour after we were married." In fact, with his decision to send her home, Jo believed she now came a miserable *third* in Peary's affections: behind his mother, with fame taking first place. She begged him to live for her as he once had. Yet despite her disappointments and daily struggles, she knew that her husband still relied on her love and support. Even in the hardest times, she willed him to continue. "The public admire you more than ever & feel convinced that if it can be done you will do it. And surely you, my darling, must *know* that my love for you & confidence in you can *never* be shaken."

Jo's strength and support would be tested more and more as time went on. Over the years Peary had made several enemies among his subordinates, John Verhoeff, Frederick Cook, Eivind Astrup and Thomas Dedrick among them. One biographer later claimed that "many in Peary's command used to return hating him in a way that murder couldn't gratify." Jo knew there were times when her husband could be heavy-handed and superior, but seeing him maligned in the press by former members of his expeditions was understandably disturbing. Always publicity conscious, Peary had befriended a few key editors, and these men now rallied around Jo. The editor of the *New York Sun* gave her prior warning when venomous articles were likely to come out and advised her not to respond to them: "I don't believe these men can hurt your husband's reputation one iota... If we have a fair sample of their ammunition, they are simply exposing the weaknesses of human nature, and exhibiting themselves to disadvantage in a pillory of their own making." Her grace in the line of fire drew compliments from Peary supporters, but from this moment on, controversy would frequent Jo and her husband's everyday lives.

Jo also had to find a way of raising money to bring her husband home. Ten thousand dollars would be necessary to fit out a ship to return to Greenland to collect him. She pressed Peary's friends to use their influence. In November, Judge Charles Patrick Daly, the president of the American Geographical Society and a firm advocate of Peary, agreed to write to his friend the secretary of the navy to ask that a government ship be sent to the Arctic to bring Peary home "as a matter of National Concern." His appeal came to nothing. Jo began canvassing scientific institutions. For a subscription of $1,000, she advised, an institution or society would be entitled to a berth on the expedition ship for its representative. The offer was open to anyone: biologists, ethnologists, glaciologists or individuals with a keen sense of adventure. She made the journey sound as tantalizing as possible, promising encounters with the "Arctic Highlanders," rare plants, wildlife and spectacular scenery, and of course time in the field with her husband—who, she asserted, would "cooperate most eagerly with the scientists."

Her persuasive arguments worked. Before long she had raised $5,000. A ship was charted and contracts drawn up for supplies, crew and equipment. Then the funds suddenly stopped. A school that had pledged considerable support withdrew its contribution, with the excuse that the professor it wanted to send to Greenland was otherwise engaged. Again Jo contacted Judge Daly, begging for help. Unable to offer much assistance himself, he put her in touch with Morris Jesup, the president of the American Museum of Natural History. After Jo had presented her appeal to the museum's board of directors, Jesup agreed to help on the condition that Jo solicit funds, give talks and do all she could to raise more support. Only then would he feel justified in covering the deficit. Steeling herself, she joined the Alert Entertainment Bureau and nervously accepted lecture engagements, even though she was terrified of public speaking.

On May 11, 1895, she made her first appearance, at the Association Hall in New York City. Her tireless advocate the newspaperman Herbert Bridgman ensured that the *Standard Union* newspaper of Brooklyn, among others, carried news of her talk. Jo was appearing before the public, the paper declared, with the sole purpose of raising funds to rescue her husband from the Far North. Her presentation, the paper continued, would appeal "not only to scientists, and those specially interested in discovery, but to everyone who can appreciate loyal and wifely devotion."

The talk was a success. The *New York Sun* reviewed Jo's first appearance in glowing terms: "To persons unacquainted with Mrs. Peary the appearance of a youthful, graceful, well-dressed woman, who had come on the platform to recite experiences that have fallen to the lot of few of her sex, was probably a surprise. Mrs. Peary spoke with distinctness, and with the experience of a veteran managed to fit her descriptions to the admirable views that were thrown onto the canvas."

In no time Jo's campaign gathered momentum. In April 1895 the *Mail and Express* offered to publicize her efforts for her husband's safe return. Should she make a personal appeal, the editor believed, "I have no doubt New York would respond in a satisfactory way in the matter of raising the necessary funds." The following month, with the encouragement of Bridgman, an article by Jo was published simultaneously in several leading daily newspapers for the fee of $5 apiece. Jo knew the value of good publicity. Her book *My Arctic Journal* had been published in 1893, and since then her story had appeared in several magazines and newspapers, including the *New York Times* and the *London Illustrated News*. Although it was usually her husband who was the focus of attention, she too had a small but faithful following, and she was hopeful that they might help.

The breakthrough for the relief expedition came on May 23 when she addressed the prestigious National Geographic Society. The evening raised almost $2,000. With the additional help from Morris Jesup, a ship would be sent to find Peary in July 1895.

TO DATE, PEARY's two-year expedition had achieved nothing new, and time was running out. He was certain that Jo would find a way of sending a ship to bring him home, but he had made no gains in attaining the Pole, and the trip had contributed very little to science. His preferential treatment in the navy had bred resentment among his peers, and to return with such meagre offerings would make him a laughingstock. Peary had to do something, and there was only one thing he could think of that would be spectacular enough to silence his critics.

The English explorer John Ross had first encountered the northerly Inuit in 1818 and found to his astonishment that the "Arctic Highlanders" were using crude knives and harpoon heads fashioned from some sort of metal. When he asked through an interpreter where they had found the metal, he was told the story of an iron "woman, dog and tent" that had been hurled from the sky by some strange supernatural power and had landed somewhere on the coast of Melville Bay. The story became a source of fascination for travellers to the region. Elisha Kent Kane, George Strong Nares and Baron Nordenskjold had all tried to discover the whereabouts of this "Iron Mountain."

Peary had realized in 1894, while Jo was still at Anniversary Lodge, that the discovery of the three meteorites would guarantee him some recognition. With a great deal of persuasion, he found a guide to take him and one of his men to the site at Cape York. Ignoring his companion's discomfort, Peary carefully measured, drew and photographed the find, then scratched a deep *P* on the surface as indisputable proof of his discovery. With ice conditions rapidly deteriorating, they turned back. For much of the return journey the men were either stormbound or forced by the rotten ice to scale cliffs and bluffs, carrying the sledge loads on their own backs before returning to pull and push the sledges and dogs to safety. Having run out of food, the three men arrived at a small settlement and were given rotten walrus meat which made Peary sick for the rest of the journey. The stories told by Aleqatsiaq, Peary's guide, of the journey back to Anniversary Lodge only convinced the Inuit of the power of the meteorites' supernatural guardian.

Peary's fascination with the meteorites deeply unsettled the Inuit; it was clear that he intended to take the sacred rocks away with him. They suspected that the white men might one day stop coming to visit, and that they would need the iron again. Moreover, they were convinced that bad things would happen if the meteorites were moved. Years before, several hunters had removed a piece of iron from the site and taken it home, to save themselves the exhausting and dangerous trip back and forth for small chippings. After laboriously removing the head of the "woman," the men prepared to take the lump of iron home. But after they had travelled for many hours, the sledge, dogs and head fell through the ice and were forever lost. Clearly the spirit of the iron woman had exacted her punishment.

Although Peary was not a superstitious man, he had to concede that there was something magical about these giant stones: "The dogged sullen obstinacy and enormous inertia of the giant against being moved; its utter contempt and disregard of all attempts to guide or control it when once in motion; and the remorseless way in which it destroyed everything opposed to it, seemed demonic." While everything else was buried in snow around the largest meteorite, snowflakes disappeared as they touched it. Even eerier: "If a sledge-hammer chanced to strike it, spouting jets of sparks lit the gloom and a deep note, like the sound of the bell or the half-pained, half-enraged bellow of a lost soul, answered the blow." Nevertheless, the meteorites were a potential key to his salvation. By their sale or exhibition, he hoped that attention would be diverted from his last two wasted years. After tremendous difficulty, Peary finally secured two of the meteorites and brought them on board the relief steamer *Kite,* which Jo had worked so hard to send up to him, and sailed home.

Peary may have had the meteorites, but it was not enough. He returned home distracted. "I have failed," he wrote unhappily. "I shall never see the North Pole, unless someone brings it here. I am done with it. In my judgment such work requires a far, far younger man than I." Jo was concerned at her husband's despondency. She confided to Jesup that Peary was filled with "gloomy ideas that he is a failure & that as he did not accomplish his main object the scientific world would always regard him as such... *You know* what a blow it is to him to find that after sacrificing everything he finds himself far from the goal of his ambition. He is completely crushed but is striving to bear it as only a strong man can bear the bitterest disappointments of his life. I will not speak of the money he has put into his plans because while we have health & each other I do not give it a thought."

Peary's moments of depression rarely lasted long, and soon his mind turned once again to the future. With remarkable tenacity he convinced the navy to give him extended leave once again to return to the Arctic, and after attempts in 1896 and 1897, he finally brought the remaining Cape York meteorite back to New York. The Inuit were deeply distressed that their last sacred rock had been taken from them. "Once the value to the Eskimos [of the meteorites] would have been incalculable," the *Illustrated American* noted. "In return for the many benefits he has conferred upon the Cape York Eskimos, Mr. Robert E. Peary has despoiled the tribe of what was once its greatest treasure."

Peary's relationship with the Inuit was fairly clear-cut. Although he was convinced of their unwavering devotion, their feelings were not reciprocated. He knew that the support of the Inuit was essential if he was to be successful in the Arctic, but he respected them only for their usefulness. Unlike Matt Henson, who took care to try to understand the Inuit culture, Peary learned only a smattering of words so that he could make his orders understood. In his writings he would write of the Inuit, or his "huskies" as he liked to call them, as "my faithful, trusty Eskimo allies, dusky children of the Pole," who were "effective instruments for Arctic work."

Peary believed that the Inuit regarded him almost as a godfather figure. He claimed that rather than helping him in return for valuable gifts such as guns, ammunition and needles, the Inuit helped him out of gratitude and respect: "I have saved whole villages from starvation, and the children are taught by their parents that if they grow up and become good hunters or good seamstresses, as the case may be, 'Piuleriaq' will reward them sometime in the not too distant future." As a people they were much like children, Peary declared, and should be treated as such.

While they were in his employ, Peary believed, the indigenous people of northwest Greenland were as much his property as his sledge and dogs. He thought nothing of exhuming the fresh graves of hunters he had known by name and transporting the remains in "five big barrels" back to New York, where he sold them to the American Museum of Natural History. In 1897 he went further. The assistant curator of the museum, Franz Boas, had suggested that if Peary could convince one of the Inuit to live in the United States for a year, it would give scientists the chance to study the individual over a length of time. Peary obliged.

On October 2, 1897, the steam barque *Hope* hove into view and moored at the foot of Dock Street in Brooklyn. The following day, twenty thousand people descended on the ship to catch a glimpse of the world's largest known meteorite and the six Inuit who were on board. Peary was not a man to miss an opportunity for publicity— why stop at bringing one individual back with him, when he could bring a group of men, women and children? In the days following, crowds numbering up to ten thousand per day visited the Brooklyn Navy Yard, where they were charged an admission fee for the privilege of seeing Peary's "curiosities."

For the public and the press, the "Esquimaux" were even more fascinating than the meteorite. As one paper reported: "Nooktah, the son of the Chief Koolootoonah of Natuluni . . . is the head of the little band. Nooktah is five feet four inches in height. His round cheeks are furrowed by the wrinkles resultant from forty-seven years of life in the ice country, but his small, bead-like eyes twinkle merrily." The photographs of the stunned Inuit at the navy yard tell a different story.

The six Inuit were overwhelmed by the size of the crowds. The full extent of their own tribe, which was scattered over a large territory, amounted to no more than 250 men, women and children. Having the attention of such a phenomenal number of people was terrifying. In the days following, the small band of Inuit became increasingly bewildered. Neither Peary nor Jo felt any responsibility for housing the group; instead, they left their care to the American Museum of Natural History. The group were housed in the museum's basement. It must have been a cheerless welcome. The rooms were clean and comfortable enough, but the world outside was disorienting and dangerous. The Inuit, so used to a life outdoors, were effectively imprisoned. Crowds thronging to the museum were disappointed when they were told that the Inuit were not on exhibition. Many resorted to lying prone on the pavement outside, peering in through a grate to the rooms below in the hope of catching a glimpse of the Arctic Highlanders.

By the autumn the Inuit were beginning to fall ill. Colds quickly turned to pneumonia. Frightened, they did all they could to cure themselves, including pleas to friendly spirits by the group's shaman, Atangana, which were regarded as "amusing entertainment" by the press. On November 1, 1897, a headline in the *New York Herald* read, "Very Sick Eskimos Have Pneumonia and Bronchitis: Are Fed on Jellies and Chicken Broth, but Declare They Would Sooner Eat Tough Meat, Hog Lard and Tallow Candles." The group had been taken to Bellevue Hospital. Atangana and her daughter were critically ill. Surprisingly, neither Peary nor Jo appears to have made any attempt to comfort the sick and distressed little band. Peary was fully engaged in preparations for his next polar expedition, and Jo was focussed on making sure her husband was healthy and happy. Their time together was precious. If she felt any shame or guilt, she allowed no one to hear of it, least of all her husband.

As always, Jo studied the newspapers to ensure that Peary was kept abreast of his public profile. Only once did she allude to the situation with the Inuit: "The clippings are only about the sick Eskimos & nothing new." In his defence, Peary would claim that he had brought the Inuit from Greenland "on their own suggestion." He had handed the responsibility for them over to the museum, and as far as he was concerned he was in no way culpable for the ensuing tragedy.

In January 1898, Jo received urgent wires from her husband as he toured the country giving lectures and meeting potential sponsors. The *New York Sun* had reported that Fridtjof Nansen was about to make a dash for the North Pole. In alarm, Jo contacted everyone she knew who might have gone to Nansen's lecture in London. They were agreed, she reassured Peary, that the reporter had it all wrong. Nevertheless, Peary could not shake off the excruciating fear that someone would attempt to rob him of the title of discoverer of the North Pole.

Less than a fortnight later, on February 17, one of the Inuit men died, leaving his child, Minik, orphaned. The group had longed desperately to go home and had woken every day in terror that one of them might have died overnight. Minik later remembered the last days of his father, Qisuk: "Every morning he would come and sit beside me until I wakened, almost crazy to know how I felt, and yet too tender to arouse me from my rest. How he would smile if I was a little better, and how he would sob, with big tears in his eyes, when I was suffering." In the hours before Qisuk died, Minik remembered his father sobbing, almost suffocating, with fear and grief. He believed his father had died of a broken heart. Within a month, Atangana, who had been very ill for some time, was also dead. The death of Nuktaq came not long after.

Extraordinarily, in his book *Northward over the Great Ice,* published in 1898, Peary mentions in the appendix some familiar names from what he described as "my uncontaminated, pure-blooded, vigorous, faithful little tribe." "As I sit here writing now I can see them," he wrote. "Qisuk, or the 'Smiler', the walrus killer of Itilleq... Nuktaq, my faithful hunter and dog driver." He mentions neither that these two men had come with him to the United States nor that they had died so far from home. Before Peary had completed his book, the two men had been dissected, cleaned, reassembled, labelled, mounted and sent to the American Museum of Natural History for display.

By the time Peary's book was published, in fact, all but two of the Inuit he had brought from Greenland were dead. Of the survivors, the only adult, Uisaakassak, had been sent back to Greenland, and little Minik had been adopted by William Wallace, the superintendent of the museum. Articles with headlines such as "Taming a Little Savage" enthused at the lucky escape the Inuit boy had made in being adopted rather than going back to the "dreary region" of his homeland. Minik, they declared, had many reasons to be thankful. One article called him "an experiment, and a promising one, in the effects of civilisation upon one of the least known aboriginal races." Minik's adoptive parents reportedly wanted to educate the boy so that he could one day return to his own people as a missionary. Whatever his future might be, Minik was loved by the Wallaces, and he seemed to be adjusting finally to his new home. For Jo and Peary it was a welcome closure to the fiasco.

Peary was often away from home on lecture tours or at meetings with potential sponsors and supporters. Jo was kept equally busy. Beyond the everyday duties of looking after her daughter and home, publishers' contracts had to be negotiated and editors of magazines and newspapers needed encouragement to write positive articles about her husband or her own Arctic experiences. Equipment and other items collected on Peary's expeditions had to be stored somewhere securely, not least some one hundred skins, including pelts from deer, seals, muskox, arctic wolves, dogs and polar bear cubs, and the three meteorites from Cape York.

It would take some years for Jo to find anyone willing to pay the
significant price she wanted for the meteorites. Like her husband,
she was not one to accept defeat easily. Astute and eloquent, she put
forward her arguments with great aplomb. She sent a flurry of letters
to the trustees and supporters of the American Museum of Natural
History with the declaration that the meteorites could become as
popular as Cleopatra's Needle, which the museum had purchased for
display in Central Park. In carefully worded letters she asserted that
the meteorites were her property, and that the money obtained for
them would not be used for Arctic exploration. Still trying to make a
sale years later, she declared: "It is all I have with which to educate &
care for my children." By that time she had both Marie and a young
son, Robert Peary Jr., to care for.

Her asking price was an astonishing $60,000—approximately
£5 million in today's money. After lengthy negotiations, she would
finally accept $40,000 from the museum.

In the meantime, there were other complications to be dealt
with. Peary had received an official order to report for duty at Mare
Island on the west coast of the United States. It was apparent that the
naval establishment was finally closing ranks on him. For years he
had enjoyed the enviable position of indulging his ambitions in the
Arctic while being on its payroll as a civil engineer. Many felt that the
favouritism should come to an end and that Peary should be posted
well away from his influential contacts in Washington. Again, Jo ran
to his rescue.

On April 6, 1897, Jo paid a visit to John Davis Long, the secretary
of the United States Navy. After being kept waiting for two hours,
she was told she would have to come back the following day, which
she duly did. Long informed her that since Peary had enjoyed five
years of leave out of his six in the navy, he ought now to be willing
to do his duty. Jo assured the secretary that her husband *was* willing
to do his duty, but she hoped the navy would postpone his transfer
until Peary had put together his reports on the scientific material he
had brought back. Her entreaties did nothing to sway the decision.
Luckily for Peary, however, a few days before he was due to leave

for the west coast, he happened to meet the prominent New York Republican Charles A. Moore, who had helped William McKinley win the 1896 presidential campaign. Moore liked Peary and decided to represent his case. Going directly to the president, Moore asked as a personal favour that Peary be allowed to continue his polar work. Two days later, Peary received notice that another five years' leave had been granted. By then, he had also secured the use of the steam yacht *Windward* and the funds to continue his polar work.

On July 3, 1898, the day the U.S. Navy won the battle of Santiago de Cuba, Peary and Jo parted once again.

Kathleen Scott

THE DREAD THUNDERCLOUD

You *shall* go to the Pole.
Oh dear me, what's the use of having energy and enterprise
if a little thing like that can't be done.

KATHLEEN SCOTT

WITHIN DAYS of their second meeting at Mabel Beardsley's home in 1907, Robert Falcon Scott was professing his love for Kathleen Bruce. "Uncontrollable footsteps carried me along the Embankment to find no light," he wrote on November 8, "yet I knew you were there dear heart . . . I saw the open window and, in fancy, a sweetly tangled head of hair on the pillow within—dear head, dear sweet face—dearest softest lips— were they smiling? . . . The thought of you means just a catch of the breath and extra revolutions within—Do you shorten life, if it is told by heart beats."

Meanwhile, Kathleen had picked up Scott's book *The Voyage of the "Discovery."* She was, she wrote enthusiastically to him, so "grotesquely" wrapped up in his narrative "that the countless people who have looked in on me for sympathy on some topic or other during the last few days, have met with [comments] such as—'yes but you've never had a frost-bitten nose.'" The thought of being party to any future grand scheme was enticing. Instead of keeping Scott at arm's length, as she had with other men when they became too attentive, Kathleen encouraged him. Love notes flew back and forth between them, and Kathleen would soon realize that her new admirer was just as sensitive and vulnerable as her more artistic friends.

Scott suffered secret bouts of melancholia and self-loathing, which Kathleen would come to call his "dread thundercloud." His moods were not helped by his unglamorous posting to HMS *Bulwark*. Although it was a natural progression through the naval ranks and brought with it an additional £100 a year, Scott found the atmosphere stifling in comparison with the challenges of Antarctic travel. Kathleen encouraged him to make the most of his situation. "Con dear," she wrote, "you must grow necessary in the navy as well as at the South Pole... You *must* have the first ship in the Fleet or what's the use of you." Scott agreed, but he worried he had deficiencies as a leader and would never be able to shake off his "black dog" moods, the "dreary deadly tightening at the heart, this slow sickness that holds one for weeks."

Scott was by no means always so unhappy—Sir Courtauld Thomson, an admirer of the explorer, later described the young Scott to J.M. Barrie as a "fair-haired English sailor boy with the laughing blue eyes... the jolliest and breeziest English naval Second Lieutenant [and] no ordinary human being." Kathleen clearly supported this view, but the stream of Scott's gloomy letters was unsettling. Believing he had little to offer her, he was frightened that she might cast him aside. Over the next few months, Kathleen tried to get him to appreciate the sunnier side of things. "Life's so thrilling just at the moment," she wrote. "I wish you were here to share it. May circles of blessing play around you, dear, to keep off the black blight." But again and again the dread thundercloud appeared. "Con dear," she responded in wonderment, "are you still and always an unhappy man? Oh what's the matter Con? What is the matter?"

The matter was Shackleton. While Scott was mooning about on the *Bulwark*, his former subordinate, with backing from William

Beardmore, a Clydeside industrialist, had returned to the Antarctic with his own expedition. Scott was deeply unsettled at the prospect of Shackleton not only beating him to the Pole but also using a route that Scott, as leader of the expedition, believed he had prior claim to. "I am astonished," Scott wrote to Scott Keltie, the secretary of the Royal Geographical Society, when he heard the news that Shackleton's plan was to reach the South Pole by way of the old *Discovery* base in McMurdo Sound. "Shackleton owes everything to me."

Scott Keltie, Sir Clements Markham and Kathleen were all subjected to a stream of emotional letters from Scott. Shackleton had agreed with Scott's demand that he not use their old base in McMurdo Sound, even though this would significantly increase the length of Shackleton's journey and diminish his chances of successfully reaching the Pole. But Scott could not rest. He was incensed when he discovered that Shackleton's *Nimrod* had, after all, landed at "his" camp. It was inconsequential that there had been no other option for the expedition. Kathleen did her best to be supportive, declaring that Shackleton's plans were likely to collapse one way or another, but Scott became increasingly childlike in his outbursts to all who would listen, something noticed by those of influence, including Arthur Mostyn Field, a rear admiral and the hydrographer of the navy, who commented on Scott's hypersensitiveness. Even Kathleen eventually tired of his complaints and self pity. "You *shall* go to the Pole," she wrote brusquely. "Oh dear me, what's the use of having energy and enterprise if a little thing like that can't be done. It's got to be done so hurry up and don't leave a stone unturned." Scott was beset by anxiety, jealousy and crushing feelings of inadequacy, and his letters bewildered Kathleen. Their meetings too were often strained. As much as they were attracted to one another, they were also repelled. The chilly reception Kathleen received from Scott's financially dependent and pious mother, Hannah, only added to her uncertainty. "I can't bear to be disliked and distrusted," she confessed, then added stubbornly: "She shall love me for I shall love her and make her."

Scott's courtship of the irrepressible Kathleen had unsettled his family, who feared that Kathleen might persuade Scott to abandon

his obligations to them. Their fears were unfounded, but the resulting coolness distressed Kathleen. Scott appealed to his mother to be
more welcoming to his bride-to-be: "All I ask of you is to get to know
the girl I love and to break up this horrid condition of strain in which
we have been living... I do so want to make for a happier state of
affairs all round." He begged his mother to be kind to Kathleen and
reminded her that Kathleen had never had a stable home or family.
When Hannah Scott acquiesced and tried to make amends. Kathleen
was delighted, but she suddenly had an attack of cold feet. It wasn't the
first time she had had second thoughts about the marriage. Six months
earlier she had written:

> Dearest Con. Don't let's get married. I've been thinking a lot about
> it & though much of it would be beautiful, there is much also that
> would be very very difficult. I have always really wanted to marry
> for the one reason & now that very thing seems as though it would
> only be an encumbrance we could scarcely cope with. I know dear
> that you will be lonely without me for a little while, but the relief
> of knowing that you need not worry or uproot your sweet little
> mother will soon compensate... We're horribly different, you &
> I, the fact is I've been hideously spoilt. I am not going to tell you to
> forget me or any such nonsense, but let's abandon the idea of get-
> ting married.

Scott replied moderately that, despite the strain their marriage
could cause, he nevertheless loved Kathleen and wanted to spend his
life with her: "Little girl, if you care, be patient and we'll pull things
straight—have faith in me. But you must work with me, dearest, not
against me." His response was so surprising that Kathleen instantly
took him back.

Other rejected suitors pursued Kathleen relentlessly. Gilbert
Cannan, a young novelist and playwright, played on her weakness
for babies by writing that he had dreamt of their newborn son closing
his pink dimpled hand around one of Cannan's fingers. Romantic but

prone to schizophrenia, Cannan was not Kathleen's ideal man. Kindly she wrote: "Corn-coloured hair and a crooked smile, maybe, but not the father for my son." Sensing that another suitor was on the scene, Scott agonized that she would throw him over for someone more free-spirited. His fears only intensified when Kathleen wrote to him of the hedonistic weekends she was sharing with her artistic friends:

> I'm in such a wild state of excitement that if I don't send the over-flow to you I don't know what I shall do. It's after midnight & we've been dancing like maniacs for the last 2 hours . . . wild impro-vised dances all of our own & oh my dear I would give you a fat hug if you were here. There are seven or eight men staying here & I'm desperately in love with several of course! But I'm being very good in spite of all the coercion! It's *so* fun! I was oh so sadly disap-pointed to get your wire, this is just the place I should like you to be, it's all so gay & happy & *good!*

Scott objected when Kathleen informed him that she was going abroad for six weeks, joined by the husband of a distant cousin. When he had not heard from her again for several days he wrote in despera-tion, his mind overrun with thoughts of her in another man's arms. Kathleen responded lightly: "Con sweet one. Everything is perfectly harmonious & will be—why not—because I let you know that I'm happy when fine natures love me & show their generosity—must I learn to be discreet & secretive—maybe . . . I just write to tell you that we are both perfect dears & that together we shall be *splendid*. Oh yes we shall—& I'm very prosaic & practical too. & if I mayn't write what I like to the man I'm going to marry a few weeks before I marry him, what *may* I do—Darling I *will* be good when I'm married."

Finally, the wedding was announced. Letters of congratulations flooded in from Kathleen's friends. On Independence Day Max Beer-bohm sent congratulations while promising some "hideous presents." Kathleen seemed strangely unexcited by the prospect of marriage. Her brother Rosslyn commented in a letter to his fiancée, Rachel Gurney,

"You cannot imagine how catching her indifference to the ceremony part is. I suppose someone will wake her up to caring about it before the day." Kathleen was even less interested in finding a bridal gown. She was adamant that she did not want Scott to give her a ring; nor would she wear the customary veil and orange blossom.

Kathleen had never been a fashionable woman. James Lees-Milne described her as the worst-dressed woman he had ever met, with a "sort of aggressive no-taste." Even her close friend George Bernard Shaw once declared: "No woman ever born had a narrower escape from being a man. My affection for you is the nearest I ever came to homosexuality." Scott may have indulged Kathleen's passion for "vagabonding," but he would not allow her to be shabbily dressed. After all, he stated, he was dreadfully sensitive to appearances. She responded by saying she would get a pretty dress, just so he could see what a "fright" she looked.

The wedding was held on September 2, 1908, in the Chapel Royal in Hampton Court Palace. To Scott's delight, Kathleen looked beautiful in a dress of white satin trimmed with Limerick lace and a bodice of chiffon with a wreath of natural myrtle. Even so, she refused to take the day too seriously. On spying Scott's handsome best man, Captain Henry Campbell, she asked her groom if she could marry him instead. Later she wrote that she hadn't enjoyed the ceremony and wished she had been outside enjoying the sunshine. The *Times* reported: "The marriage will make no difference to Capt. Scott's future plans with regard to Antarctic exploration."

ON MARCH 24, 1909, Scott heard the news that Shackleton had dramatically beaten Scott's farthest-south record. No matter that Shackleton had been forced to stop ninety-seven miles short of the South Pole; it had been a remarkable achievement, not least because of his extraordinary bravery in putting the lives of his men before glory and turning back when the Pole was within in his grasp.

In the shadow of Shackleton's achievements, Scott set about trying to raise the finances for another Antarctic expedition. He enjoyed the loyal support of men such as Sir Clements Markham, but others, including Admiral Sir Lewis Beaumont, the vice-president of the Royal Geographical Society, were loath to become embroiled in another sparring session between Scott and Shackleton. Furthermore, Shackleton had so far proved himself the more worthy explorer. News of the competing claims of Peary and Cook for the North Pole had swept through Europe. After an illustrious history in polar exploration, the British had lost a major geographical prize to the Americans, and there were rumours that Peary was planning a South Pole expedition.

Scott wanted the South Pole, and Kathleen wanted it for him. For the next few months, she was at his side, cajoling, pressing and inspiring potential sponsors. She accompanied him to Norway to test the caterpillar-tracked motor sledges that he planned to use in the Antarctic. Together they met Fridtjof Nansen, who advised that skis and dogs would be vital for the success of the expedition. Scott disagreed but consented to meet Tryggve Gran, an accomplished young skier who was planning an Antarctic trip of his own. Before long, Kathleen and Scott had convinced Gran that he should abandon his plans and join Scott's expedition. Gran later recalled that when he finally agreed, Kathleen grasped his hands enthusiastically with hers.

With Kathleen beside him, Scott felt empowered and courageous—by rights, he believed, the South Pole would be theirs. He needed to raise £40,000 (about £3.5 million in today's money), and Kathleen advised he should take advantage of the patriotism running high in the country. "The main object of this Expedition," he wrote in his public appeal, "is to reach the South Pole, and to secure for The British Empire the honour of this achievement." It was rousing stuff. Scott began a tour of Britain to drum up support. It was not something he was naturally good at, and the strain took its toll, particularly as Kathleen, now pregnant, was unable to join him. In Wales he raised nothing. Audiences in other areas were more sympathetic to his ambitions and collected £20 to £40, but still he was well short of his target. Kathleen had more success; she charmed Sir Edgar Speyer into giving £1,000 and agreeing to become treasurer of the fund.

Kathleen was unused to being the one left behind. To assuage her unexpected feelings of solitude, she went to dances and flirted with sailors. Yet the thought of her husband's expedition filled her with pride. She loved him "desperately, deeply, violently and wholly." She was ecstatically pregnant, knowing that her child would be born in the autumn. Whenever possible she escaped to the country, where she would eat wild raspberries and mushrooms, sleep on the beach and swim in the moonlight.

As the expedition was announced, Kathleen went into labour. The following day, on September 14, 1909, Peter Scott—large, healthy and perfect—was born. The effect of the birth shook Kathleen:

> Then a very strange thing happened to me. I felt for the first time gloriously, passionately, wildly in love with my husband... Until now he had been a probationer, a means to an end. Now my aim, my desire, had been abundantly accomplished. I worshipped the two of them as one, father and son, and gave myself up in happy abandonment to that worship. Now my determined, my masterful virginity, sustained through such strong vicissitudes, seemed not, as I had sometimes feared, mere selfish prudery, but the purposeful and inevitable highway to this culminating joy and peace.

Although she now had the son she had always craved, Kathleen desperately wanted to be involved in the great adventure. She could not go to Antarctica, but she could go as far as Australia to see her husband off. She knew that it would be painful to leave Peter for four months, but she had made her decision. In "agonies and ecstasies of reciprocated love," she left her son with a nurse and followed her husband to the other side of the world.

Marie Herbert

TILTING AT ICEBERGS

Sometimes it seems as though we are
the only three in the whole world who see
the point of what you are doing.

MARIE HERBERT

IN CONTRAST to the "agonies and ecstasies" that Kathleen
Scott experienced as she began her journey to
New Zealand with her husband, the next journey Marie and Wally
Herbert would take together would be regarded by Wally as just
agony. A temperamental caravan and a demanding four-year-old
passenger were just the start of the challenges Wally and Marie would
face on their journey to Lapland. It was winter, and no one in their
right mind would attempt the journey from Oslo to Jokkmokk by
road. The major roads were kept reasonably clear, but snow was
banked so high on either side that it was impossible to pull off the
road to rest. One would have to walk many tens of miles for help if
the vehicle broke down. In addition, Marie became bedridden with
a flu virus in Oslo. So it was decided that she and I would go north

by train and rendezvous with Wally in Jokkmokk. Still feeling weak and fuzzy-headed, Marie fought back the tears as we waved goodbye through the train window.

"From the very start this trip has been backfiring like a car full of peas, and I'm really not sure why," Wally wrote to friends. On the morning of January 19, 1975, after a hearty breakfast, he had set out along the deserted snow-covered roads "to the accompaniment of Bach suites 1 and 2 . . . and the purring of a happy and thoroughly self-sufficient man." By the end of the day his mood had changed. When passing through a customs post he had declared with disarming honesty that he had ten pounds of St. Bruno Flake tobacco in a bag behind the driver's seat and would be very happy to pay the duty. Officials promptly confiscated the entire stash and stamped on his passport "smuggler." Being labelled a smuggler was bad enough, but for Wally, who hadn't had one waking moment without a pipe in his mouth during the past twenty-one years, having no tobacco was an untold disaster. "Without my tobacco the bad dreams came rolling in like an endless regiment of frothing policemen and each night was the same."

The reunion with my mother and me several days later was some relief, but even then things didn't improve. In contrast to the reception my parents had had in Greenland, the Lapps were at best unhelpful. As this was Marie's project, not his own, and he had agreed to take a back seat, Wally felt increasingly frustrated.

Compared with the warm and generous Inuit, the Lapps appeared suspicious and aloof. Any attempts at friendship were rebuffed. "If Marie stayed up here for ten years she could never get a *Snow People* out of these insular bunch," Wally noted, "but of course she is trying—and I think she is a very brave girl."

Marie wanted to move in with a Lappish family and make the winter reindeer migration with them to the coast, but it was difficult enough persuading a family to take even one outsider; they would never consider a family of three, even if one was an experienced polar traveller. With no useful role, Wally felt his resolve to stick around and help weakening by the hour. They agreed that he would return home with me, and Marie would stay on. With the decision made, Wally wrote to their closest friends: "You'd better put your hands together for that lonely little figure walking across the snows who, in spite of her courage and wonderful way of getting along with people, will probably be as out of place as a diamond in a bucketful of s**t. But now I am getting coarse so I had better stop."

After a breathtaking journey over a frozen river and tundra, Marie was taken to meet a family who might be willing to take her with them on the reindeer migration. Opposite her sat an elderly grey-haired man, the head of the house. Two young men sprawled on chairs with their legs wide apart. Two other men sat observing her from the shadows. Marie was ordered to "siddown" by her negotiator, Hans, while the men talked. "I could not have been given more scrutiny if I had been a prized mare," she later recalled. After some discussion, however, they agreed to take her. She would leave the following night with the old man, Mathis, and a group of other men. Marie was startled. She had understood that there would be other women on the journey and had been cautioned strongly against travelling with only men. The journey could take weeks to complete and would take the group over isolated and trackless mountainous country. Travelling with men she didn't know had obvious dangers, but Marie felt it was too late to turn back.

It was dusk when Marie and Hans set out for the rendezvous. Hans had joked that Mathis would be drunk and singing to himself by then. Marie grew nervous. "Mathis, not dangerous," Hans said sheepishly, "only singing." She had to take his word for it.

There was no one at the agreed-upon spot, though they could see reindeer tracks and signs of a fire not long lit. After an adventure-filled evening that culminated in Hans attempting a passionate clinch, Marie was given a safe place to stay by a gentle old man. The following morning, the group was waiting for her.

There were no reindeer to be seen at first, but after a few hours of travelling, one of the men pointed excitedly:

I felt my heart miss a beat, for there, moving slowly in a great broad swathe, were the reindeer, six hundred of the magnificent creatures. It was all that I had been waiting for, and I acknowledged his gesture with a whoop of delight, smiling broadly back at him.

At the camp, Marie put up her own tent, then joined the men in the large communal tent where a fire burned brightly. To her relief they were welcoming and in good spirits. She was offered a hunk of blackened meat covered almost completely with reindeer hairs while the men watched her anxiously. After she had produced her penknife, Mathis grumbled and then threw a large knife at her feet, where it stood upended and quivering as a challenge. Respectfully Marie plucked it out of the ground, cut a piece of the meat and ate. The men nodded appreciatively. The ice had been broken. In the days to come, Mathis told her they would need to protect her; some of the people they would meet on their route, such as the men from the nearby fishing village, were untrustworthy and rough. Only three women lived in the village, which was why the men were so dangerous. "They're a strange lot," he added. "All they think about is fish."

By the end of their journey Marie saw her companions in a very different light. With them she had plowed through challenging territory, and she had witnessed the passion they had for their animals and environment. Although she felt nothing like the bond she had had with the Inuit, nevertheless she had been given the privilege of being part of the Lapps' way of life.

AS SOON AS Wally returned to England with me, he began making plans for his next expedition, the first circumnavigation of Greenland. By 1977 almost everything was in place, and he was raring to go.

At RAF Lyneham, the years of planning and anxious waiting came to a head. On the surface everything seemed positive; exciting, even. But although Marie tried to smile as she waved goodbye, when she drove away from the air base on that grey October morning, pregnant with their second child, she felt as though she had just buried her husband.

The house in Welford-on-Avon was desolate and cold by the time she returned. She tried to distract herself with two abortive attempts to light the fire. A neighbour knocked on the door: "Now that you are all on your own, is there anything I can do to help?" Her response was one she would remember for years: "That just about broke the last little dyke I had banked up and I stood at the door a blubbering idiot till she fled in embarrassment."

The British North Polar Expedition aimed to be the first to circumnavigate Greenland—the largest island in the world—a journey of seven thousand miles following a coastline famed for its hazardous terrain and unpredictable sea and ice conditions. Accompanying Wally would be Allan Gill—a vital companion on all his expeditions—and John "Jumper" Bitters, an ex-commando with several years of polar experience. The circumnavigation, which could take a year and a half to complete, would be by umiak—a traditional Inuit skin boat—and dog sledge.

Many people thought the journey not only impossible but suicidal—a common criticism had been levelled at Wally's crossing of the Arctic Ocean—and this was a far more obscure proposal. Few people even knew where Greenland was; why bother going around it? Potential sponsors were on the whole unexcited by the proposition: there were too many risks and too little potential return in the form of public interest. Yet for Wally it was a journey he felt compelled to make. Marie could not admit to anyone that, as she left the air base, she truly believed that her husband would not return.

There was plenty to distract the mind from such things. As with most expeditions, someone had to be the liaison in England, and Marie was the only person Wally could trust implicitly. Suppliers bombarded her with questions, bills and problems. These were tasks enough without the added pressure of writing a book, looking after a demanding seven-year-old daughter and a fragile mother-in-law, and preparing for another child who was on the way. There was nothing for it but to meet the problems head-on.

Letters and telexes of encouragement from Wally punctuated the chaos. He was riddled with guilt that Marie should be bearing the brunt of the difficulties at home, but the expedition was on a knife edge, and unless funds and support came in on time, it would have to be cancelled before it had begun. "You could try the technique (if you can bear it) of doing a Lady Franklin—i.e. getting in touch with the big shots ... and tell them you need help. What you must definitely NOT do under any circumstances is to take all the full weight of this responsibility on your own shoulders. Remember you are pregnant (not that you need much reminding) ... Roll on when it's all over," Wally wrote, "when we can look forward to an easy old age with no more 'last great journeys.'" A month after he left, a bouquet of flowers arrived for Marie with a telex: "I know these things are always a reminder of how much longer we will be apart but it is [also] now one month less than when I left and I think this is worth celebrating."

Wally's book *North Pole* was due to be published in his absence, but it was still unfinished and had to be completed in the Arctic. When he was not writing, he was working to ensure that equipment and logistics were all in place. It was difficult to keep on top of such things so far from home.

Two major sponsors were still hesitating over their contracts, and the BBC, which was to make a film of Wally's journey, was getting cold feet at the expense involved. A technicians' strike then made the project impossible. In desperation Marie considered trying to see the head of the union, to plead her case, but she doubted that would have any impact. Trying to keep Wally's spirits up, she wrote: "Don't be disheartened we will do what we can this end. I love you my explorer man." He responded enthusiastically, "I have obviously got the perfect wife! ... Our time will come you see when we have our little house by the sea (and a *warm* sea that's for sure!!) I am a part of you & you of me always."

Wally had also run into some unforeseen challenges. On his arrival at Dundas in northwest Greenland, he had discovered that theirs would be just one of three major expeditions in the same area. One of them was being led by his respected friend the Japanese "super adventurer" Naomi Uemura, who was planning a solo expedition to the North Pole and back before travelling the full length of the Greenland ice cap. "Crazy sod!" Wally wrote in wry affection. "He will have seen enough ice to last a lifetime that's for sure." Marie's reply eventually found him: "The Arctic is far too crowded now, you will have to go into space."

Even though Wally had goodwill on his side from his years spent travelling and living in the area, the hard cash being flaunted by his competitors put him at a distinct disadvantage. It was essential that his team get to Qaanaaq to secure the best dogs for their expedition. Then, as he and Allan Gill made their way by dog sledge from Qaanaaq to our old family home on Herbert Island, Wally finally began to relax. After a few hours they noticed a light in the distance, bobbing toward them. A sledge gradually became visible, and when it stopped fifty yards ahead of them Wally instantly knew it was his old friend. The hunter Avatak had heard on the radio that Wally and Allan were headed for Herbert Island and had come out to meet them.

> We had a marvellous reunion out there in the dark—big hugs and lots of laughing and joking—it really made me feel that the whole thing was worthwhile... It was a home-coming and I shall never forget it as long as I live... To see the old familiar landmarks looming out of the darkness, and to spot and name the lights and see the old hut profiles, the cove and the meat racks—it was all very, very exciting—and I wished very much that you could have shared it with me.

As the three men tore over the buckled ice of the tide-crack into the village, people poured out of their huts in excitement. "But all the time, not thirty yards away I could see out of the corner of my eye, our old hut—dark and forlorn-looking, and I felt an overwhelming loneliness because you were not there with Kari." Anticipating this, Wally's old friends warmed the two men with tea and pointed out the pictures of our family that had been pinned to the walls in pride of place. Then Avatak took them to the place where he had stored Wally's rifles, woollen clothing, ice axes, whips, ammunition and other equipment in perfect condition, just in case Wally one day returned.

After a few happy days in Qaanaaq, Wally and Allan drove their dogs back into Dundas at 2 AM on Christmas Eve. After a celebratory breakfast of bacon and eggs, Wally wrote to Marie: "It is our wedding anniversary—remember! You better never forget it because I love you... It really is a wonderful thing to have a wife and family—it gives me a whole new strength; a whole new dimension to life."

Back in England, Christmas came and went for Marie as if it were any other day. She wondered whether Wally was as lonely as she was.

THE EXPEDITION LEFT Dundas on January 27, 1978. "The trip is ON, ON, ON—and *nothing* will bloody well stop us from having a crack at it," Wally wrote in elation to his friend Geoff Renner before their departure. "We have got stacks of dog food; some fantastic gear, and the prospect ahead of us of a journey of a lifetime... Only 7,000 miles to go!" The excitement of the first few days of sledging disappeared as men and dogs ran into unmanageably bad weather and ice conditions. Open water leads appeared where they shouldn't have. As the party crossed Inglefield Land they discovered there was no snow—a situation never before seen by the local Inuit hunters. They had to push their sledges thirty miles over rock and tundra before encountering a hard layer of ice over snow on the Humboldt Glacier, which made sledging treacherous. Rope brakes, usually used only in emergency, had to be deployed for much of the way.

Beyond the glacier the travellers were greeted with more open water and fragile ice pans that broke under the sledges. They had to move fast, staying aware and awake at all times—sleep was a luxury they could not afford. It soon became apparent that they would have to take drastic action. Their only hope of success was to reduce the team to two men and share the dogs between them, so that they could travel much faster. Jumper, already suffering from exhaustion and frost-nip, volunteered to go back. Forty-two hours after he left them, Wally and Allan were hit by a hurricane-force wind. It screeched across the six inches of ice on which their tent was precariously pitched, threatening to blow them straight out to sea:

> With the ice bending visibly under our weight, we expected to survive no more than ten minutes. But that blizzard raged for thirty-six hours and by the time it had blown itself out, Allan and I were near total wrecks. For thirty-six hours we had not been able to speak to each other because of the noise of the flapping tent, which had also given us splitting headaches, and made it impossible to light the stove, or to have anything to eat or drink. We had no choice but to sit there shivering—convinced by the reflected fear that we could see in each other's eyes that we had only minutes to live. Small wonder then that when the wind finally eased enough that we were able to shout above it, the first spoken words were: "never again—never, ever again!"... How we envied Jumper who was at that time relaxing in the comfort and safety of Eigil Jensen's house at Dundas and eating like a Lord.

The going would not get any easier. In front of them lay an almost impenetrable regiment of pressure ridges. For the next hundred miles at least they would have to hack out a route with their ice axes.

Even with their accumulated knowledge of the polar regions—five years apiece in the Antarctic, several winters travelling with the polar Inuit, the sixteen-month journey across the Arctic Ocean and two years of living and travelling in the Arctic—Allan and Wally floundered in the abnormal weather and ice conditions. Pilots informed them that forty to fifty miles of open water lay ahead of them, where there should have been a solid pack. Any ice that had remained was buckled and thrown up in hellish confusion. "Today Wally called me and told me that he has never, never seen such rough ice conditions before in his whole life. And that means something," Eigil Jensen, the expedition radio operator and liaison, confided to the journalist Peter

Dunn. Jensen would become a pivotal person during the expedition. He had years of experience in the Arctic and had travelled across some of the most remote areas of Greenland. He understood more than most the difficulties Wally and Allan might encounter, but their run of bad luck was astonishing. He admired their tenacity, but even he was beginning to wonder whether they might have to quit the expedition.

As the end of March approached, Wally's mind turned to the imminent birth of his second child. There had been no letters from Marie since February 13, and he was concerned. He sent telexes to his contacts at the *Sunday Times* and to Eigil Jensen and even tried to get information through the Canadian High Commission in London. Eventually he discovered that labour was to be induced on March 30. Pascale arrived after a difficult birth, but she was happy and perfect. Wally's cheery messages of congratulation disguised the misery he felt at being very far from home. More than ever, he questioned his motivations for this journey. But for now they had to press on.

No sooner had Wally and Allan started on the trail again than towering pressure ice stopped them in their tracks. At one stage it took them six hours to advance only thirty yards. They were cold, bone-weary and weeks behind schedule. They climbed the five-hundred-foot summit of Cape Rawson only to see that the chaos of mountainous ice ridges extended in all directions seaward. Never before in the historical record had the pack ice in that area been under more pressure from the drift of ice. This was no consolation. After days of futile hacking with ice axes they had to call for assistance and were airlifted over the towering death trap of moving, squealing ice. It was discouraging. To be a genuine circumnavigation, the point from which they now started would have to be the official start point of the expedition, and the hard haul of the last seven weeks would count for nothing. It was, as Marie later described, a monstrous journey.

As radio operator for the expedition, Eigil Jensen had been inundated with messages from the press asking for news. He tried his best before telegraphing back in frustration: "Please be patient, take it easy. I can understand that many people want to know what is going on, but this is not Piccadilly Circus, Hyde Park or something similar. This is North Greenland... I will give you news when it arrives." At home, Marie was also trying to handle the press. Wally had been sending beautifully written reports, but the press wanted straightforward, hard-hitting copy. Coverage was essential to keep their sponsors happy.

In despair she telegraphed Wally, "Important you realize there is strong competition for media space—lyrical messages unfortunately not usable suggest give details of adventures and terrain at home trying to cope with sponsors and daughters finding my hands very full." But at that moment, there was simply no news to be had from the two miserable men. They had been struck down with flu on top of all their other problems and were dosing themselves with antibiotics. "Believe me my sweetheart," Wally finally wrote, "I will do my damnedest to get out of here & make it the rest of the way back to Thule & the sponsors—all of them—will get their stories & pictures... My poor darling—you must be so tired. I miss you all terribly." Even though they felt wretched, Wally wrote, they wouldn't give up: "I could of course go on for ages discussing the many reasons why we *must* continue, but you know them all because you know me better than anyone (perhaps including myself!). What I really want to say especially to you my love, my darling, is that I really *want* to go on." He longed for a drop of letters, photographs of the baby and tapes so that he could find comfort in the voices of home.

Finally Wally and Allan were able to move again. As they reached the Thule District, memories came flooding back. The result was a telex from Wally to the *Sunday Times:*

> There can be few polar explorers who have set out on a journey the first 200 miles of which were in the footsteps of their wives. In this male dominated profession, the wives by tradition wave goodbye cheerfully and return to a home which seems empty, while their husbands, bearing the full weight of their strange ambition and their secret hope of fame and fortune carry their loneliness without admitting it to anyone except of course to their diaries which are published when they die.

But in my case, and on this expedition, every mile we have sledged so far and every Eskimo we have met has reminded me of the two years that I spent travelling these well worn routes with my wife and baby daughter... [Soon we'll be] beyond the furthest point north that I travelled with Marie five years ago—I shall miss her companionship then for sure, but one consolation in any journey is that it must eventually end and this, the longest and most hazardous one that I have ever attempted will surely be my last.

Nonetheless, support for the expedition was waning. Eigil Jensen, the expedition's most vigorous supporter, found it hard to conceal his distaste for those who criticized the expedition and its leader: "I will put Wally Herbert up beside men like Francis Drake and the pioneers that started out on the Mayflower with a lot of courage and determination. What he is doing now, out there in a tent, with Allan and the dogs in cold weather (below -40°F) is calling for respect and admiration from every Englishman... It is a great thing he is doing. Nobody can fight nature only make a try and they are for sure trying, that I can tell you." Jensen was shocked at the lack of patriotism being shown and angered by the demanding messages from sponsors. "To hell with [them]," Jensen declared.

The lead newspaper sponsor for the expedition wanted to withdraw its sponsorship and considered asking for its money back. The BBC film appeared to be a non-starter. With the odds stacked so heavily against them, their only reserve was their pride and the faith of a few loyal friends.

Cruelly, Wally's expedition was once again stymied: another channel, another towering impasse of ice. On Sunday, May 1, a bank holiday, a telegram was delivered to Marie: $8,000 Canadian had to be transferred immediately into the account of a small airline that had agreed to pick up the men and dogs and take them to Station Nord. A short telegram written with such urgency could only mean that Wally and Allan were in deep trouble. Marie had no way of knowing if it was a life-or-death situation, and with it being a bank holiday she felt utterly helpless. The money was found and transferred just in time, and a relieved telegram came a few days later: "Arrived Nord... We live to fight another day because of you and for you." Now the men suffered the humiliation of being cheek by jowl with a Japanese expedition at Station Nord that had almost too much money to spend. The spotlight shining brightly on the other expeditions cast a deeper shadow over their own underfunded, increasingly unpopular journey.

Marie wrote to Wally saying she had decided that she must fly to Greenland with the children. "To hell with the expense—life is short and we have been away from you long enough... We are starting a totally new & exciting life together when you finish." She could not know that the two men were about to descend into one of the most colourful episodes of misery either of them had ever encountered.

As midsummer approached, the men reached a peninsula that had been named Hold With Hope by Henry Hudson. Although they had covered sixteen hundred miles, they were running out of both time and food, and the stretch of coast that lay before them had nightmarish qualities. The sea ice was broken and mud-stained. The beach, Wally wrote, was a "strip of ooze into which we sank up to our shins and from which it took us several hours to extricate ourselves... Every item of equipment and clothing, every dog and every exposed square inch of human flesh was covered in wet mud and blue-grey slime." After five miles of torturous travel they made it onto the sea ice, only for it to break up and peel away from the coast. Rain fell in torrents and melt streams roared down the hills, dislodging boulders that would smash anything that happened to get in the way.

Feeling their way along the ice-starved beaches, Wally and Allan hauled their sledges short distances over rocks and through slime, then repeated the journey with another load of equipment—if the sledges were too heavy, they would not budge at all. Day upon day was spent enduring this murderous toil across steaming tundra before they made it to the baked mud flats of Badlandal.

We had been eaten alive by the swarms of mosquitoes and half drowned in the thundering rivers. We had been blasted raw by choking sand storms which even in Tolkien's Middle Earth would hardly have seemed more sinister, for what we had come through had been, in truth, a real and damn-nearly lethal nightmare in which we were tormented and reduced by fatigue to the very brink of insanity. In our fight to defend our breathing space there had been times when we thought the end had come and the mosquitoes in their blood-filled millions finally had won; but in our spluttering and near-hysterical defiance we had cursed and raged and staggered on, flailing the air with arms and whips and hacking a pathway through those mosquitoes until the wind-blown sand had swept down the valley and blown them all to Hell. But by then we were so tired and hungry, and so sick with smoking dried tea leaves, that this seemed like the end of the road.

Their extraordinary journey across the top of the world nine years earlier, which should have been rewarded with lasting recognition, had not received its due. If this circumnavigation of Greenland, the swan song for these two great polar travellers, was not completed, it would compound their sense of failure. They had reached a point where a decision would have to be made: should they abort the journey, or try against all odds to soldier on? Marie made her position clear in language that sounded remarkably reminiscent of Jo Peary seventy years earlier: "I am all for you giving the project everything you have got at the moment—but if you have to abandon it—then I would like you to put it behind you and to come to terms with the new life that must lie ahead."

For Marie, seeing Wally in the flesh in Greenland two months later was heart-rending. He was full-bearded, exhausted and emaciated, the trials of the last few months etched on his face and body. Later that night he dozed sitting upright in a chair, listening to the eager chattering of his seven-year-old daughter as three-month-old Pascale slept peacefully in his arms. Seeing the family again changed everything for Wally. His heart was no longer in the project.

Shortly after, with sea ice blocking their way out of the fjord, the expedition came to a grinding halt. There was nothing for it but to begin a new chapter.

PART THREE

DARKEST
DAYS

12

Eva Nansen

A MAN IN A MILLION

Poor him, he will come too late.

EVA NANSEN

ON OCTOBER 10, 1893, Fridtjof Nansen came down with a fever. Confined aboard the *Fram*, powerless to influence the currents and ice that held the ship captive on the Arctic Ocean, he felt as though he had led his men directly to purgatory. It was his thirty-second birthday, and he was so shrouded in gloom that none of his companions could cheer him. In his diary he wrote:

> So far far away from Eva. Eva, Eva, you are thinking a lot about me today, I feel that, and you are miserable. Why should we be separated ... but what is the point of all this—don't complain, in time, we will meet again.

His only consolation was the distant gleam of Jupiter, which he imagined represented his wife: "Ah how I love that star ... It shines over our journey, it is your eye, no evil can befall us as long as I have it." Constant yearning for his soulmate and the boredom of entrapment were affecting him deeply. It was increasingly unlikely that the *Fram* would ever successfully drift to the North Pole. Nansen took to walking out on the ice alone. He stood for hours gazing skyward. "Parted, parted," he exclaimed, "for no one knows how long from the only one I love." He had become a difficult companion. One minute he was "extravagantly cheerful and pleasant, almost to the point of puerility," the next argumentative or withdrawn.

The following year, having made little progress, and with the darkness of yet another five-month-long winter descending upon them, Nansen gathered his men together and announced his new plan. He, together with Hjalmar Johansen—one of the strongest skiers in the party—would leave the ship as the light returned and use dogs and sledges to reach the Pole, then continue on to Franz Josef Land or the west coast of Greenland. The *Fram* and the rest of the men would continue their drift until the ice released them to return home. This, Nansen reasoned, was their only hope for success.

On February 17, 1895, with the preparations for his attempt at the Pole on skis finally complete, Nansen wrote a letter of farewell to his wife:

> Now it seems a journey towards the sun and summer; towards the only thing that life holds for me... All the time the image rises up before me vividly and beautifully where you receive me when I arrive... And if it should happen that this journey is no bridal dance, you will know that your image will be the last I see... when I go to the eternal rest, where we will meet some time and rest for ever safely in each other's arms. Ah Eva, my Eva, if it should happen, do not cry too hard. Remember no one escapes his fate.

By April 2, Nansen was beginning to have serious reservations about pushing farther north. He and Johansen were still 240 miles from the North Pole, and even farther from the closest known point

of land. Even if they miraculously made it to the Pole, they would not
have the supplies, or the energy, to return to safety. Compounding his
emotions was the daily task of writing in his leather-bound journal,
into which he had pasted a photograph of Eva and their first child, Liv.
Each time he opened his journal he read the lines written by his wife:
"My beloved boy, God grant that happiness, health and good luck will
follow you." These words, which had once inspired him, now made
him want to turn back all the more. On April 6 —a date that in years
to come would be irrevocably written into the history of the North
Pole—Nansen recorded that the chaotic impasse of ice had brought
him to the brink of despair. After many hours of gruelling hauling
and hacking, he and Johansen had advanced barely two miles. The
following day, after sledging ahead and climbing the highest pressure
ridge he could find, Nansen made the decision to turn from the Pole.
To continue north would certainly cost them their lives. That night, he
and Johansen celebrated their new farthest-north record of 86°10' N.
They were, finally, homeward bound.

To the explorers' surprise and delight, no sooner had they turned
south than the heaved-up ice gave way to a smooth frozen sheet that
seemed to reach to the horizon and beyond. "Day and night the
same marvellous ice," Nansen recorded happily. "We sweep over
plain after plain... If it continues like this, the journey home will
be shorter than I thought." Their elation did not last long. To their
dismay, Nansen and Johansen discovered that both their watches had
stopped, and knowing the exact time was the only way they could
precisely fix their position. Making as educated a guess as possible,
they continued south, hoping that they would find land.

Toward the end of May the conditions underfoot changed
dramatically. The snow cover was so loose that the men found
themselves either sinking up to their thighs or ramming into
sastrugi—hard, wind-whipped hummocks of ice that they couldn't
see because of a perpetual whiteout. With the warmer weather came
the porridge-like mush ice. The miserable travelling conditions were
alleviated briefly by the sounds of birds and seals and the distant

blowing of whales—the unmistakable signs of nearing land—but joy was fleeting. Even though game was starting to appear, neither man had successfully shot a morsel. Their supplies were exhausted, and they had been forced to start slaughtering their huskies, feeding dog to dog to survive. It was a bloody, depressing and distressing business. Midsummer's Day, June 24, was the second anniversary of their departure from Christiania. "When I think back to this day, two years ago, dismal and grey as it was, it does not seem long since," Nansen wrote thoughtfully. "I would not go through that day again for anything in the world."

A month later, Nansen wrote again in his diary. They were finally eating fresh meat, and his spirits were soaring. "At last we have seen land! Land! Oh wonderful word!" That evening they celebrated with a hot stew of pemmican with dried sliced bear, seal and bear tongue, with bread crumbs fried in bear fat for dessert. But land itself was elusive. The ice heaved itself up into a glittering barrier or dissolved into belts of treacherous mush ice. Any stable-looking ice was at the mercy of winds and currents, and it appeared to cruelly take them farther from their objective. As autumn fog surrounded them and the ice was stained with the blood-red and gold hues of the waning sun, Nansen miserably realized that the prospect of arriving home that year was slipping beyond their reach. On August 11, the sixth anniversary of his engagement to Eva, he wrote: "Ah, my Eva, today you are surely longing grievously. If only you do not have to wait yet another long, long year." Without being able to calculate their longitude correctly, Nansen and Johansen were undeniably lost. As their third Christmas away from home came and went, Nansen imagined Eva sitting in lamplight sewing a child's dress, with a pretty blond, blue-eyed girl by her side: "She looks tenderly at the child... but her eyes become moist and heavy tears fall on its hair." His tragic image of his wife, however, was not Eva's reality.

Eva had long since refused to become the lonesome, voiceless, stay-at-home wife. She continued to entertain regularly and had begun to perform in public once again. By the time Nansen had built his winter quarters, Eva had given recitals in Copenhagen and had embarked upon a concert tour of Sweden, leaving her daughter in the care of a childhood friend. Re-embracing her career was not simply a panacea for the years of loneliness and anxiety; it was a means for her to regain her sense of self and step out from the shadow of her husband. As the wife of the nation's hero, Eva was constantly under the scrutiny of the press. Some rumoured that she had taken lovers in Nansen's absence; others nicknamed her "the Nordic Penelope," a label she defiantly ignored. If she had to endure being fodder for the newspapers, she preferred that it be on her own terms. Through music, she hoped she could be respected once again as her own woman—as the singer Eva Sars.

Although her performances were well received, the level of Eva's celebrity had significantly changed. It had been two and a half years since her last public appearance, and her reputation as one of the best performers in Norway was largely forgotten. While some critics praised her "rare talent," many others openly wondered whether she was exploiting her husband's name to arouse interest in her recitals. Her performances drew audiences that included King Oscar II of Sweden and Norway and one of his sons, Prince Eugen, and were said to inspire thunderous applause. Nonetheless, with every unsubstantiated report of her husband's success or failure, Eva was held up as a symbol of the long-suffering explorer's wife.

Each year since Nansen's departure, new, often fabricated stories had emerged in the European press. In April 1894 the French newspaper *Figaro* suggested that Nansen had reached the Pole—it turned out to be an April Fool's trick. In September 1895 another report claimed that a police chief in northern Norway had discovered a bottle containing two notes signed and sent by Nansen from the North Pole. By early 1896, a rumour was circulating that Nansen would return successful in March. A *Lokal-Anzeiger* reporter asked whether Eva was overcome with astonishment, hope or joy at the news. She was "unmoved," she replied, "for I did not believe it. I regarded it as a canard, and it left me perfectly composed and cool." The reporter persisted: "Do you not believe in your husband's success, then?" She responded with a sigh: "Only this much I can tell you. I believe in my husband's return, but not now. It is too soon. Besides, the statements are so vague. There is nothing positive and decided in them. They are all unauthentic reports. How could I place any hopes in them?"

In many ways, Eva had lost hope and faith. Enough time had passed for her to question her husband's motives for embarking on such a long and dangerous journey, and she began to doubt his love for her. Dwelling on such thoughts plunged her into a depression verging on the suicidal: "At any rate, I went round and thought out the easiest way of killing myself." Profoundly unhappy, she confessed to a friend that, as a result of such despair, the memory of her husband had all but disappeared.

ON MAY 19, 1896, after enduring eight dreary months trapped in their squalid, primitive winter quarters, Nansen and Johansen began to head south. They had barely started out before blizzards forced them to make camp once more. Johansen recorded miserably:

> To know that one cannot advance, while time passes, and summer goes by... To feel imprisoned here in the unknown, while longing causes one's heart to thump in one's chest—that feels heavy after having lived in this desert of ice for over a year like beasts, and not like human beings.

For Nansen there were other concerns. Surely the *Fram* by now was free from the ice and making her way home—if the ship arrived before them, Eva would no doubt assume that her husband was dead. The thought of such pain being inflicted upon her was almost too much to bear. Taking advantage of a spell of favourable weather, the men made astonishing progress, using sails on the sledges when the ice was firm enough and lashing their kayaks and sledges together as a makeshift catamaran to cross open water. Then providence, of sorts, appeared in the form of an enraged walrus. Walruses are notoriously unpredictable mammals, and this one attacked without warning, puncturing

Nansen's kayak with its tusks and threatening to drag man and craft underwater. Nansen beat the walrus away with his paddle and desperately made for the shore. With his kayak badly damaged, and their remaining equipment soaking wet, the men were once again grounded. On June 17, just as they were about to relaunch, Nansen stiffened and said, "I hear dogs barking inland." Leaving Johansen in charge of the kayaks, he skied quickly toward the elusive sound.

> With strange thoughts hovering between doubt and certainty, I went on, and out of the misty land of doubt, certainty began to dawn—a stream of dogs' barks reached my ears, more distinctly than ever... Suddenly I was certain that I heard a strange voice, the first for three years; what a stream of emotion flooded the soul; how my heart hammered. I jumped up on a hummock and shouted with all the power of my lungs. Behind that single human voice in the middle of this wilderness of ice—this single message from the south, with its pulsating life—lay home and she who was waiting at home for me, and I saw nothing else as I forged ahead between floes and hummocks as fast as my skis could carry me.

In the distance Nansen made out a dark shape moving between the hummocks. It was a dog, and beyond, the unmistakable figure of a man waving. Finally the men faced one another. Nansen immediately recognized the young British adventurer Frederick George Jackson, who had once volunteered to join the *Fram* expedition. Having been turned away by Nansen, Jackson was attempting to discover the North Pole by his own means. On the fateful day of their reunion, Jackson was taking dinner at his expedition headquarters at Cape Flora when one of his men rushed in to say they had seen a man approaching from the south. Later, Jackson recorded the encounter:

> As he approached I saw a man on ski with roughly made clothes and an old felt hat on his head, covered with oil and grease and black from head to foot. His hair was very long and dirty... At first... I... imagined that he was a walrus hunter who had come to

grief in some sloop . . . His complexion appeared to be fair but dirt prevented me being sure on the point. I, having examined his features, came to the conclusion that it must be Nansen.

For the next six weeks, Nansen and Johansen enjoyed the hospitality of their hosts at Cape Flora while they waited for Jackson's expedition support ship, the *Windward*, to take them home. Since leaving the *Fram* they had travelled seven hundred miles—the longest journey so far over the polar pack—and had survived by sheer ingenuity.

On August 13, the *Windward* dropped anchor at Vardø on the Norwegian coast. Within minutes, Nansen and Johansen were making their way to the nearest telegraph office. The first telegram was to Eva: "Here you have your boy at last All well Expedition successful as expected." Five days later, Nansen arrived to a hero's welcome at Hammerfest aboard a modest mail ship. Norwegian flags decked the streets, and residents crowded the quayside to glimpse the explorer. A few hours later, Eva arrived in a small steamer to a salute of guns and the fierce embrace of her husband. "At this ecstatic moment," a German journalist reported, "there was a wonderful expression of happiness in Frau Eva's flushed cheeks and in her gleaming eyes." All vestiges of Eva's depression and fiery independence were for the moment gone. "It is all like a dream and I am in the seventh Heaven," she confided to a friend. "Who could ever have dreamt of such happiness? My man looks wonderful, well-fed, fat and strong. I had expected to find a skeleton."

With remarkable timing, the *Fram* and her crew arrived in Norwegian waters just two days later, then steamed to an emotional reunion with Nansen in Tromsø. Nansen, with Eva by his side, finally sailed into Christiania on the *Fram* on September 9, with an escort of warships pushing through the flotilla of private sailing vessels that had turned out to greet them. A triumphant procession of carriages took the couple to the royal palace to be received by the king and, most important, by Nansen's daughter, Liv, who had stayed at the palace to be reunited with her father. It was perhaps the most rapturous welcome the city had seen.

ONCE THE HEADY days of Nansen's return had faded, there was naturally a period of readjustment to routine. When Eva's independence of spirit rose to the surface, Nansen was bewildered by her need to indulge it. "You have talked about your singing and everything you had done while I was away," he wrote sadly, "and ... I understood that in some ways it was a good thing for you that I left, you could ... devote yourself entirely to your art. Then I understood that in one way you were afraid that this would finish when I came home." Nansen was quickly engrossed in writing the narrative of his journey, *Farthest North,* for which he had been paid a handsome advance. Disenchanted with her preoccupied husband, Eva undertook a concert tour to Stockholm and Helsinki, all the while writing emotionally charged letters back home. In one she threatened to take up the offer of a Russian impresario to continue her tour to St. Petersburg or the United States, rather than come home, unless Nansen proved his love for her.

For the next few years the Nansens' emotional turmoil continued. Often he was away on lecture tours, making the most of his farthest-north record and colourful adventures before they were superseded. Sometimes Eva would join him, but she invariably found the tours tiring and dreary; it was not a little insulting when she was clearly regarded as little more than decoration on the arm of the hero of the hour. Some of the receptions, she complained, were "so boring you could weep tears of blood." On every occasion she knew what people were going to say, she confided to a friend: "Weren't those 3 years horrible? ... You, who knew how to wait, are a far greater hero than your husband, etc. etc. It makes you sick."

For now, Nansen was the darling of Europe. Gold medals were struck in his honour; he was made an honorary professor, and his lectures were applauded with standing ovations. The British in particular took him to their hearts. He was "a Man in a Million," according to the legendary mountaineer Edward Whymper; others called him a "true hero of the century" and even "our popular gladiator." In the United States too he was received with interest, but Nansen was far happier with the more familiar culture of Europe. A rumour that Jo Peary was "furious" with him made him all the more uneasy. Jo's anger, he wrote to Eva, was as a result of "my dedication [of *Farthest North*] to you [who] 'had the courage to remain behind'... She thinks... this is aimed at her. What self-delusion." Eva's courage to remain behind, however, was about to be tested.

Eva had heard, to her dismay, that one of the reasons her husband had gone to the United States was to raise money for an expedition to Antarctica. "Is that true?" she challenged. "You might tell *me* how matters stand." In fact, Nansen had been considering mounting an expedition to the South Pole for some time. However, since Eva had told him that if he embarked on another expedition their relationship would be over, he had been reluctant to share his plans with her.

Eva knew that her chance of accompanying her husband to the Arctic was long gone. Perhaps aggrieved at the lost opportunity, she asserted that no wife of an explorer should be allowed to join a polar expedition. Such adventures, she declared to a journalist, were "outside the sphere of [a] woman." On being reminded that Jo Peary had accompanied her husband to the Arctic, Eva countered: "Yes; and so much the worse for the expedition. It must have been a great burden to carry her along, although Mrs. Peary certainly showed much courage."

Her dismay at the prospect of another long separation was heightened by rumours that her husband was having an affair with Dagmar Engelhart. According to the latest gossip, Eva challenged Nansen, "you and I are going to be divorced, because you are so in love with The Treasure that we can no longer hold out. What is more, you two have been seen alone." Feverishly she continued: "I feel as if we were no longer man and wife, and as if I can only be unhappily in love with you." Nansen responded sadly: "We two are made for each other [yet we] are made to destroy life for each other." Another letter wounded Eva even more deeply. Nansen confessed he had been seeing Dagmar as a means of forgetting that Eva's love was now shared with their two children. "No longer [was I] the only one [and it] tortured me." Eva cabled back in alarm: "Do you love me or The Treasure. Life depends on reply." As always, letters of remorse quickly followed. Eva promised that when Nansen came home he would find her a changed woman and that she would live only for him. In turn he responded, "If you will show some tenderness to me and not just violent emotions . . . that will be enough to make me happy. It is tenderness that I have missed."

FOR A TIME, life at their family home Polhøgda near Fornebu was calmer and sweeter. In the spring, Nansen took his children for long walks, urging them to find the first wood anemones, violets and lilies of the valley for their mother. On summer evenings, the children could hear the distant splash of oars as their father rowed out into the fjord with Eva and the songs she sang back to him.

Such happy times came and went. Acutely aware that young, ambitious explorers would soon challenge his farthest-north record or win the South Pole before he had his chance, Nansen became restless and despondent. "The great emptiness envelops me again," he wrote. "It is my lot to desert what means most to me in order to seek out that which is cold and hard." Family life was sometimes a welcome distraction from such thoughts. In quick succession, Eva gave birth to a further three children, and Nansen focussed his considerable energies on building them a home "where we can shut [out] the whole world" and on returning to his first love, science.

Nansen's celebrity, however, drew him time and again into the limelight. For some years the Swedish Union had been unravelling, and in early 1905 Nansen was conscripted to represent the interests of an independent Norway and to campaign for the royalists. His crucial negotiations behind the scenes in London and elsewhere helped place King Haakon VII on the throne, and it was clear that Nansen would have a significant role in the new Norway. On April 15, 1906, he was once again in London, this time as an ambassador. On his arrival he was greeted with the headline "The Minister from the North Pole" and the comment: "I suppose Dr. Nansen was sent to us because King

Haakon knew from personal experience the rigours of an English spring, and decided that only an Arctic Explorer could stand it."

It was an interesting post, but it meant another separation from Eva and the children. "The King and Queen [of England] both say that you must come over soon," Nansen wrote to his wife, hoping that she might consider joining him. "Everyone is asking after you, and feel sorry for me, having to be here alone, and I heartily agree."

In truth, being in London was a chance for Nansen to distance himself from an uncomfortable situation that had emerged at home. He had begun an affair with the wife of a neighbour, the artist Gerhard Munthe. Sigrun Munthe was an elegant woman with whom both Nansen and Eva regularly went horse riding. Nansen's meetings with her at first were innocent, but as time went on, Sigrun became more persistent in her attentions. When Nansen carelessly sent her some verses by Tennyson, she demanded that he leave Eva and the children, then threatened suicide when he refused. It was not long before Eva became aware of the scandal. "There is much talk about Mrs. Munthe," she wrote to her husband, "and they say that she is unhappily in love with you and has become another person since you left." Although ordinarily confident, when it came to Nansen, Eva had always felt insecure. How could she, plain Eva, compete with the allure of a woman like the Treasure, and now the handsome Mrs. Munthe? She wondered how she could have been so blind to the temptations surrounding her husband.

> I often felt as if you were naturally fond of me in one way, and were sorry for me, but could not withstand the temptation of being together with her. I have borne this unpleasant and destructive [feeling] since she fell off [a horse] last year, and I saw you holding her in your arms, looking down at her with a strange expression.

Nansen admitted that he had acted badly and desperately wanted to make reparations. He begged Eva's friend Ingeborg Motzfeldt to intercede on his behalf, which went some way to ease the pain. "Had Ingeborg not come... and told me that she knew you loved me,"

Eva wrote, "I think I would have gone mad and taken my life, I was already looking in the medicine cupboard." Remarkably, Nansen managed to heal the rift, and Eva became convinced that their love was stronger than ever: "I discovered... when I thought that I had lost you for good—that I care more for you than for the children— Heaven help me it is horrible to admit it, but that is how it is."

Feeling the distance between them acutely, Nansen submitted his resignation as ambassador to London on November 15, 1907. The prospect of his departure left many in England feeling bereft. Nansen had become an integral part of the royal court and high society; King Edward VII in particular objected to Nansen's wish to return home and forbade the explorer to leave. Nansen was polite but immovable. His place now should be home, with Eva and the children. The king conceded but insisted Nansen stay for the visit of Queen Maud from Norway.

A fortnight later, while at the royal country retreat of Sand- ringham, Nansen received a letter from his family doctor. Eva had been taken ill with a persistent cough and a troublesome pain in her right side that could be relieved only with morphine: "There are absolutely no disturbing symptoms, but your wife asked me to write to you, as she is not able to do so." In response, Nansen wrote light- hearted letters to his wife, which cheered her enormously. Hearing that he had been persuaded to dance with Queen Maud between the bridge tables at Sandringham, Eva replied: "Now don't you go and fall in love with Queen Maud! Or let yourself be tempted by her flirting—just you remember!... Flirt as much as you like, but don't go too far. Amen!"

By November 21, Eva's illness had worsened. Bedridden, she still managed to write to her husband: "We must make sure we enjoy ourselves in future... not go our separate ways too much... Won't you try?" A few days later she continued:

I have become so thin, and am glad that I have time to put on weight before you arrive, I so want you to be in love with me again as in the old, long vanished days. You will see I will be pretty for your sake... Now and then, if you are dissatisfied with me, say so straight out and not put on your stiff, cold immovable face and silence, because then we will be back in the old misery again, and I will become old and irritable... I don't think we have always been sensible and shown confidence in each other; not I in any case. I have often been afraid of you, and on that account failed to say many things... And then that repulsive woman came between us, which made me more and more bitter and less fond of you with each passing day. Ugh, one can't go through such things without being marked. But everything will be better when we both show good intentions and much love.

Having been charged with the care of King Haakon, who had joined Queen Maud, Nansen remained at Sandringham, reassured by letters from Eva that she was feeling better. On December 7, Eva's birthday, he telegraphed her with love and his hopes for her speedy recovery. His telegram crossed with another from the doctor, reporting his wife's sudden decline. In distress, Nansen raced toward Norway. At Hamburg a telegram intercepted him. Eva had died from pneumonia.

Numb with shock, Nansen continued homeward. For days he sat silent and immobile alone in a room, too removed by grief to respond even to his children. He was haunted by guilt and incapacitated by longing and loss, and it was weeks before he was able to allow his feelings to surface. Finally, in his diary he wrote:

So kindly from her heights, where nothing more can reach her, she smiles down on my misunderstood striving, which separated me from her for a time. Now all is shattered...

One of the last things she said was: 'Poor him, he will come too late.' Ah yes, he came too late, and now all is lost. The only great thing that life gave has gone.

Ah what have I possessed—now I am poor and alone.

Here everything is so cold and inconsolably forlorn.

Out there in the night the moon is shining down on the frozen, snow-covered ground.

Life? Confused sleep-walking.

What a nightmare, and I wanted only to wake. Now I want to sleep.

13

Jo Peary

COLD AWAKENING

These are the darkest days of my life.

JO PEARY

O N A COLD March day in 1900, Jo Peary began the last of five identical handwritten letters. The letters would be sent with separate whaling vessels bound for the Arctic, in the hope that one might reach her husband. She was used to the lengthy, uncertain process of trying to get news to him, but this time she had to draw on deeper reserves of strength as she repeated the same excruciating words. "My Darling, My Husband," she began once again:

> For the first time in my life it seems a hard task to write to you as I ought. If only the time since last August has not been as hard for you as it has been for me is all I ask & pray for nightly. Surely, surely, we ought not both to suffer & I have suffered for both. Our little

darling whom you never knew was taken from me on August 7 [1899], just 7 months after she came. She was only sick a few days but the disease took right hold of her little head & nothing could be done for her... Oh my husband I wanted you, how much you will never know. I shall never feel quite the same again part of me is in the little grave.

Confounded by grief and loneliness after the death of her seven-month-old daughter, Francine, Jo was plunged into renewed fears for her family when her older daughter, Marie, was quarantined for several weeks with a vicious bout of measles, followed by scarlet fever. "Surely," Jo wrote hopelessly, "God will not take her from me too. She is all I have left to live for. I mean the one to whom it makes any *real* difference."

The turbulent twelve years of marriage had taken their toll. Jo had married Robert Peary knowing that there would be long periods of separation, but the loss of Francine on top of all the other pressures of being an explorer's wife was too much to bear. The news that her husband had lost several toes to frostbite and was still refusing to come home was yet another blow.

The news of your terrible suffering... nearly prostrated me but you know I am strong & can bear, & bear & bear. Oh Sweetheart, husband, together we could have shared it but alone it is almost too much. You too will carry the scars of your sufferings all your life & not only physically.

Her last remark echoed the concerns of some of Peary's supporters and friends that his desire to conquer the North Pole had become an obsession. Should he fail to reach the Pole this time, he planned to try the following year, and so on until his goal had been accomplished. Peary was supremely confident that he would be victorious, as long as another competitor did not beat him to the prize. However, when he had boarded the *Hope* at Sydney, Nova Scotia, on July 7, 1898, he was aware that another veteran polar explorer, Otto Sverdrup, was sailing toward the same part of the Arctic in the *Fram*.

Sverdrup had accompanied Fridtjof Nansen on the first crossing of the Greenland ice cap, had lived with the Inuit of western Greenland and had captained Nansen's *Fram* on the ambitious attempt to drift across the Arctic Ocean via the North Pole five years earlier. Although Sverdrup insisted that his goal was only to reach the northern part of Greenland and to map the surrounding areas, Peary was convinced that the Norwegian was secretly planning to bag the Pole. Both explorers were to be in the same area at precisely the same time, with the *Fram* anchoring just forty-three miles south of Peary's second ship, the *Windward*. Their proximity increased Peary's paranoia. Determined not to lose his chance of a northern base to a competitor, he insisted that his team fight their way to Fort Conger, on Ellesmere Island, dangerously early in the season. It almost cost him and his party their lives. Suffering from starvation, exposure and exhaustion, they would not have survived had they not found the remote hut.

Fort Conger was an eerie place, littered with the remnants of the Greely expedition of 1881, which had ended in disaster. Eighteen out of twenty-five of Adolphus Greely's men had died of starvation, hypothermia or drowning. One man had been executed for stealing rations. Those who survived were accused of resorting to cannibalism in the last desperate days before their rescue. It was there, at the Greely expedition headquarters, that Peary noticed a suspicious wooden feeling in his right leg. As Matt Henson cut away Peary's sealskin boots, he discovered that both Peary's legs were bloodless white to the knee. As Henson ripped off the undershoes, several of Peary's toes from each foot clung to the hide and snapped off at the first joint. "My God, Lieutenant! Why didn't you tell me your feet were frozen?" Henson cried. "There's no time to pamper sick men on the trail," Peary replied tersely, adding, "Besides, a few toes aren't much to give to achieve the Pole." The surgeon Thomas Dedrick, using primitive tools and medicines, then performed the grim task of removing parts of seven of Peary's toes, with no anaesthetic.

For six weeks Peary lay at Fort Conger, his broken body and a savage winter holding him and his men hostage. The forced inactivity, constant pain and his humiliating dependence on others for his daily needs plunged him into depression. To urge himself on, he scrawled a quotation from Seneca on the wooden wall beside his bunk: "Inveniam viam aut faciam" (I shall find a way or make one). It was a motto that would forever be linked to him.

Even after a prolonged convalescence, Peary was unable to stand unassisted. It was clear that he had to return to the ship, but that was a grim prospect. Weather and light conditions were poor, the men were weak, and Peary would have to be lashed to a sledge as the party negotiated a route over jagged ridges of ice. On one occasion, loyal Henson bent down and let the others guide the sledge over his back down a drop, so that the invalid would not be jarred too much.

On returning to the ship, Peary had a second operation to remove all but the little toes. Within five weeks, with the stumps still raw, he was once again on the move. His attempt to continue with the expedition was a disaster. He was a mere dead weight on the sledge, and his unhealed right foot assumed an unhealthy appearance. Again he had to return to the ship. When the relief ship *Diana* arrived, Peary locked himself away to read the letters from home. Tragically, unbeknownst to him, just five days before he read the happy letter from Jo telling him of their daughter Francine's birth, the fragile child had died of infantile cholera.

As Jo mourned alone, Peary found strength and solace in her scent, which still clung to the letters, supplies and gifts she had packaged up for him a few weeks earlier. On August 27, 1899, he wrote: "Never was a man more fortunate in his wife than I . . . never a wife more loving, tender, delicious, yet with it all, clear and level headed. Your letter was like an exquisite soft warm breeze of spring in this lonely desert." Discarding his old furs, he bathed and dressed in the clothes Jo had sent, put her letter in his inside pocket and devoted the day to her. "Ah sweetheart," he wrote longingly. "If only I might really have you if only for a day."

Then he told her of his recent struggles. Knowing the reaction the news of his mutilated feet would provoke, he lightly dismissed the situation:

The past year has been particularly free from annoyances with the exception of the one unpleasant episode... viz the frosting of my toes. This gave the doctor an opportunity to trim them up a little, and as a result when I come back I shall be able to wear a size shorter shoe. The mishap is of no importance. The toes were slow in healing because I did not give them rest. They are well now and cause me no trouble, and no one will be aware of the mishap unless they are told.

Brave as always, Jo made light of her feelings in her letters. But as she saw her youth fade, she tried to reconcile her husband's ambitions with the wish to have him back as husband and father. Peary agreed:

You are right dear, life is slipping away. That cannot come to you more forcibly than it has repeatedly to me in times of darkness and inaction the past year. More than once I have taken myself to task for my folly in leaving such a wife and baby (babies now) for this work. But there is something beyond me, something outside of me, which impels me irresistibly to the work. I shall certainly come back to you. I believe I shall accomplish my object and then hand in hand we will meet the days and years until the end comes... If I succeed well and good. If not, this is not everything in the world by any means.

His letters to Jo completed, Peary handed them to Herbert Bridgman, the commander of the relief operation, and informed Bridgman that he would remain in the Arctic for another year. Bridgman was aghast. As a newspaperman he knew the value of heroic stories, but this was going too far. Horrified at the wreck of the man he had found, and filled with doubt that Peary could survive another year in the Arctic, let alone conquer the Pole, Bridgman urged him to return home. Peary refused.

Bridgman's reports of the explorer's emaciated body and mutilated feet prompted a wave of concern from Peary's supporters. Rumours circulated that the explorer was at best showing a distinct lack of objectivity, and at worst exhibiting early signs of megalomania. Increasingly, Jo found herself under pressure to use her influence to bring her husband back. But, dutiful to his dreams as always, she continued to encourage him.

> Your mother, Mrs. Jesup & others think I will induce you to return this year if you have not succeeded. But you need have no fears, I am far too proud of my husband to want him to waive duty for inclination. You have involved others in this scheme & as long as you have health & can see your way clearly it is a matter of *duty*. If at the end of your leave you have not succeeded I know you will gladly return but I know too that you will *never* be satisfied with yourself & it is that which I dread more than your failure.

Jo knew that only she could judge what state of mind and body her husband was in. She had to return to the Arctic and, if possible, convince him to come home. She would raise the money to take the *Windward* back to Greenland, in the hope that she would find him alive and well.

While Jo and Marie were making the final preparations for their journey north, Peary was enjoying one of his happiest periods in the Arctic. His feet were in far better condition. Mentally too he was far stronger—proven by the extraordinary journeys he had completed during the summer. In May 1900, after overcoming considerable hardships, he had discovered the northernmost tip of Greenland, proving the insularity of the island. At the cape, which he named after Morris Jesup, his chief benefactor, he had built a small cairn and sealed within it a small square cut from the Stars and Stripes that Jo had hand-stitched for him.

Fort Conger had taken on an entirely new complexion. There was plenty of fresh meat—in two months the men had killed no less than one hundred muskox, and Arctic hares were so plentiful that from a distance the barren summer landscape looked like a vast field covered in snow. Peary had the old Greely headquarters demolished and built a series of smaller huts, which were easier to heat and afforded him some privacy. On July 12, 1900, he wrote in his journal: "Wonderful this cabin... this mellow life, this warmth... this freedom from care or annoyance, this freedom to do as I please; it will unfit me for [later] life I fear."

ON JULY 21, 1900, the *Windward* left the sun-warmed docks of Sydney, Nova Scotia, and headed north with Jo and Marie on board. Newspaper headlines congratulated the intrepid Mrs. Peary on her mission to rescue her famous Arctic explorer. "Mrs. Peary is a woman who will have her way," one claimed:

> Arguments and entreaties have been powerless to dissuade her from attempting the journey... She is fathoms deep in love with him, and she says she would follow him to the ends of the earth. She has proved her faith by doing it on three previous occasions. "They are so devoted to each other," said Mrs. Diebitsch, Mrs. Peary's mother, "that they think nothing they can do for each other a sacrifice. My daughter is a fearless woman. The only thing that ever seems to make her afraid is the thought of losing her child."

As Captain Sam Bartlett steered the ship toward Greenland they found themselves confronting the first marker of the northern boundary: fog. "Thick, damp, white fog," Marie later wrote, "the curse of the sea, the secret dread of every sailor, no matter how experienced. Fog so dense that you felt as if you could take hold of it. Fog blowing into your eyes, dripping from the rigging, holding the smoke down to the decks so that it stung your nose with every breath." Suddenly, a shout rang through the ship: "ICEBERG DEAD AHEAD!"

With a terrific lurch, the ship spun on her heel and keeled over. Jo flung one arm around a stanchion and the other around her daughter. Everything movable on deck crashed about them. They expected at any moment to feel the shock as the berg struck them, but slowly the ship righted herself. Missing them by inches, a jagged tower of ice swept by. Before it was out of sight the giant berg split and capsized, throwing up vast waves in its wake.

In the following days, Jo and Marie made preparations for the expected reunion. Jo hung new undergarments over the stove so that they would be warm and soft for her husband, then put out bottles of Yquem, sparkling Moselle and Maraschino. Marie brushed out the cabin and decorated it. After an exhausting month-long journey through Melville Bay, the *Windward* limped into the waters at Etah, on the far northwestern coast of Greenland. Peary's flag was not flying as it should have been. Marie's first impulse was to run to her mother and cry, but one glance at Jo stopped her short. "She was standing very still, gazing off into the distance with such a strange, frozen look upon her face that I realized at once that she was feeling even worse than I."

Quickly, Captain Bartlett had a boat lowered and went ashore. It was not long before he returned, vigorously waving a piece of paper above his head and shouting repeatedly, "He's all right, Mrs. Peary." When Bartlett was within reach of the ship he shouted up, "He's just moved across to Cape Sabine and wants the ship to join him there." Jo's relief was tempered: it was clear Peary had not received her letters advising him that she and Marie were heading north, or that Francine had died.

Although she was a whaling vessel, the *Windward* had not been built for the High Arctic. Already there were signs of an early winter, and heavy pack ice was pushing to the south, giving a clear indication of troubles to come. Even though by now the decks of the ship were filled with Inuit hunters and their families and dogs, Cape Sabine was not a spot to be stranded upon.

It took them eight long days to cross the sound—under normal circumstances it would have taken them just a few hours. At times the ice floes crowded in so much that the ship groaned with the pressure. Eventually the *Windward* anchored at Payor Harbour near Cape Sabine. But Peary was not there, either. He was farther north at Fort Conger, and there were 250 miles of impenetrable ice between them. With such bad conditions Jo and the rest of the party could not afford to press on. They would have to bed in for the winter or make their escape. Although the thought of returning home without seeing her husband was excruciating, Jo was aware that there were others to consider. In addition, if they remained, the crews' fees over the winter would have to be met. "I therefore take the responsibility of ordering [the *Windward*] home," she wrote sadly in a note to be left for her husband, adding: "If I am going against your wishes, I shall be more than sorry for believe me I am doing what I believe to be the best for your interest. It is like death to me to go back." The following day provisions would be offloaded for Peary, and the *Windward* would sail south. Heartbroken, Jo tucked Marie into bed and succumbed to a restless sleep.

While the exhausted crew and passengers tried to rest, swollen seas edged with ice crowded in on the *Windward*. In no time, fast-running currents dragged the ship from her mooring, and she was driven against the craggy shore. Jo and Marie, already dressed in their warmest clothes, were hauled onto the deck and quickly bundled into a smaller boat waiting to take them ashore. Around them a snowstorm raged, chilling them to the core. They clung to each other for warmth as they watched the crewmen frantically removing goods from the *Windward* as she bucked and shrieked, her strained timbers giving voice to the pressure she was under. As the tide went out the ship was left stranded, balanced precariously on the rocks.

For a short time the company thought they were saved. With the turn of the tide, the *Windward* was released from the rocks and floated into deeper waters. Their relief was short-lived. The violent weather had wedged a large iceberg at the entrance to the harbour, blocking their escape. The next high tide, instead of carrying the berg away, ground it deeper still. Attempts to blast it with dynamite achieved nothing. They were prisoners for the winter.

Upon arriving in the Far North, Jo had received another blow. Among the young Inuit women on board was a girl she had met on a previous expedition to Greenland. Aleqasina, still in her teens, was the wife of a skilled hunter. On her back she carried a baby boy called Anaukkaq. Peary, she innocently informed Jo, was the boy's father.

Long before Peary had set foot in Greenland, he had written in his journal that he believed the presence of women on an expedition was essential: "It is asking too much of masculine human nature to expect it to remain in an Arctic climate enduring constant hardship, without one relieving feature. Feminine companionship not only causes greater contentment, but as a matter of both mental and physical health and the retention of the top notch of manhood it is a necessity." Five years before he had added: "If colonisation is to be a success in the polar regions let white men take with them native wives... Then from this union may spring a race combining the hardness of the mothers with the intelligence of the fathers." It is unlikely that he shared such thoughts with his wife, but an "ethnological" photograph of Aleqasina posing naked in his book *Northward over the Great Ice,* published years before, in 1898, must later have been a painful reminder to Jo of his infidelity.

Peary had begun a program of making ethnological records of the Inuit during his first expedition to northwest Greenland. His request to photograph the Inuit nude understandably puzzled his subjects. "It was interesting to observe the modesty both of the women and the men," he noted. "I told them that we wished to compare their bodies with those of other people in the world." Peary had first met Aleqasina when she was just ten years old at Anniversary Lodge during his 1893–94 expedition with Jo. He recalled that Aleqasina, who was just beginning to develop into a woman, evinced extreme reluctance at having her picture taken, and only a direct order from her father accomplished the desired result. In 1896 Peary described "Ally" as "the belle of the tribe."

Jo had suspected that her husband had a mistress in the Arctic, but the prospect of being trapped with Aleqasina and Peary's illegitimate son for an entire winter was agonizing. "These," she confessed, "are the darkest days of my life."

Just before the *Windward* became imprisoned, Jo had begun a letter to her husband, which she expected to leave for him before returning home with her daughter. Remarkably, the twenty-six-page letter still exists and is now privately owned. With the loss of her daughter still so raw, Jo poured her grief, anger and fierce sense of betrayal onto paper: "You will have been surprised, perhaps annoyed, when you hear that I came up on a ship . . . but believe me had I known how things were with you here I should not have come." It took five pages of expedition business for her to gather the strength to confront the issue that had broken her heart:

> I have looked out for Allakasingwah and your boy & allowed them in the cabin with Marie. It is a great concession for me to make . . . It cut me like a knife to hear her tell Marie all about you . . . To think she has been in your arms, has received your caresses, has heard your love-cries, I could die at the thought . . . Have you, my husband, ever thought what these years have been to me since I bade you farewell?
>
> During these hungry years I have been consoling myself . . . with the thought that it was just as hard for you, & I must be brave for your sake . . . On reaching Etah I find you have probably never given me a thought & a creature scarcely human has the power to make you forget everything except her. Oh my love, why do I live?

Jo continued with other pressing news from home until she could no longer stem her grief. "Everything is gone from me & I can't remember my child's name at times. Oh my sweetheart my love how can I face the future without you. You who have given me more pain & more pleasure, more sorrow & more joy than any one else in the world. I can't give you up. I can't. You gave me three years of the most exquisite pleasure that can be had after that the pleasure was pretty evenly divided with the pain until now it is all pain except the memory of what has been." Astonishingly, she promised she would continue to do everything she could to support her husband and his work, but added, "I have the strongest feeling that I shall never see you again. I have felt this way all along but never so much as when I buried my baby & now... I shall not hear you I shall not feel your touch nor look into your eyes. *My darling, mine,* in spite of anyone."

Marie later recalled her mother during this time:

> Just by closing my eyes, I can even now call up the picture of that tiny comfortless cabin on the *Windward* and Mother singing "Swanee River" and "Old Black Joe," and "The Blue Alsatian Mountains"... while tears rolled down her cheeks. I thought then that she was crying because the songs were so sad. But that is the only time that I can remember having seen Mother cry. She was never sad and she never complained. It was as if she had determined that my childhood should not be clouded by griefs and worries which I was too young to understand.

The *Windward* was a working vessel, and the quarters Jo shared with Marie were so cramped that only one of them could dress at a time. The only escape from the confines of the ship was to walk outside, but in winter there was twenty-four-hour darkness and polar bears were likely to be in the vicinity. The area of Payor Harbour was bleak and soulless. It seemed as though the land itself was echoing Jo's powerful sense of desolation. Even so she did her best to mask her feelings, even when Aleqasina fell desperately ill. Remarkably, Jo took it upon herself to nurse her, although she remarked she was only doing so for her husband. By the end of August the woman's condition had become serious. "I am much afraid you will lose your 'Ally,'" Jo wrote to Peary on August 31. "This morning she was a pitiful sight." Knowing that the Inuit custom was to strangle a baby who was orphaned while still being nursed, Jo elicited a promise from the other Inuit on board that the boy would be spared if his mother died. In her letter to Peary she added, "I hope for your sake the woman will recover." Aleqasina did recover and bore three more children. One, a boy named Kale born a few years later, was also fathered by Peary.

To take her mind off the situation, Jo tried to encourage a happy atmosphere on the ship. She ensured that Marie's seventh birthday was celebrated, and when Christmas came, she ingeniously created a Christmas tree with the help of the on-board taxidermist, using a broomstick, wire, candle wax, coffee grounds and green-painted strands of hay. Her only outlet for her thoughts was through her letters to Peary, but she kept her emotions under control:

> Should this reach you, you must *not think of coming down* ... [Ally] has told me how very tender your feet are and you must do nothing that would in any way interfere with your work ... You wrote me that *failure* would not affect you seriously. I want you to know that whenever you return your friends, who are many, will think you the bravest, pluckiest explorer that ever went into the field ... Whatever you do you must take care of yourself ... Sometimes I think you are a physical wreck. If this is so, come home and let Marie and me love you and nurse you. Don't let your pride keep you back. Who will *even* remember it ten years from now? ... Oh, Bert, Bert. I want you so much. Life is slipping away so fast— pretty soon all will be over.

Together with Captain Bartlett, Jo took an inventory of their stores, and a rationing system was drawn up to avoid having to break into the supplies that had been brought up for Peary. The ship was bedded down for the winter using banks of snow blocks against the sides, with canopies laid over the decks to conserve warmth. Knowing the importance of fresh meat to keep them healthy, Jo offered the hunters every inducement to stay, but she could not persuade them to travel to Fort Conger with news. The journey was notoriously dangerous at that time of year. Besides, the hunters insisted, it was bad luck for the living to go among the dead.

Oblivious that his wife and daughter were so close, Peary wrote to Jo that over the last weeks he "had but one thought, an intense unevadable longing for you and my babies":

> How blind, blind, blind, I was and how clearly you saw it all. A great slice out of our lives, apart from each other, and for what, a little fame. I would exchange it all for a day with you . . . I woefully overestimated my strength when I thought I could remain away from you three or four years. Two years is the utmost limit, and I should not be equal to that again . . . I carry the pictures of you, and my babies, and your last letter, with me everywhere. They will be very threadbare when I bring them back to you.

Another attempt at the Pole had come to nothing. It seemed as if Peary's every effort was thwarted, and that his goal was unattainable. Dispirited, he continued: "The past runs black, the future blacker . . . I feel at times I am going mad. I have lost my sanguine hope, my élan, I am an old man, I think at times I have lost you."

Finally, on April 17, Peary turned south toward home. Within two weeks, he encountered a party from the *Windward*. With the return of the light, Jo had finally persuaded some hunters to relay a message to Peary.

According to Matt Henson, Peary winced at the news. Strangely, instead of rushing to the *Windward*, he instead made for a small hut nearby at Cape D'Urville and secluded himself there to gather his thoughts. Had he left immediately he could have reached the *Windward* easily in one or two days, but it took him six. His hesitancy perhaps was due to the twenty-six-page letter the Inuit hunters from the *Windward* carried with them. A letter from his mother must have also found its mark:

> Bertie Mine . . . Oh my child do come home give up this pursuit— which has resulted in so much suffering and privation to you and sorrow and anxiety to those that love you. Every night dear Marie

says dear Lord watch over my dear father and bring him safely home to me... My heart ached for Jo when she had to give up her baby. She needed you in her greatest sorrow. No one could fill your place.

Peary's arrival at the *Windward*, on May 6, 1901, was perfectly timed. It was his forty-fifth birthday, and knowing Jo's particular observance of such occasions, he knew that would be some distraction from the issues he would have to face. Marie recalled the reunion:

On May fifth, the day before my father's birthday, I was allowed to help make a magnificent birthday cake. Mother had decided that we would celebrate in Dad's honour even if he could not be there to enjoy the feast with us... I have wondered since what Mother really thought as she looked at it.

Very, very early the morning of the sixth, I was awakened by a thud above my head, as if someone had jumped from the ship's rail on to the deck. Then there was the sound of hurrying feet coming down the companionway. Mother sat bolt upright in bed, with her eyes shining like two stars, and said in a quiet little voice: "It is your father!"

Scarcely had she spoken when the door burst open to admit a fur-clad giant who made one rush straight for Mother. He never turned in my direction at all until I piped up in a hurt and abused voice: "I'm here too, Dad!" Then what a bear hug I received!... Mother had known his step, even in her sleep!

Reunited with her husband after almost three years, Jo resolutely fell again into the role of wife and support. She could not consider life being any other way.

Later that summer the ship *Erik* arrived, sent by the Peary Arctic Club, a group of the explorer's wealthy supporters. Frederick A. Cook, the doctor from Peary's first polar expedition and the man who would become his greatest rival, was also on board. Herbert

Bridgman had requested that Cook accompany him to gauge the fitness of the man the club was funding. The doctor by no means held back in his assessment:

> The first impression was of an iron man, wrecked in ambition, wrecked in physique, wrecked in hope... Peary was worried, anxious, discouraged as I have never seen him before. In desperate overreaching he had frozen both feet. Dr. Dedrick had removed eight of his toes leaving only the two small digits and painful stubs with which he could barely walk.

Cook advised that Peary was suffering the early symptoms of pernicious anemia and prescribed a diet of raw meat and liver. Peary is said to have replied, "I would rather die." Cook retorted that his old commander was "through as a traveller." Peary, outraged at the effrontery of this man—a man nine years his junior whom he had once regarded as a friend and who clearly had ambitions to rival his own—refused to dignify the doctor's statement with an answer.

Perhaps it was Cook who gave Peary the impetus to stay on in the Arctic. Perhaps it was his crushing sense of defeat and embarrassment that he had not achieved all he had set out to do. There was one person to whom Peary felt he needed to prove himself: his mother. Or her spirit, at least. Among the letters from home was one informing Peary of his mother's death.

In a surprisingly candid interview published by the *New York American* years later, Jo confessed that she had finally challenged her husband: "Why don't you tell them that you have found [the Pole] and let it go at that?" She recalled his reply: "Because there are a hundred ways in which I would be found out."

Squaring up to Peary's stubborn resolve, Jo gave him an ultimatum. She would do everything she could to support him during the five years he had set aside for Arctic exploration. After that time, she believed that he owed it to himself and his family to return, unless he intended to make the Arctic his home. Certain now that he had

Jo's unconditional love, despite his infidelity, Peary headed once more toward the Pole. Ten months after they had arrived, his wife and daughter boarded the *Erik,* watching sadly as Peary disappeared from view.

14

Kathleen Scott

I MAY BE SOME TIME

I watched his face radiating tenderness
as the space between us widened,
until I held only my memory of that upturned face,
but held it for a lifetime.

KATHLEEN SCOTT

ON VALENTINE'S DAY 1910, Robert Scott wrote to his wife: "I was lying abed thinking last night, and all you've done and are doing for me spread itself out—and I saw all the brave attempts to conquer the horrid parts of me ... When things look bad, when I'm tiresome or petulant, don't think your care is wasted. When I'm away on the snows it will be bad to remember that I've grieved you, but it would be infinitely worse if I thought that you didn't know that I understood your sacrifices. My dear, my dear, my heart is very full of you in spite of the hard crust which you find it so difficult to get through."

Five months later, on July 16, he and Kathleen boarded HMS *Saxon* and, along with the wives of Bill Wilson and Teddy Evans, left England bound for Cape Town for a rendezvous with the *Terra Nova,* which had sailed ahead of them. From there, Scott took command of the *Terra Nova* and assigned Wilson to the task of chaperoning the wives on the liner *Corinthic* to New Zealand. Neither Wilson nor Kathleen was happy with the arrangement. Wilson, used to the all-male company on the *Terra Nova*, didn't much care for the company of the women. After all her support so far, Kathleen thought it unfair to be treated as an outsider in regard to expedition affairs.

Kathleen was even less impressed with Wilson's wife, Ory, and the other "polar wives": "If ever Con has another expedition," she wrote, "the wives must be chosen more carefully than the men—better still, have none." Kathleen made little effort to be popular. Unlike Hilda Evans, who seemed to be universally liked, the team member Birdie Bowers reported, "Mrs. Scott is another sort . . . Nobody likes her in the expedition & the painful silence when she arrives is the only jarring note in the whole thing. There is no secret that she runs us all now & what she says is done—through [Scott]." Bowers, like many others on board, did not like to see "women out of their provinces." "Mrs. S. is very ambitious," he continued, "& has too much say with the expedition for my liking . . . Certainly she appears to influence her husband & to make this apparent is a crime." When away from his wife, Bowers observed, Scott became just another man aboard ship.

Wilson certainly had his hands full with Kathleen. When finally the *Terra Nova* came into Melbourne on October 10, 1910, she demanded to be taken out in wild seas to greet the ship. Wilson protested that the other women were cold and hungry and that it was too dangerous to risk their lives, when they could easily wait for calmer conditions. Kathleen persisted. After enduring a rough crossing, a near capsizing and some hysterics, they reached the *Terra Nova* and saw their husbands holding lanterns above them. "It was for them on board, Capt Scott and Lieutenant Evans, to say whether I should risk drowning their wives now," Wilson reported. He hoped that in the future "it will never fall to my lot to have more than one wife at a time to look after, at any rate in a motor launch, in a running sea, at night time."

For Kathleen, seeing Scott again made the world far brighter. But the joy of the reunion ended abruptly. Also waiting in Melbourne was a telegram sent from Madeira on September 9, 1910, by the Norwegian explorer Roald Amundsen. "Beg leave to inform you *Fram* proceeding Antarctic. Amundsen." The cable was dated October 3 and had been sent from Christiania, even though the *Fram* had left Norway with Amundsen on board three months earlier. It was mystifying.

Amundsen was a diligent, inspired explorer who had planned to reach the North Pole. On hearing that both Peary and Cook were claiming priority there, he decided to turn his attentions to the South Pole. He had felt it unnecessary to inform anyone of his plans: not his financial backers; not Nansen, who had lent him his ship the *Fram;* nor even the majority of his crew. Burdened with this audacious secret, Amundsen had sailed from Christiania on course for Buenos Aires. From there, the *Fram* was supposed to head up to the Bering Strait and beyond. However, when the ship docked in Madeira, Amundsen finally revealed his intentions. The situation had to be handled tactfully—he couldn't risk a mutiny, and his respect for his benefactor, Nansen, made the disclosure uncomfortable. Nansen had been Amundsen's trusted supporter for years and had provided him with one of his own ships, *Gjoa,* as well as valuable supplies and the financing that had enabled Amundsen to be the first to successfully traverse the Northwest Passage four years earlier. The astonishment of Amundsen's men at the news quickly gave way to excitement. "Before going North," wrote one of the men to his wife, "we will make a small excursion to the South Pole." "Hurrah," cheered another. "That means we'll get there first!" Letters and orders for the strategic announcement of Amundsen's change of plan were entrusted to his brother, and the anchor was quickly weighed. The *Fram* slipped away toward Tasmania, and then to Antarctica.

This unexpected turn of events struck a devastating blow to Scott. Initially he kept the news to himself, confiding only in Kathleen. But Amundsen's sensational announcement had already made Norwegian headlines. When the *Daily Telegraph* reported the story, those in London became aware of the challenge. With Kathleen beside him, Scott reiterated to the newspaper that the primary reason for his own expedition was scientific research, not the quest for the Pole. But further reports that Amundsen might try to forestall Scott on his own base were unsettling. There was nothing for it but to leave as soon as possible.

Kathleen and Scott travelled on to Lyttelton to oversee the remaining preparations for the journey south. The *Terra Nova* was painstakingly loaded with a vast array of equipment: 3 motor sledges, 460 tons of coal, collapsible huts and an ice house, along with 162 carcasses of mutton, 35,000 cigars, 32 tons of pony fodder, 5 tons of dog food, 15 ponies, 35 huskies, 3 rabbits, a fantail pigeon, a guinea pig and the obligatory ship's cat (with its own hammock). Kathleen sat on a crate and sewed name tags onto the clothing. In between their tasks she and her husband spent happy hours together on a cliff jutting out over the sea with snow-capped mountains in the distance.

So much time, energy and emotion had gone into her husband's endeavour that Kathleen refused to believe that anything could go wrong. Simply put, she believed that it was Scott's destiny to claim the South Pole, and that she had been placed beside him to help him attain the prize. Such a high opinion of her role did not endear her to the other expedition members or their wives. Tensions increased as the women struggled to contain their concern for their men. Hilda Evans constantly aired her fears, working her husband, Teddy, "up to insurrection." Kathleen was exasperated by what she saw as Hilda's destructive childishness. Hilda Evans thought Kathleen was insufferable and heartless, and when Ory Wilson interjected, they all exploded. Titus Oates described the scene: "Mrs. Scott and Mrs. Evans had a magnificent battle, they tell me it was a draw after 15 rounds. Mrs. Wilson flung herself into the fight after the 10th round and there was more blood and hair flying about the hotel than you see in a Chicago slaughter house in a month, the husbands got a bit of the backwash and there is a certain amount of coolness which I hope they won't bring into the hut with them." "May it never be known," Birdie Bowers wrote, "how very nearly the 'Terra Nova' came to not sailing at the last few hours."

Kathleen and Scott spent their last day alone together, walking over the hills and gazing out at the sea. On November 29, the women stayed on board the *Terra Nova* as she sailed out of the harbour to resounding cheers from crowds gathered at the docks. Once the ship was out of sight, a tug drew alongside to take the women back to shore.

"I didn't say goodbye to my man," Kathleen wrote, "because I didn't want anyone to see him sad... On the bridge of the tug Mrs. Evans looked ghastly white & said she wanted to have hysterics but instead we took photos of the departing ship. Mrs. Wilson was plucky and good." Quietly the men watched as the tug took the women away. Wilson wrote of the departure of his wife: "There on the bridge I saw her disappear out of sight waving happily, a goodbye that will be with me till the day I see her again in this world or the next." Determined to keep spirits high, Kathleen mustered the women "for tea in the stern and we all chatted gaily except Mrs. Wilson who sat looking somewhat sphinx-like." Meanwhile, on board the *Terra Nova*, Teddy Evans described the mood:

> Personally I had a heart like lead, but... there was work to be done... and the crew were glad of the orders which sent them from one rope to another and gave them the chance to hide their feelings, for there is an awful feeling of loneliness at this point in the lives of those who sign on the ships of the South Pole trade.

Hilda Evans was lucky—because of a severe case of scurvy, Teddy Evans would be sent home on the *Terra Nova* in March 1912. Kathleen Scott and Ory Wilson never saw their husbands again.

"POOR LITTLE KATHLEEN!" Kathleen later wrote in her autobiography. "My babe at one end of the earth, my lover just off to the other, and I to stay primly at Admiralty House at Sydney for a week, until my P. and O. should convey me back to England." That evening she wrapped herself in a rug and lay for hours under the stars before deciding that she would go off into the bush. Kathleen had met a young, intelligent South African man who she believed could be trusted to fall in discreetly with whatever plan she suggested. Together they headed off into the Blue Mountains, where they wandered aimlessly until they were lost. It was the first time she had been anything approaching happy since Scott left.

According to her autobiography, Kathleen "journeyed home as countless sad wives have journeyed before." This was not strictly the case, as she made a leisurely trip home, taking in as many sights as possible and enjoying her freedom. In Sri Lanka she observed "the play of the back muscles of my rickshaw driver [which] caused me much pleasure," and at the Temple of the Tooth in Kandy she found "ridiculous frescoes of tortures." She watched as an Indian magician hung weights from his eyes and made a snake and a mongoose fight. On hearing there was smallpox in the vicinity, Kathleen and the other passengers made quickly for their ship. That night a man by the name of Captain Blair said at dinner: "It seems rather absurd for me to drink this soup because I'm going to drown myself directly." He promptly disappeared overboard. The ship tried to find him for an hour, then finally had to continue on its way.

Scott's expedition had begun like any great classic saga. As the men saw in the dawn of December 2, 1910, everything began to go wrong. They had crossed into the Furious Fifties—the latitudes between 50° S and 60° S—and been greeted with hurricane-force winds that whipped the sea into swells thirty-five feet high. The overladen *Terra Nova* pitched helplessly on soaring mountains of froth, then plunged into black chasms. With the pump broken and the engine stalled, the men desperately bailed water in two-hour shifts as they vomited—some managing to sing as they did so. Stacks of coal sacks and petrol cans were torn from their lashings and smashed from side to side. Dogs and ponies slid back and forth, gulping for air.

The storm finally broke, but then came the ice. The *Terra Nova* was frozen into a barrage of ice floes that at times were so obstinate "one would almost believe [them] possessed of an evil spirit." The ship, Scott wrote, seemed "like a living thing fighting a great fight." It seemed an eternity before they reached Antarctica, but the sight that greeted them was magical. As they steamed up the sound toward Cape Royds, the crew were mesmerized. Instead of sleeping, the men wrapped themselves in blankets and sat drinking in the extraordinary sight in front of them. "Many watched all night," the assistant biologist, Apsley Cherry-Garrard, later wrote, "as this new world unfolded itself, cape by cape and mountain by mountain."

Kathleen, for her part, was beginning to feel guilty about her adventures. Perhaps it was time that she returned to England and her baby, "the only authentic thing in my life." Looking back many years later, she wrote, "I can think of nothing that hurt more hideously than unlocking the sturdy fingers that clung round mine as I left the laughing, tawny-haired baby Hercules for four months, four months of enchanting change and growth that I should be shut out from and would never come again." Yet the lure of travel was simply too much for her to resist.

At Port Said, Kathleen decided that she shouldn't waste the opportunity of seeing Egypt, which she had always longed to do. She would indulge her freedom speedily, though it left her frustrated: "It seemed most impertinent to attempt to see these things in one day. Each wall merited a week's study." She was entranced by camels: "They fold up like a telescope for you to get on and then unfold again when you are ready." She travelled up the Nile and helped an amiable archaeologist open an untouched sarcophagus within a Second Dynasty tomb dated to about 3600 BC:

> I was of course most awfully excited. Together we descended a shaft . . . and there was the sarcophagus, a large wooden box, much eaten by white ants. We had to prop up the sides with sods before he dared lift off the lid. We found three mummies inside, greatly

decayed and indeed little left but bones... One set was to be sent
to a professor at the museum at Manchester. He numbered each set
of bones. I helped him. As I was lifting out one of the heads he said
"I suppose you know how to prevent the teeth falling out of the
lower jaw?" As though I'd been at it all my life!... We hope to find
jewels or papyrus in our tomb, but there were neither. Mr. Bruce
sat at the top of the hole, smoking and regarding us as harmless
lunatics. I did enjoy myself.

En route home she allowed herself one last visit—to Paris—and
spent time revisiting old friends and memories. Then she crossed
back to London and was reunited with Peter, who she thought looked
a little lumpy and dull but healthy.

Kathleen returned to her work, but money was still tight. She
was forced to take in a lodger and contemplated doing public talks.
She distracted herself from these annoyances by spending time with
Prime Minister Herbert Asquith and having lunch with people who
had influence in expeditionary circles, such as Sir Clements Markham
and Douglas Mawson. On one occasion at the Royal Geographical
Society, Shackleton sat beside her and said, "You know, I know your
husband very well, perhaps better than any man... He is the most
daring man I ever met, extraordinarily brave." Kathleen responded
pointedly, "Yes, he is brave morally as well as physically."

On March 27 she filled her studio with daffodils and invited
fifty-two guests to her birthday party. In the midst of the frivolities
a message came through from a news agency: "Ship sighted all well."
Kathleen was delighted. The following day, more messages came
from New Zealand: "A state of frenzy all day... I was of course
bombarded with reporters... I told them we still wanted money!!!
And nought else." When the messages were deciphered it appeared
that a party of Scott's men had run into Amundsen. His camp was
sixty miles nearer to the Pole than Scott's. Clearly this was going to
be a race to the Pole.

By the time the sun had set in Antarctica on April 22, flaws were
beginning to show in Scott's plans. Ten of the nineteen ponies were

dead, and the few dogs they had were ill trained. One of the motor sledges had been lost through the ice, and there were doubts as to whether the machines were suited for the expedition. Nevertheless, they pressed on.

As time drew on, Kathleen alternated between being her usual strong, vibrant self and falling apart. She avoided going to plays as she frequently found herself sobbing loudly throughout them. The only cure she could think of was to throw herself into an exhausting round of lunches, dinners and dances. On one evening she went to a show, danced until 3 AM at a fancy-dress party, then drove directly to Hendon airfield to watch a flying race at dawn before returning home to have breakfast with Peter. Later she wrote that she had probably been the second British woman to fly a plane; she had piloted with dual controls with the young pioneering aviator Tommy Sopwith, the inventor of the Sopwith Camel and Pup, which helped win the First World War. Flying became her new passion. Aviation was in its infancy; the Wright Brothers had successfully flown their first powered, heavier-than-air flight just seven years before. Aviators were explorers of the skies—pioneers and heroes—and Kathleen needed pioneers and heroes in her life. Scott's family disliked the idea of Kathleen being involved in such an outlandish activity. They beseeched Scott's brother-in-law, Gerald Ellison McCartney, to talk some sense into her. Kathleen found this enormously entertaining, considering that McCartney went flying himself without telling his wife.

Her hectic social schedule eventually began to pall, and in the summer Kathleen retreated to a small coast guard's cottage on the beach at Sandwich in Kent. She sat with her bare toes in the sand, imagining her husband lighting his pipe and looking out over the marshes. She wondered if he would be with her the following year. Far to the south, Scott remained positive: "All going well and everyone in splendid spirits . . . I fear to be too sanguine, yet taking everything into consideration I feel that our chances ought to be good."

On September 20, Kathleen woke having had a bad dream about Scott. Later that morning two-year-old Peter said to her, "Daddy won't come back." She comforted herself by imagining her husband saying contentedly: "Silly little maid." At that moment, Scott was making preparations for the long final trek to the Pole. "The future is in the lap of the gods," he wrote in his diary. "I can think of nothing left undone to deserve success." The night before his departure he wrote, congratulating Kathleen on being "the antithesis of a pathetic grass widow. Bless you."

Her sturdy independence was essential for facing the challenges at home. "An infuriating thing has happened," she wrote to Scott on October 24. A cinematograph company she had hired to film Peter for his father had used the images as advertising without permission. Pictures of their son had appeared in all the broadsheets, with the result that he was being recognized in the park by the public. "The whole thing is so vulgar and horrid, and I cannot bear him to be lent to this sort of thing. It's beastly and I want to cry." She was in an uncomfortable position—the expedition still needed money, and she needed the press to help her raise it. The *Daily Mirror* offered up to £4,000 for the expedition—a tenth of the fundraising goal—if she would allow them to publish a picture of Peter, but she balked at the suggestion. "My dear," she wrote, "I do humbly beg your pardon if I have done wrong, but I said 'No!'"

As winter pulled in, Kathleen felt the sense of loss acutely. By November 20, she was immobilized by depression. To make herself feel better she planted hundreds of bulbs at the cottage in Sandwich and at the family home on Buckingham Palace Road, just in case Scott came back the following spring. To raise more money for the expedition, she tried the chancellor of the exchequer, then the Treasury, but had no success. Like Jo Peary, Kathleen would have to face up to her fears and speak in public. On December 15, she went to Manchester, where she spoke about the Antarctic at the opening of a new theatre. "My dear," she wrote later, "I have never before done so great a thing for you. It was sheer, unmitigated agony until I began and then it wasn't so bad." Unbeknownst to Kathleen and Scott, on December 14, 1911, the day before she gave her talk in Manchester, Amundsen had reached the South Pole.

Kathleen's moods swung wildly. One moment she would feel on top of the world, the next floored with loneliness. The cottage was a welcome refuge, though it offered temptations:

> I rather need a man down here, but hesitate to ask one because I am afraid I should make love to one if I had one. One has so much time here, and I am so overflowing with vitality; so though it seems rather a waste to impart one's pleasure to no one, maybe I'd better not.

Kathleen's vitality was not lost on her male acquaintances, and the fact that she was married seemed to make no difference to the stream of advances. At first she enjoyed the attention, but soon she thought the persistence of some of her admirers rather vulgar. There was one exception: Nansen.

Kathleen had met the explorer with Scott while they were preparing for the expedition. Nansen was elegant and intense, a gentleman widower and a statesman. Given that he had been so supportive of her husband, she felt compelled to go to his lecture in London. Despite Nansen's stiff delivery and strong accent, Kathleen was riveted. Using the lunch afterwards as an excuse to press Nansen on what he knew of Amundsen's intentions, she found him not only generous with the little information he had, but wonderful company. The consummate diplomat, Nansen confided his hopes that Scott and Amundsen would join forces and reach the Pole together. After a second lunch date, Nansen spent the entire afternoon with Kathleen. "He is the most charming individual imaginable," she wrote. "We talked about the most unexpected things… He is so simple and straightforward in his views. I told him it is a year tomorrow since you left me."

The following day Kathleen received "an amazing letter" from Nansen. He was clearly smitten. "I do not understand what you have done to me," he wrote. "You are continually in my thoughts, and I am always thinking of our meeting and wondering, and that did frighten me a little." Over the next few weeks a flurry of letters arrived from Norway. Kathleen was delighted. "I worked hard and well all day. It does my work good to have the admiration of a person like Nansen."

Since the death of his wife, Eva, in 1907, Nansen had withdrawn emotionally from the world, but Kathleen made him feel reborn. "I am trying to gaze into the mists of the future, but can find no path leading anywhere," he wrote to Kathleen on November 30, 1911. "I am thinking of how different things might have been, if we had met years ago. Of course, in my conceitedness I take it as possible, that you might have really loved me, if you had learnt to know me... Though I thought I had lost all power of really loving a woman feeling as if life and all that was gone, I now feel as if it would have been possible to love you with body and soul, and it seems as if in your arms life might still have been worth living... It is best as it is, and that it remains only a sweet dream... After all, what would life be without its dreams?"

Nansen believed that Kathleen could be his soulmate, and although he was fully conscious that she was another man's wife, he could not suppress the feelings that overwhelmed him. "Do not think that I lived away from the world for so long now, that I fall in love so easily," he insisted. "No, there are many women in the world, but well, need I say it again? You are very different from the others;—it might sound conceited to say it, but it was like meeting an equal and I felt it, as if here at last, [I had] met something of that which I had always been looking for without knowing it."

> Sometimes it is possible for a man and woman to be absolutely real with one another, to stand naked souled to each other, unmasked and unafraid, because of the natural all-glorifying love between them. I feel like that with you. I feel as if I could not possibly be ashamed of anything before you, there was absolutely nothing I would care to hide from you, not a corner of my heart... You would see and understand a naked soul, as you would a naked body, with the eye of an artist.

His memories of their afternoon in London filled Nansen with exquisite memories—even though it is perfectly clear that nothing physical happened between them.

> I cannot get away from our last meeting, cannot forget, though I try to,—it is as if hundreds of threads pull me gently back to something lovely and warm, into a soft caressing embrace,—I see you still near me, I look into those mysterious eyes lifted towards mine, their depths I never was quite able to read—I see your lips which I never touched, they have such a strange smile—it was as if something important depended in that moment.

Kathleen's letters to Nansen have not survived, but his responses indicate that she too was confused by the sudden strength of their feelings for one another. But even in the face of such passion, she refused to cross the forbidden line.

Kathleen's letters sent Nansen into "a bubbling chaos of changing feelings and sentiments," but the force of his attention did not trouble her—she had plenty of experience with lovelorn friends. She travelled to Berlin to join Nansen at the launch of the German edition of his book *In Northern Mists* and had a glorious time in the city, going to concerts and meeting strange new acquaintances, including a woman who had inherited a vast income with the proviso that she spend every penny of it each year. Together she and Nansen also visited the king and queen of Norway. Queen Maud, Nansen wrote to Kathleen after her visit, "always talks to me about you. I believe she has found out that I like you very much."

A recent biographer claims that Kathleen and Nansen consummated their affair in a hotel room in Berlin, though this assertion has been hotly contested by her descendants. Kathleen always insisted that she had been completely faithful to Scott. Although Nansen would nurse his love for her for many years, he had accepted that there would be no romantic future for them. "For you, your splendid husband and baby are above everything in this world, and will remain so . . . I wish for you to love your husband as much as you do, and would not for my life do any harm there."

Scott, meanwhile—after travelling for a body-shattering seventy-seven days over almost eight hundred miles of sastrugi, crevasses and wild white desert—was confronted with a terrible discovery. On January 16, Bowers spotted what he thought was a cairn. "We marched on, found that it was a black flag tied to a sledge bearer; near by the remains of a camp; sledge tracks and ski tracks going and coming and the clear trace of dogs' paws—many dogs." The Norwegians had arrived before them and were first to the Pole.

The following day Scott wrote in his journal: "The Pole. Yes, but under very different circumstances from those expected. We have had a horrible day . . . We started at 7.30, none of us having slept much after the shock of our discovery . . . Great God! This is an awful place and terrible enough for us to have laboured to it without the reward of priority."

15

Emily Shackleton

A BIT OF A FLOATING GENT

I looked after the small things
and they rather stifle the soul.

EMILY SHACKLETON

FOR THE SHACKLETONS, the summer of 1909 was a
continuous round of celebratory lunches, garden
parties, dinners, receptions and electrifying oratory. Although Emily
was at the side of her husband throughout many of the celebrations,
the public were vociferous in their demands on his time. She felt
increasingly sidelined as Shackleton became consumed with his
new-found fame and the wealth he believed should materialize with
it. She longed for the days when her husband used to lazily recite the
poetry of Tennyson, Kingsley and Browning to her from memory.
Looking back, she mused, "But there was never time—and he was
doing bigger things and making his own bit of History after all. I never
got him again to myself, but that is a selfish way of looking at it."

As autumn drew in, the parties became less frequent, and
finances began to weigh heavily on their minds. Certain that he

had struck a seam of good luck and potential wealth, Shackleton had been donating the fees earned from his appearances and talks to good causes, without attending to his own family's future needs or the debts of the expedition. "His heart was always bigger than his pockets," commented one of his men. "He never worried about money... not for one moment." Shackleton had also made it clear that his wife's small allowance must not in any way be used to pay off expedition debts.

As fortune would have it, the Shackletons were introduced to the well-respected political journalist Sir Henry Lucy and his wife. Responding to her hostess's kindness, Emily confided her concerns about her husband's financial position. Lady Lucy informed Sir Henry, who immediately published a statement in the *Daily Express* of his consternation that Shackleton should be saddled with the costs of an expedition that had brought such honour to the country. With public sympathy running high, Prime Minister Asquith summoned Shackleton the same day to assure him that he would be relieved of some of the burden. A fortnight later, Shackleton was advised that the government would make him a grant of £20,000 (worth £1.75 million today). "The Government have been induced to take this course," Asquith wrote, "as they are much impressed, both by the great value of the discoveries made in the course of your voyage and by the efficient and economical manner in which the whole of the enterprise was conducted, as is shown by the fortunate return of your entire party." Shackleton fired off an ecstatic note to Emily: "Isn't it splendid! Just think of your Boy getting £20,000 from the Country: What Oh!!" "What Oh!" was an exclamation Emily had heard many times before when her husband believed that he had found a surefire answer to their financial woes.

Unlucky in business and hopeless with finances—one of his early employers noticed that Shackleton had forgotten to claim his wages for five months—the explorer was infinitely positive that his luck was about to change. The far more prosaic Emily could do little but endure her husband's ever-growing catalogue of failed enterprises and pray that circumstances might improve.

Just three months after Shackleton's glorious return to London from setting his farthest-south record, the *New York Herald* reported that the American explorer Frederick Cook had allegedly reached the North Pole on April 21, 1908. Five days later a cable from Labrador announced that Robert Peary was making a rival claim, with the declaration that he had reached the North Pole on April 6, 1909. In the midst of this sensational news, Robert Scott announced his intentions of an expedition to the South Pole at an elegant reception in honour of Shackleton and the *Nimrod* expedition at the Savage Club, concluding: "All I have to do now is to thank Mr. Shackleton for so nobly showing me the way."

Although Shackleton was surprised and disappointed by the announcement, his popularity was in no danger of being so easily eclipsed. On September 27, he gave a lecture before the king at Balmoral, and on November 4, his much-awaited book *The Heart of the Antarctic* was released simultaneously to good reviews in England, France, Germany, Italy, Hungary, Finland, Sweden and the United States. Five days later it was announced that Shackleton was to receive a knighthood. For the next twelve months he would undertake a dizzying lecture tour that would involve twenty thousand miles of travelling and audiences that totalled a quarter of a million people.

For a time, Emily shared the warmth of the spotlight on her husband. She accompanied him on a tour through Scandinavia and Europe that brimmed with royal and diplomatic receptions. His lecture at the Geographical Society in Copenhagen was attended by the king and queen of Denmark, Queen Alexandra, the dowager empress of Russia and other royals from Denmark, Russia and Greece. In Christiania they were greeted by Nansen and given an enthusiastic welcome by Amundsen and crowds of students who carried Shackleton shoulder-high in a cheering, torchlit procession to the lecture hall. Emily recalled seeing a mystical look pass across Amundsen's face at a subsequent banquet, and she later came to believe that hearing her husband speak inspired Amundsen to also make an attempt on the South Pole.

In North America, the Shackletons met President William Howard Taft at the White House. Taft later presented Shackleton with the

Hubbard Gold Medal of the National Geographic Society in front of an audience of five thousand. Shackleton's charisma was undeniable. "I think of all the explorers I have met," commented the respected journalist Philip Gibbs, "Shackleton is the one who belongs most closely to the type which has been pictured for us in old tales and sea romance... When [he] comes into a room he brings a breeze with him, and smiles to the company." There were many who were just as impressed by Emily. The American press enthused about her "distinctly original personality" and her "unusual force and intelligence." Yet she was not always comfortable sharing the limelight, and the tours were exhausting. At the end of a lecture in Winnipeg a member of the audience called, "Three cheers for the girl he loves." Shackleton replied, "She's down at the Royal Alexandra, sound asleep."

"Pole fever" had gripped North America. Shackleton's tour coincided with the tussle of public opinion over who had been the first to reach the North Pole. Like the majority of polar men and the public, Shackleton doubted the integrity of Cook's claim and supported Peary. He did so before he had even met the man. On March 29, Peary presided over a celebration at Carnegie Hall, with Shackleton as the guest lecturer. It must have been an electrifying evening. Not only was Peary at the height of his celebrity, but there were rumours that he was planning an expedition to race Scott to the South Pole. The previous month the *Daily Mail* had wondered whether Shackleton might also join the competition. Shackleton appealed instead for funds to be directed to Scott and his British expedition.

The Americans had already annexed the top of the world and were bent on being first also to the "bottom end." The British saw Shackleton, not Scott, as their champion. Shackleton still held the farthest-south record and had won the hearts of the British public with his engaging character and conscientious attitude to his men.

> Poor Sir Ernest Shackleton is not yet clear of the financial troubles which he incurred by his last expedition. But there ought to be no difficulty about drying up those anxieties and equipping him afresh for another trial, unless the sporting classes have become

infected with that dismal Little Englandism which some of them are fond of imputing to other people.

For now there could be no thought for Shackleton of entering this race, particularly given Scott's public intentions. Both he and Emily knew he would lead another expedition, but it had to be entirely separate from a race for the Pole—an even more ambitious plan. For now they had to concentrate on the present. The tour was losing its momentum. Although Shackleton had charm, wit and the farthest-south record, Peary was claiming the North Pole itself.

They returned to England exhausted. For a time, everything was blissful. Shackleton was still buoyant from his success and was intent on spending time with his family. After a brief respite, he continued on to Europe, but the tour felt joyless and lonely. In Germany he was discomforted by the increasing anti-English feeling: "When the picture of the Queen's flag is shown there is a stony silence and altogether it seems different: there are no social arrangements and this may be due to the lack of my lady's gracious presence." The strain of separation from his family was compounded when Emily discovered that she was pregnant once again. His reassurances in response to her fears for the future were heartfelt:

> Sweetheart the greatest thing in all the World is Love: of that I am more than ever convinced: and as long as we two have each other: whether the days are bright and all is fair: or whether the times are dark and cloudy with worries we ought to be happy... I am more and more in love with you my wife than I can say... Where would my life have led had it not been that for you I wanted to make good.

But all was not so rosy, and despite the arrival of their third child, Edward, 1911 would be a time of unhappiness for them both. With no expedition on the horizon and frequent disappointments in business, Shackleton became increasingly argumentative and began spending time with acquaintances Emily did not altogether approve of. He frequented the Marlborough Club and developed a habit of hiring taxis and keeping them for the day, asking them to wait outside friends' houses while he paid hurried visits. He was, as the British skiing pioneer Sir Harry Brittain put it, "a bit of a floating gent."

Isolated and miserable, Emily made her children and their domestic routine her main focus. Shackleton began looking for comfort and support elsewhere. He started to confide in Elspeth Beardmore, the wife of one of his sponsors. Another patron, Janet Stancomb-Wills, who had composed a poem for him and was a generous supporter of his expeditions, also became a confidante. Emily was fully aware that Shackleton had wealthy female devotees, and their generosity could not be taken lightly. In later years she was advised by her husband to nurture her friendship with Stancomb-Wills; the woman was charming, he insisted, and her support was vital. So too was the continued patronage of Elizabeth Dawson-Lambton, whose funds were used in part for the support of Emily and the children.

In recent years, some biographers have claimed that Shackleton was a serial philanderer—an opinion that many regard as fact since the release of Kenneth Branagh's popular film about the explorer, in which Shackleton is depicted as having a long-standing affair with the American actress Rosalind Chetwynd. Although there is little doubt that Shackleton loved the company of women, this particular assertion is based on thin evidence.

Emily dutifully kept up appearances even when later her husband admitted that though he hated to be false in any way, he had "committed all sorts of crimes in thought if not always in action and don't worry much about it." In a surprisingly frank interview in the United States, she had confessed she did not believe in reading her children stories that ended with "And they lived happily ever after." Doing so might encourage a girl to think that marriage was the only option, and she added wistfully, "How wrong that is."

SHACKLETON COULD NOT forever trade on the achievements of the *Nimrod* expedition. Yet, when news broke on March 9, 1912, that Amundsen had reached the South Pole in December 1911, there was renewed interest in the Antarctic, and Shackleton was called upon again for lectures. He knew he had to pioneer a more ambitious quest if he was to maintain his profile as one of the world's leading explorers. By the end of 1913, his focus was concrete: he planned to cross the continent from the Weddell Sea to the Ross Sea. The venture would be called the Imperial Trans-Antarctic Expedition. It would utilize two ships: the *Endurance* would carry the main party into the Weddell Sea, and the *Aurora* would take a support team to the Ross Sea and lay depots across the Great Ice Barrier. These depots, to be used in the latter part of the trek, would be essential to the survival of the crossing party.

On July 16, 1914, the *Endurance* was visited by the Dowager Queen Alexandra, her sister Empress Marie Feodorovna of Russia, Admiral of the Fleet Lord Fisher, Earl Howe and Princess Victoria. As she had done for the *Nimrod* expedition, the queen presented Shackleton with a Union Jack; this time she also gave him a silk replica of her own standard, two bibles and a St. Christopher medallion for the ship. But the future of the expedition was uncertain. On August 3, it was announced that a general mobilization had been ordered. The First World War had begun. Immediately Shackleton put the resources of the expedition at the disposal of his country, only to be advised by Winston Churchill, first lord of the Admiralty, to proceed. The following day the king gave the expedition his blessing. Although he was uncertain, Shackleton felt duty bound to continue with his plans.

By the time Shackleton left Liverpool on September 25, bound for Buenos Aires, he was a nervous and physical wreck. The news of the war, the struggles for funds and the tensions at home had prompted a quarrel with Emily just hours before he left. Their hurtful exchanges were far from the heart-rending parting from Dover on his previous voyage. In Buenos Aires he wrote his wife a letter which must have been very hard for her to read:

I am just glad to have the worry over and get out to my work and my own life: it seems a hard thing to say but this I know is ... the one thing that I am suited for and in which I yield to no one; I know full well that . . . for some time past we have not seen eye to eye and that the fault lies with me . . . I wonder if you know me really: I am not worth much consideration if I were really known and I have shown you that or rather tried to show it to you only you think differently don't you? . . . I have tried to look at things [from] your point of view as well as mine and all to no purpose: and I go round in a circle . . . I am just good as an explorer and nothing else, I am hard also and damnably persistent when I want anything: altogether a generally unpleasing character: I love the fight and when things [are] easy I hate it though when things are wrong I get worried . . . Now I am on my own work I will be better and more at peace and I don't think I will ever go on a long expedition again.

ON DECEMBER 5, 1914, the *Endurance* sailed out of the whaling station of Grytviken on South Georgia Island. Within just three days the ship ran into a belt of heavy pack ice considerably farther north than Shackleton had anticipated. Their battle with the southern pack ended when on February 21 the *Endurance* was beset at 76°58' S. Attempts to chip out a channel for the ship with chisels and ice picks failed, and Shackleton instructed his men to prepare for a winter on the ice.

Shackleton worked tirelessly to keep spirits up during their imprisonment, but by the end of July the ice was rifting alarmingly and pressing toward the listing ship. On October 18, the *Endurance* was picked up by a pressure ridge and was thrown over to her port side. On October 27, the order was given to abandon ship. The men were 360 miles from the nearest depot of food. The nearest inhabited piece of land was a thousand miles away by boat. After five months of camping on drifting, splitting and rafting ice floes, the men saw their chance to escape and took to their three lifeboats. On April 15, 1916, after battling heavy-running seas and frigid conditions, the men finally set foot on the desolate shores of Elephant Island. It had been over sixteen months since the twenty-eight souls had felt anything but ice or keel under their feet.

As the men made landfall, Emily was engrossed with writing letters to those who might be able to save her husband. There had been no news for some time, and she was desperately worried. To Prime Minister Asquith and Australia's high commissioner she wrote impassioned letters reminiscent of those written by Jane Franklin. Two relief ships would be needed to rescue the men, since they were marooned on opposite sides of the Antarctic continent. The *Endurance* still had not appeared, so a ship would have to be sent to the Weddell Sea, and news had reached New Zealand that the Ross Sea party, in the *Aurora*, had been stranded after setting up depots. Emily hoped that the British government would help her with one ship, but she desperately needed the support of the Australian government for a second.

Some newspapers had condemned the expedition from the start; now they printed strongly worded objections to the prospect of a relief operation when so many men were sacrificing their lives for Britain in the war. Emily answered every criticism politely but firmly. The reports were incorrect and unfair, and in her eyes they questioned her husband's patriotism.

With no means of communication, Shackleton could not be sure that Emily or his other supporters would be able to mount a search operation. Even if a ship was sent, it was unlikely he and his men would be found. Their chance of survival on the island for any length of time was slim. An ocean voyage in the small open boats with all the men was impossible. The only hope, and a slim one at that, was for him to take some of the strongest in his team and seek help before winter was upon them once more. Such a prospect would have terrified most men, but not Shackleton. Later, Emily was unsurprised: "He was always at his best when leading a forlorn hope, it brought out reserves of patience and tenderness, which were the 'superman' part of him, at least I thought so."

Leaving Frank Wild in charge of the shore party, Shackleton, Tom Crean, Harry "Chippy" McNish, Timothy McCarthy, John Vincent and Frank Worsley clambered into the twenty-two-foot whale boat the *James Caird* and set out on a harrowing eight-hundred-mile journey toward South Georgia. Their fifteen-day crossing of the storm-whipped southern ocean is one of the most astonishing in polar history. Those on board had already endured a brutal winter on the ice. Their skin was blistered and torn; they were suffering from exposure, hunger, thirst and exhaustion. They could not lie down comfortably in the boat, nor stand for more than a few moments. Innumerable times the boat threatened to capsize as it pitched and careered through the towering waves. When the seas briefly calmed, ice was hastily chipped away or the boat was bailed. On May 5 at midnight, Shackleton believed he saw a line of clear sky:

> A moment later I realized that what I had seen was not a rift in the clouds but the white crest of an enormous wave. During twenty-six years' experience of the ocean in all its moods I had not encountered a wave so gigantic. It was a mighty upheaval of the ocean, a thing quite apart from the white-capped seas that had been our tireless enemies for many days.

After a seemingly endless moment of suspense, the boat was hurled into seething walls of tortured water. "We bailed with the energy of men fighting for life . . . and after ten minutes of uncertainty we felt the boat renew her life beneath us."

On May 8, after brilliant navigation by Worsley, South Georgia came into view. Still, they were far from safe. Hurricane-force winds were smashing waves onto the rocky shore, and any attempt to land would end in disaster. Powerless, they had to ride out the storm. Finally, on May 10, the *James Caird* entered King Haakon Fjord. Although they had reached land, the men found themselves on the opposite side of the island from the whaling station where they could raise the alarm. Two of them were too weak to move, and it was too dangerous to attempt another boat journey around the island. Shackleton would have to cross the island on foot for twenty-two miles to reach safety. Along with Crean and Worsley, he set out over the chaotic interior of South Georgia's ragged mountains, crevasse fields and glaciers. They were hopelessly ill equipped for such an endeavour. Their clothes were thin and ripped; they had no sleeping bags and had to make do with battered boots with screws from the *James Caird* hammered through the soles as makeshift crampons. Each man had to carry his food in a canvas boot strung about his neck with lamp wick.

On May 20, the three men arrived at the whaling station of Stromness. They had staggered over extraordinarily tough terrain continuously for thirty-six hours. The first inhabitants they met were two boys who fled in terror at the sight of them. Wild-eyed and emaciated with blistered, blackened skin, the men finally made it to the manager's office. The manager, Thoralf Sørlle, demanded to know who they were. Shackleton replied quietly, "My name is Shackleton." The manager's assistant, Mansell, turned away and wept. Sørlle was dumbstruck. He knew Shackleton well and was amazed at the apparition before him.

On May 31, the Admiralty in London received a cable from Port Stanley that Shackleton was safe. That evening Emily was entertaining Tryggve Gran, who had been on Scott's British National Antarctic Expedition, and Shackleton's friend and sponsor Campbell Mackellar at her home. At midnight, the two men rose to leave. As their cab arrived, the telephone rang. "We bade a hasty goodnight as Lady Shackleton went to the telephone and it being raining we ran down the steps and jumped into the cab. They tried to stop us, [Emily's maid] even running after the cab, but we were gone. It was the news of Shackleton."

The following morning Shackleton's safe arrival in the Falklands was front-page news. The story of his miraculous journey sped through Europe. In the midst of war, an interview with Emily made it into the Berlin press, which commented on the character and perseverance of her husband. Even Kathleen Scott could not help but remark: "Shackleton or no Shackleton, I think it one of the most wonderful adventures I ever read of, magnificent." For Emily, the news brought indescribable relief. She had already accepted that it might be another year before she heard the fate of her husband.

Shackleton, Crean and Worsley were safe, but others from the expedition were stranded and in mortal danger. McNish, Vincent and McCarthy, who had been left to rest on the other side of South Georgia, were immediately picked up, and Shackleton pressed for an urgent rescue campaign to be mounted for the men marooned on Elephant Island. The Admiralty, clearly focussed on the demands of war, was agonizingly unresponsive. A committee suggested Shackleton simply rest for two months in Port Stanley. It was not an option, as far as he was concerned; there was nothing in Port Stanley, he grumbled, except that the main street in the port connected the slaughterhouse to the graveyard, which only reminded him of the peril his men faced. Worsley noted that "the Boss" had been cast into deep despair. "For the first time in three years I saw him take a glass of whisky. He was unaccustomed to it and it affected him at once." To Shackleton's relief, help came from elsewhere, as the Uruguayan and Chilean governments mobilized a rescue operation.

After four attempts at rescue, hindered by unnavigable ice and atrocious weather conditions, the *Yelcho* appeared through the mist surrounding Elephant Island on August 30, 1916, to the band of castaways who had been marooned for 137 bleak days. As the ship neared the shore, Shackleton shouted to the men: "Are you all well?" Wild waved back, "All safe, all well!" "Thank God!" the Boss cried.

The men were taken safely to Punta Arenas and greeted with a roar of sirens and cheers. Flags flew from every public building in the city, and police were forced to form a barrier to keep back the surging crowds. The men ate and bathed, although all were asked not to shave until publicity photographs had been taken. They were entertained in Chile, Shackleton wrote to Emily, "as if I had made a triumph instead of the Expedition having failed."

Still his men from the Ross Sea party were in the Antarctic and needed rescuing, and Shackleton soon discovered that plans had been made in Australia for a relief expedition that would sail with another man in command. He was astonished. They were, after all, *his* men. "I *know these men's hearts*," he declared. Emily tried to temper his fury, to which he replied, "I *will* be tactful in Australia but I am very sore about it all." On January 10, 1917, two of Shackleton's men cried out "Ship ho!" in surprise and relief as the *Aurora* appeared at Cape Evans. Other than three from the Ross Sea party who had died, Shackleton had saved all his men.

Mentally and physically exhausted, Shackleton focussed once again on his family. Home was still a long way away, and he longed for Emily and the children. "My Darling Little Cecily," he wrote to his daughter:

> Two years have gone by, child, since your old Daddy has seen you, and I am just longing to see my little girl again... It has been a time full of work and danger, so that I want to come home and rest, and I want to... hear all you have been doing, everything about you, darling... I know you will be a comfort and help to Mummy all the time I am away.

Emily needed comforting. While Shackleton was away, her eldest brother had died, with her sister Daisy following him to the grave the year after. Now, with their disagreements forgotten, his letters were filled once again with promises: "I do not think that ever again will I venture far from the homeside and your love." Life from then on, he imagined, would be peaceful. "I don't suppose for a moment that the Antarctic will ever see me again," he wrote. "I must settle down and I want to."

Finally Shackleton was coming home. The thought was both glorious and frightening to Emily. She worried that she had aged and was not as beautiful as she once had been. Shackleton reassured her: "You must not mind [being] older," he wrote. "We are all that: I am quite grey at the temples and threads throughout... Anyhow, you & I have the children who live our lives over again and that should help a good bit."

TOP | This portrait shows Emily Shackleton circa the 1920s. Shackleton loved his elegant wife as "truly and purely and as dearly as a woman can be loved." *Athy Heritage Centre*

BOTTOM | Emily and young Ray Shackleton are shown here with some of the crew aboard the *Nimrod* before her husband's departure on his British Antarctic Expedition, 1907. *Athy Heritage Centre*

FACING | This 1916 front page of the *Daily Mirror* headlines Shackleton's remarkable story of survival in the Antarctic. Emily and the children told reporters of their excitement to hear that he was safe. *Private Collection*

ANZACS AND AEROPLANES CHASE AND ROUT FOE IN EGYPT

The Daily Mirror

CERTIFIED CIRCULATION LARGER THAN THAT OF ANY OTHER DAILY PICTURE PAPER

No. 3,934.   Registered at the G.P.O. as a Newspaper.   FRIDAY, JUNE 2, 1916   One Halfpenny.

SIR ERNEST SHACKLETON SAFE AFTER A MIRACULOUS ESCAPE: EXPLORER'S THREE WEEKS' VOYAGE IN AN OPEN BOAT.

Lady Shackleton and two of her children walking through the Park yesterday.

Last photograph taken of Sir Ernest before he left for the South Pole.   Sir Ernest's elder son.   "Hurrah! Daddy's safe!" And the terrier barked with joy.

Sir Ernest Shackleton is safe. Grave apprehensions had been felt about the safety of the explorers, and this dramatic news was received in London yesterday with the greatest pleasure. The expedition, it appears, had a miraculous escape. Following the foundering of the Endurance, which was badly nipped by great bergs, the party, which suffered terrible privations, reached Elephant Island after a journey of great hazard.

As there was a considerable scarcity of rations, Sir Ernest decided to leave his men in an ice hole and, setting out to seek help in a small boat, he reached South Georgia after a three weeks' voyage of extraordinary peril, which must be unique in the annals of Antarctic work. No member of the expedition has been lost, but urgent help is needed for the marooned men.—(Speaight.)

FACING | This photograph by Herbert Ponting shows Robert Falcon Scott on his last expedition. Scott would make it to the South Pole only to find Amundsen had beaten him to it. *Private Collection*

TOP | Kathleen Scott works in her studio at Buckingham Palace Road in London with her son, Peter, in 1912, the year that Scott died. It wasn't until 1913 that she learned of her husband's death. *Scott Family Archive*

BOTTOM | The *Daily Mirror* ran this commemorative front page when news reached London in 1913 of Scott's death in the Antarctic. Kathleen, travelling in the United States, would not hear the news for another week. *Private Collection*

FACING | Marie and Wally Herbert are shown here on their wedding day in London, Christmas Eve, 1969. Wally had recently returned from his crossing of the Arctic Ocean via the North Pole. *Herbert Collection*

ABOVE | Marie checks on Kari during a long sledge journey in the five-month winter night of the polar north, 1972. *Herbert Collection*

ABOVE | In 1975, Marie travelled with Sami reindeer herders in Lapland on their winter migration. The journey was documented in her book *The Reindeer People*. *Herbert Collection*

FACING TOP | Kari and Marie Herbert pose in northwest Greenland in 1972, where the family lived with a remote hunting community of Inuit for two years. *Herbert Collection*

FACING BOTTOM | Wally Herbert, shown here with daughter Kari in northwest Greenland, 1972, believed it was only natural to take his family with him on this expedition. *Herbert Collection*

PART FOUR

A HERO,
MY HUSBAND

16

Marie Herbert

HEALING QUEST

All of a sudden, I felt inordinately
burdened—not only by the cares of home,
but also by the cares of the world.

MARIE HERBERT

IN THE FINAL DAYS of his attempted circumnavigation of
Greenland, Wally Herbert felt as Shackleton had
done after his attempt to cross Antarctica: lonely and exhausted.
Wally returned from the harrowing journey emaciated and broken
in spirit. It grieved him deeply that he had had to call the expedition
off. Time had run out, and neither he nor Allan Gill could afford
another protracted journey. Although Wally wanted desperately
to salvage the expedition and return to Greenland the following
year, the need to be with his family and make a living outweighed
any other consideration. The next obvious step was for him to write
about the experience, but although the expedition had been the most
colourful of all his polar journeys, he could not face committing it to
paper. It would be a very long time before he could look back on what

he had achieved during the expedition, let alone the disasters. "As a perfectionist," Marie noted, "he made no concessions to failure."

Wally knew that his time as an active explorer was drawing to a close, and this change of direction was profoundly unsettling. The last few months had also taken their toll on Marie. The demands and anxieties involved in juggling motherhood, writing about her experiences in Lapland and keeping abreast of expedition affairs had drained her resources. "All of a sudden, I felt inordinately burdened—not only by the cares of home, but also by the cares of the world. The strife in N. Ireland, and the constant threat that the Cold War engendered affected me deeply. I began to seriously question the role of religion in my life, railing inwardly at a God who could allow such misery to exist on the planet."

She was strangely forgetful and unable to finish the simplest sentences. When she consulted her doctor, he laughed, saying that he was forgetful too and she shouldn't worry. But she feared that she had pre-senile dementia. In fact, what she had was mental and physical burnout, and the best remedy was complete rest and relaxation. Marie booked herself in to a "stress farm" in Devon. After gentle counselling, wholesome food and twenty-four hours of isolation and meditation, she felt positive for the first time in months, and she was determined to discover more about meditation and the power of the mind.

My parents had an unwritten agreement that whoever had the greatest need in any endeavour would have the help and energy of the other. When Wally was away on an expedition, Marie would assist him in any way she could. Likewise, once he was back, it was understood that he would take over the duties at home and provide her with the freedom and financing, wherever possible, to travel or work on other projects. One such project was an opportunity in 1981 for Marie to visit the Tukak Theatre in Denmark, the only Inuit theatre school in the world.

The creator and artistic director of the school was Reidar Nilsson, a charismatic Norwegian actor who was known for his innovative approach of drawing on Greenlandic and Norse mythology to produce groundbreaking theatre. Through him, a lost generation of Greenlanders who had been educated and brought up in Denmark were reconnected with their own culture.

Tukak was situated on the rugged Jutland coast. It was an elemental place, battered by winds and high seas. It was a place for change—the coastline itself was forever changing shape as voracious seas swallowed great chunks of it. While Marie was there, several houses were wrenched clean away from the land. It was the perfect setting for drama and rebirth. Marie's eight weeks at the Tukak Theatre—albeit tough at times—stretched her physically, mentally and spiritually. She now embarked on a quest to find a healer who did not want his gifts, as the basis for a novel. Over the next year, with Wally's full support, Marie travelled extensively to research her novel and found in Australia a mentor who was willing to help her. Her guide to the unfamiliar world of healing was Andrew Watson, a troubled but brilliant man whose involuntary urge to heal had become more a burden than a gift. He had done all he could to rid himself of what he described as "a disease" but eventually had had to accept his unconventional talents. Through him, Marie was introduced to revelatory wisdom that was light years away from conventional religion. But after months away from Wally and the children, Marie began to question whether she could continue with her project. The family longed for her return, and she was torn between being a writer in the field and being a mother, wife and ally.

Marie returned from Australia to find Wally in turmoil. He had been commissioned by the National Trust to prepare a feasibility study for an Explorers' Museum to be based at Buckland Abbey in Devon, once the home of Sir Francis Drake. Characteristically, he had thrown himself into the task. His proposal was that the outbuildings of the sixteenth-century abbey be transformed into an experiential museum—one of the first of its kind in Britain—that would take visitors on a journey through the polar environment and expedition history. It was a visionary concept, but perhaps too radical and expensive compared with the more straightforward museum the trust had in mind. After two years of work, his proposal was rejected after a cursory fifteen-minute glance. The subcommittee went on to use his blueprint, with certain modifications and with no credit for his work.

The rejection of the proposal had implications for the whole family. Although by now both Wally and Marie had several books in print, the royalties from sales barely covered the rent. To their intense relief, Wally was approached by the National Geographic Society with a fascinating project that, in the short term at least, appeared to be the perfect antidote to the disappointments and struggles of the past few years. The request was for Wally to write an assessment of Robert Peary's North Pole diary. As an expert navigator and polar explorer, the society believed, he would be able to judge better than anyone whether Peary had reached the North Pole. Wally regarded the assignment as a privilege. The stories of Peary's exploits had inspired him as a boy, and ever since he had regarded the American explorer as a remarkable traveller and pioneer. Marie was less convinced. She knew how sensitive the subject was and knew it could easily make Wally a target for criticism. Although he appreciated her misgivings, he could not bring himself to turn the project down.

For the next nine months Wally immersed himself in Peary's papers and astronomical observations. As time went on, he became aware of the expectations some had of his project. He was deeply touched by the co-operation of the Peary family, who had been welcoming and helpful, but naturally they expected him to conclude that Peary had, without doubt, reached the Pole. For their sake, Wally wished that he could find irrefutable proof; instead, he was faced with discrepancies, navigational errors and glaring unanswered questions.

Some of these questions had presented themselves within hours of his first look at the diaries. To his surprise, Wally discovered that the pages for the most critical dates either were blank or had been inserted as loose, separate sheets. One of these loose sheets was Peary's entry for the attainment of the Pole on April 6, 1909. It appeared to have been written well after the event. There could of course have been an innocent explanation for this. More difficult to defend, however, was Peary's lack of longitude readings and his records of daily speeds on the ice that Wally, from his own experience on the Arctic Ocean, thought impossible for a sustained period. However much he tried to ignore them, doubts crept in about the validity of Peary's claim. Then there was the issue of Frederick Cook. Wally was tempted to investigate Cook's material, too, although he knew that would likely complicate matters.

At home, Marie's soul-searching and the ever-present financial pressures were bringing her fears about the future to the surface. We were a close-knit and loving family, but the alternating absences of one or the other partner and the day-to-day pressures on both my parents made it a confusing time. We had visited my father during his research in the States, but returning home without him was almost unbearable. He had looked so forlorn and troubled when we left. The responsibility of his project was enormous. He was concerned that his family not share his burden, but I wanted to carry it for him.

The experience of delving into Peary's papers, so exciting at the start, had become a harrowing process. Wally realized that neither Peary's claim nor Cook's passed scrutiny. To contest Peary's title of discoverer of the North Pole was particularly difficult; it was as though Wally were blowing the whistle on a family member. He felt that the project was too important to be confined to just a written assessment for the National Geographic Society; to be fair to the subject, he must also write a book. What was to be a year's assignment became an all-consuming project lasting four years. Meticulous in his research, Wally identified with the two rival explorers so strongly that at one stage he confessed he felt as if he were both men. The pressure of his empathy caused two heart attacks. The resulting book, *The Noose of Laurels*, was truly a labour of love and heartache.

While receiving critical acclaim and great support from the exploration community, the book prompted an outcry among both Peary and Cook supporters. After initially endorsing Wally's findings that Peary had not reached the North Pole, the National Geographic Society went back on its decision, having been lobbied by patriots who could not bear the fact that their hero had failed. Although the Peary family were dignified in their response, others poured vitriol not only on the book but on Wally's character and achievements. Some questioned his motives, believing he wanted to discredit Peary and Cook so that he could claim priority for the Pole himself. This was never the case. "At no time, ever, did the subject of Wally being the first to get to the Pole come up, as either a consideration or a desire," Marie insisted. The crossing of the entire Arctic Ocean had been a far more difficult and satisfying challenge.

Wally had always understood that if neither Peary nor Cook was first to the North Pole, then Ralph Plaisted—who travelled by snowmobile—would have the next claim to be the first to have reached the Pole by surface crossing. Nevertheless, the criticisms came: letters swearing retribution were sent to the Herbert family, and personal attacks were broadcast. While Wally and Marie had anticipated that his book would attract debate, the fervour of some critics was disturbing.

Many respected historians and polar experts backed Wally's findings, but the strain of writing the book and the distressing fallout had affected his health. He was unable to lie down at night because of severe edema and was dangerously short of breath. He was advised that he needed an emergency quadruple heart-bypass operation. For a man who had always been self-sufficient, the realization that his life depended on a surgeon's skill was unnerving. Wally was concerned that he would not survive the operation, as were the rest of the family.

By now, Marie had learned the techniques of meditation and was training as a counsellor. Over the years, she had noticed that in times of crisis, Wally seemed to have a direct line to his intuition. She offered to take him through a guided meditation to see if he could get some helpful insight into the outcome of the operation.

I suggested that he imagined himself entering his body through a doorway into his heart, from where he would see a lift which could take him to the floor above. The lift would open to a large airy room where he could speak directly to his "mind". In the middle of the room he would see a table with a large open book on it, and I inferred that the book might have something to say to him.

Wally followed the process as I suggested, he told me afterwards, but on entering the "room of the mind" he had felt nervous, because he could see the open book propped up on the table in front of him, and he was fearful of what he might read. Finding courage he approached it, and saw that written in big bold letters across the middle of the two opened pages was the word *"DEATH"*. His heart missed a beat when he saw this, but then he noticed that there was a huge X scoring it through. And written all around the central word were smaller words, all saying, *"live, live, live, live, live!"*

Thankfully Wally survived the operation, but, as Marie recalled, "all doors seemed to close on Wally's professional life." He had always had a gift for drawing, which was perhaps one of the reasons why his years of map-making in the Antarctic had been so enjoyable. Inspired by a dream in which Wally had seen a preview of artworks he would one day create, Marie suggested that he start painting. Wally was reluctant to try, thinking it would be a waste of precious time. Eventually she convinced him to take a pastel in his left hand and simply make some marks on the page. Frustrated with his clumsy attempts, he began to use his dominant hand, and never looked back.

The first painting was a watercolour of our friend Avatak looking out over an Arctic scene that the men had visited during a walrus hunt. The painting was a triumph, and Wally went from strength to strength in his new profession. As Marie recalled, "This ability of Wally and myself to be the catalyst for each other's creativity lasted our entire marriage."

ON NOVEMBER 4, 1993, the telephone rang in my student house in Portsmouth. It was my father. My beautiful sister, Pascale, had died in a freak electrical accident at home. As my parents were out walking, she had moved a floor lamp toward a desk to do her homework and put her hand on the wall to steady herself as she did so. Unbeknownst to any of us, there was faulty wiring in the old house. The shock was so great she would have felt nothing.

I was too stunned to move. Over and over again the image of the last time I had seen my sister ran through my mind. Just a few days earlier I had gone home for the weekend. I had stayed on for an extra day, and when Pascale got home from school she hurtled into the living room and gave me the fiercest hug. We spent the evening under a duvet on the sofa watching films. It was the tightness of the hug I remembered, and it would be the last she would ever give me.

The next few weeks were a blur. We went through the unreal process of arranging the funeral, of encountering everyone else's grief as we battled with our own, of trying to comfort one another when the pain was so overwhelming it seemed as though the sun was gone forever. There is very little that can compare to the blinding anguish of losing a radiant young person who has everything to live for. She was only fifteen.

We tried to deal with the unbearable loss in various ways. My father tried to bury his broken heart by immersing himself in painting and in lectures on ships going to the Arctic and the Antarctic. I tried to piece my shattered world together by illustrating my confusion in artworks for my finals at college. My mother was the bravest of us all; she sought out the pain and journeyed into the heart of it.

I left her at the airport in Albuquerque. Six weeks earlier we had all travelled to the United States together, before my mother and I said goodbye to my father in Denver, Colorado, as he left for the Antarctic. The two of us then travelled through the southern states together by car. After a month on the road I was due to fly home, and my mother was going to embark on a quest for healing. I felt desolate leaving her. She told me later that she only just managed to get back to her beaten-up Cadillac before sobbing uncontrollably.

Marie had already met the first of a string of remarkable healers who told her there was no severance in death, nor ownership of anyone, family, friend or lover. She was reminded of Kahlil Gibran's words in *The Prophet:* "We do not own our children or even beget them, but... we are loaned them, while serving simply as a channel, or vehicle, through which a soul can incarnate." Jamie Sams, of Seneca and Cherokee descent, was the custodian of an ancient spiritual legacy, and she had worked tirelessly to maintain the traditions and stories of her people and those of other indigenous people around the world. Marie was awestruck at their first meeting: "I had never met anybody quite like this towering legend of a woman." Jamie brought out a packet of Fortnum and Mason tea and told one of the rudest jokes Marie had ever heard. They became instant friends. Under her guidance, Marie learned the value of a retreat. She joined a women's healing quest, through which she experienced a deeply moving healing ceremony, learned sacred teachings and began to mend her wounded heart.

The healing quest and the wise people she met during her time in the United States had such a profound impact on Marie that she decided to become a guide in wilderness rites of passage for others who were dealing with trauma or life crises. The training took place in the Mohave Desert, and her mentors were living examples of their philosophy. "After years spent in such places as the Inyo Valley, the Mohave Desert, and Death Valley, there seemed no separation between them and the land they loved so much. Their faces were weathered by wind, heat, rain and cold... There was no one so wretched they could not love, nor anyone so brazen they would not help: Although they were endlessly patient while you were learning to walk, they would unhesitatingly boot you up the backside when you were ready to fly."

As part of the training, Marie had to undergo eleven days of ceremony and quietness in nature, with four days and nights of fasting alone in the desert. During this time, if one was open enough to receive it, nature would present a subtle vision or experience that would have great significance to the person on the quest. Marie felt completely unprepared when her moment of inspiration came.

Walking out alone, she climbed up a hillside between the twisted trunks of bristlecone pines and stood in wonder, allowing the heat and the sweet scent of sagebrush to envelop her as she gazed at the desert stretching out to the horizon. Then, in a split second, she felt her heart leap into her throat. Some two hundred yards away she saw two dark shapes that looked like a bear and her cub. She wanted to turn and run, but instead stood rooted to the spot—perhaps it was a test? She remembered from her time in the Arctic how the combination of distance and light could confuse the eyes, transforming rocks into animals or humans, convincing you that they were moving or stalking you from behind. She decided she must confront her fear, using all necessary caution, or she would never know if she had run from a mirage. She laughed when after creeping silently toward the bears she realized that they were nothing more than a couple of unusually shaped boulders.

As she turned around, the world suddenly seemed to fall away from her, and she stared in astonishment at an eleven-thousand-foot precipitous drop in front of her. She began to hear a strange, unearthly sound:

Rich and dark, it was a sound containing many overtones. At once intimate, and at the same time universal, it filled the spaces in and around me with a kind of celestial music. It was a sound I recognized, carrying both the ache of abandonment, and at the same time the comforting voice of being "called home."

I looked around, wondering what could act as an instrument for something so divine. I expected to see some amazing geological equivalent to organ pipes or pan pipes. Then I noticed that as I turned my head that the tone kept changing and that it was me the wind was sounding. The tones and overtones were way above my natural vocal range. They would have been impossible for me to create, yet *I* was the instrument that was being played. With this realisation, I felt a sense of overwhelming acknowledgement and acceptance, and with tears coursing down my cheeks, I stood there and allowed myself to be sung.

It was a pivotal moment. The quest had become the catalyst for Marie to explore indigenous wisdom from around the world and find a whole new way of working with people. It also encouraged her to look at exploration and her explorer husband in an entirely new light. She had always thought that Wally had "a touch of greatness" about him; she had observed how his intuition and his dreams had guided him through many life-threatening moments and how he was able to read signs in nature. Other pioneering explorers had had similar experiences and skills. This intangible guidance has been called many things: providence, intuition or destiny. But put simply, it appeared that almost every pioneer before my father had been in touch with something bigger than himself. Intrigued, she started writing a book called *The Way of the Explorer*—a guide to travelling safely and creatively through the journey of life. As she came to this epiphany, Wally was also entering a new phase of his life.

Thirty-one years after completing his journey across the top of the world, Wally was awarded a knighthood "For Services to Polar Exploration" in the Millennium Honours. He was deeply moved; doubly so, since the last man to receive this honour had been Sir Ernest Shackleton. It was a tremendous boost to Wally's morale.

He was no longer able to travel in the Arctic or the Antarctic. His health had been deteriorating; heart problems, together with the debilitating effects of diabetes and the unexpressed grief over Pascale's death, had taken their toll. He and Marie had moved to a crofter's cottage in the highlands of Scotland, which had breathtaking views across the Upper Spey Valley to the Monadhliath Mountains beyond, but before long his walking distance had slowed to a painful hundred yards, and he was no longer able to climb the much-loved neighbouring hills. It was heartbreaking for a man who loved being out in nature. So although the knighthood would make no material difference to their lives, it was welcome recognition of the value of Wally's work in the polar regions. For months after the investiture, my parents smiled happily at each other when any post arrived addressed to Lady Herbert or Sir Wally. Every evening there were giggles at bedtime when they said, "Knight, Knight—Lady, Lady" to one another.

Together they had been on many journeys, and this last one was perhaps the most difficult, as Wally grew increasingly frail. Their love for one another had become deeper, quieter and completely unconditional. They trusted each other implicitly. Together they had conquered many fears. Marie had faced the darkness in Greenland because of Wally's love and understanding, and now she helped him to try to be unafraid of the inevitable end. Her guidance was absorbed in a powerful recurring dream of his that, as always, had a polar theme.

"In this dream," my father recalled, "I was in a tiny hut in the middle of the Arctic Ocean, in the dead of winter. It was a familiar place, and with me were the same three companions with whom, in 1968, I had drifted through the long polar night—six black months of isolation, cold and constant danger. Suddenly in the dream there was a noise. It appeared to come from outside the hut and, strangely, the noise was made up of several sounds which produced the most terrifying scream that I had ever heard. Whether it was the sound of ice breaking, or the wind, not one of us dared to guess, nor did it really matter, for what happened next almost stopped the heart beating. There was an 'explosion'—an almighty BLAST! But the door was not blown in by the wind, nor even by the crescendo of sound. It had been blown in by LIGHT."

17

Jane Franklin

LADY FRANKLIN'S LAMENT

A freezing climate seems to have
a wonderful power in bracing your nerves
and making you stronger.

JANE FRANKLIN

THE FRANKLINS returned to England from Tasmania in 1844 licking their wounds. The recall of Sir John from his position as governor had disturbed him greatly, and Jane was anxious that she would be judged as the cause of his disgrace. No sooner had they set foot on home soil than she set her mind to making reparations. As luck would have it, the Admiralty was planning to send another expedition to the Arctic in search of the Northwest Passage. Even though it had been seventeen years since his last Arctic journey, Jane decided to do everything in her power to ensure her husband was awarded the command of this high-profile enterprise.

If successful, the leader of such an expedition stood to gain £10,000—almost £500,000 in today's money—and would be hailed as one of the greatest polar explorers of all time. Competition for the assignment was fierce. Polar greats such as Sir James Clark Ross and Sir William Edward Parry were being considered for the position. Younger men with ambitions to prove were also vying for the job.

Since the early days of their marriage, Jane had tried to encourage Franklin to return to polar exploration, convincing him that a polar climate had "a wonderful power in bracing your nerves and making you stronger." "All the world knows what you can do," she had enthused, "and England has acknowledged with shouts which almost drowned the declaration, that,—'in the proud memorials of her fame, stands linked with deathless glory, Franklin's name.'" Now powered in equal parts by pride and an acute sense of self-preservation, Jane focussed her considerable energy on generating support for her husband. To her friend Sir James Clark Ross, she confessed that she was deeply concerned about Franklin:

> At the present crisis of our affairs & being treated so unworthily by the Colonial Office, I think he will be deeply sensitive if his own department should neglect him . . . I dread exceedingly the effect on his mind of being without honourable and immediate employment, and it is this which enables me to support the idea of parting with him on a service of difficulty and danger better than I otherwise should.

Her request that Ross lend weight to her husband's campaign she felt was a fair exchange—after all, she had bought a 640-acre estate on his behalf in Tasmania. Ross's response was instant. He would do everything in his power to smooth the way for Franklin. With persuasion from some of its more influential members, the Royal Geographical Society grandly backed Sir John's candidacy. Parry also pledged his support, then urged Thomas Hamilton, Earl of Haddington, first lord of the Admiralty, "If you don't let him go, the man will die of disappointment." Under intense pressure from all sides, the Admiralty officially appointed Franklin the leader of the Northwest Passage expedition. The Irishman Francis Crozier was his second-in-command, and James Fitzjames, Sir John Barrow's choice for leader, was assigned as third-in-command.

Before Franklin left for the Arctic, Jane busied herself with last-minute arrangements and—just as Eleanor, his first wife, had done—sewed a silken British flag to give to her husband as a talisman. A few days before his departure, Jane gently placed the flag over her husband as he slept. Stirring, Franklin suddenly exclaimed in horror: "Why there's a flag thrown over me!" He leaped to his feet and bellowed at Jane, "Don't you know that in the Royal Navy we lay the Union Jack over a corpse?" Jane left the room in distress, and Franklin immediately followed to apologize. "Forgive me, Jane. I was half asleep." Quietly she replied: "As if my loving gesture, John, could be anything but a harbinger of your success."

ON MAY 19, 1845, two steam-powered bomb vessels, the *Erebus* and the *Terror*, set sail from a village near Gravesend in Kent amid a cacophony of brass bands, cheers and tearful flutterings of handkerchiefs from a crowd estimated at ten thousand. "Never, no never shall I forget the emotions called forth by the deafening cheering," Charles Osmer, the purser aboard the *Erebus*, wrote of their departure. "The suffocating sob of delight mingled with the fearful anticipation of the dreary void... could not but impress on every mind the importance and magnitude of the voyage we have entered upon. There is something so thrilling in the true British cheer." For weeks, national newspapers had been building up the momentum for the departure of Britain's most significant and impressive expedition to date.

Beneath the pomp, however, was an undercurrent of uncertainty about whether the expedition could fulfill its task. Although the ships were well equipped, some argued they were too bulky and heavy to navigate some of the trickier channels that wove between the unmoving fast-ice and the countless islands of the North. The choice of Franklin as commander was also open to criticism. The veteran explorer was overweight, unfit and, frankly, too old for such an assignment.

Among the doubters was Sir John Ross, who had made two attempts himself to discover the Northwest Passage, only to be locked in ice and stranded for four years on the second attempt. He openly questioned several aspects of the expedition, and when he learned that Franklin had made no contingency plan, he was horrified. If Franklin had not returned by 1847, Ross declared, he would go looking for the expedition himself. Dr. Richard King, an ambitious naturalist and surgeon who had coveted Franklin's post, was even more disenchanted. Later he wrote: "I told Sir John Barrow publicly at the time Franklin sailed that he was sending him to form *the nucleus of an iceberg.*"

The officers and crew of the *Erebus* and the *Terror* left England feeling invincible. Franklin had rarely felt more content. His ships were the best of their class, and they had enough food on board to last five years or more. God willing, with the power of modern technology driving them through any problematic ice, they would complete their task quickly and without the least strain or danger. As he focussed on the journey ahead, the words of Roderick Murchison, the president of the Royal Geographical Society, were still ringing in his ears. The expedition, Murchison enthused, would be a grand success. "The name of Franklin alone," he declared, "is, indeed, a national guarantee."

Franklin was regarded by his men as an amiable yet somewhat eccentric uncle. Polar exploration, he believed, need not be an uncivilized affair. On board they had an extensive library of seventeen hundred volumes. Evening classes were held, and Franklin conducted regular services and prayers. Overall, he made a great impression on his men. "I have never felt the Captain was so much my companion with anyone I have sailed with before," wrote James Fairholme, the ship's most junior lieutenant. "We are very happy. Never was more so in my life," reported James Fitzjames, Franklin's third-in-command. "You have no idea how happy we all feel . . . and how anxious to be among the ice. I never left England with less regret." On July 28, 1845, the *Erebus* and the *Terror* passed two whaling ships and disappeared into Davis Strait. Sir John Franklin and his crew of 129 were never seen alive by their countrymen again.

NOT LONG AFTER Franklin sailed, Jane too began travelling. It was necessary, she declared, for her continued health and that of her stepdaughter. The remainder of the summer she spent in France; then she visited Madeira. From there they travelled through the West Indies to the southern United States, then northward in the hope that Jane would be able to rendezvous with her husband as he emerged triumphant into the Pacific. That was not to be. She returned to England to find that nothing had been heard from the expedition since they had rounded the coast of Greenland. By December 1846, she was concerned. She confided her fears to Sir James Clark Ross, who told her not to worry; the expedition was adequately provisioned, and there was no reason to believe they were in trouble.

Others thought differently. True to his word, early in 1847, Sir John Ross presented himself at the Admiralty with plans and charts for the rescue of the expedition. His proposal was quickly dismissed, as was a proposition by King that he should lead a relief expedition down the Great Fish River. Sir James Clark Ross and Sir William Edward Parry agreed that it was "perfectly absurd to entertain the smallest degree of alarm on [the expedition's] account." Edward Sabine also advised patience. Franklin had written to Sabine with his instructions in the event of just this situation, making his feelings quite clear:

> I hope my dear wife and daughter will not be over anxious if we should not return by the time they may have fixed upon—and I must beg of you to give them the benefit of your advice and experience when that [time] arrives—for you know well that even after the second winter without success in our object we should wish to try some other channel if the state of our provisions and the health of the crew justify it.

The belief of such men in Sir John's ability cheered Jane enormously, so much so that she took off to southern Italy for almost five months with her stepdaughter, Eleanor, and Sir John's niece Sophy. Nonetheless, as autumn approached, she felt compelled to return home: "Sir John Richardson tells me that if they do not return by December there will be reason to fear some disaster." By November 1847 Jane had obtained a copy of her husband's original orders and had gathered together a coterie of advisers who attended meetings at her home to discuss a potential relief operation. Finally, the Admiralty had to do something.

In May 1848 a three-pronged search operation was launched. Sir James Clark Ross was dispatched with orders to search the shores of Lancaster Sound and Barrow Strait. Two more ships would attempt to rendezvous in the Bering Strait to search the western Arctic, and Franklin's friend Richardson would lead an overland expedition, following the Mackenzie River to the Arctic coastline. Richardson's team included the seasoned Arctic expert John Rae, who was skilled at using methods of travel and survival learned from Indian and Inuit peoples.

Jane sent letters with the expeditions, praying that her husband would receive them. "I try to prepare myself for every trial which may be in store for me," she wrote, "but dearest, if you ever open this, it will be I trust because I have been spared the greatest trial of all." She considered travelling with one of the parties herself, but finally accepted that she could do more if she stayed in England.

Jane was fully aware of the difficulty of the search. The northern coastline of the Canadian and Alaskan Arctic is a constantly changing, shredded maze of passages and dead ends. A route that is ice-free one summer can be impassable the next. Even though Franklin had clear orders, there was no knowing if his ships had deviated from the planned route because of unforeseen changes in the ice. The problem of finding the expedition would be doubly hard if the ships had been wrecked and the men forced to travel overland.

Jane could not sit idle. Later that summer she and Sophy travelled to the Orkney and Shetland Islands in the hope that one of the whaling ships returning from the Arctic might have news of her husband. The whalers and their wives were naturally sympathetic to her cause. Besides, she made quite an impression: she was so unperturbed by a rough crossing in a small fishing boat between the islands that a crewman was said to remark, "If the woman be such a man, what must the husband be?"

In November 1849, while in Edinburgh, Jane heard news that plunged her into a "fearful crisis." Sir James Clark Ross and Sir John Richardson had arrived back in England just days apart, and neither had found any sign of her husband, his ships or his men. Distraught but undeterred, she declared she would send a private expedition. Fitting out a ship for the Arctic, however, was well beyond her means. She needed assistance from elsewhere, and she was prepared to ask for it. Letters flew to the president of the United States, Zachary Taylor, and to various royal families of Europe.

Soon the search for Sir John Franklin became an international affair. The emperor of Russia, moved by a letter from Jane, sent a search expedition to the Asiatic coast of the Bering Strait and the northern reaches of Siberia. The American financier Henry Grinnell pledged to fit out two American vessels and forwarded Jane's appeal to Congress along with a petition signed by numerous ship owners. Jane offered £3,000 as a reward to any ship that found the expedition or dedicated itself to the search. After considerable pressure, the Admiralty followed suit with the offer of a reward of £20,000— over £1 million in today's currency—to any ship that lent "efficient assistance" to the lost party. As a salutary afterthought, £10,000 was offered to anyone who could ascertain the fate of the expedition.

By now a massive publicity drive, instigated by Jane, ensured that the plight of Franklin's men had become a national issue. The public began to regard Jane as the torchbearer of hope. She was more than a devoted wife: she was becoming a champion of lost souls. In sixty churches across the country, public prayers were said for the safety of the expedition. Soon, the fate of the Franklin expedition had embedded itself so firmly in the public imagination that clairvoyants, cranks and even everyday folk started to offer Jane a bewildering range of information that had come to them in dreams or from "beyond the grave." Sophy Cracroft, Jane's constant companion, wrote to Franklin

about the effect Jane was having on the British people, in the hope that
the letter might one day reach him:

> An active spirit of sympathy is aroused throughout the whole
> nation. It is to my dear Aunt's personal influence and most won-
> derful efforts that the existence of the feeling is mainly due.
> Throughout the length and breadth of the land she is honoured and
> respected and sympathy for her has been expressed and conveyed
> to herself by all ranks, from the Queen down to the lowest of her
> subjects—and this, notwithstanding the most shrinking anxiety
> to avoid notice, or comment or observation. You could not find in
> all England a woman more universally honoured and admired and
> respected than your own wife.

Jane was powerfully aware of the influence the press had over
public opinion. She drew on her most influential friends, encourag-
ing them to write appeals and articles in journals on her behalf, then
penned many herself under various pseudonyms, prompting an "Arctic fever" to sweep the country. Books about heroic polar adventures,
dioramas showing Arctic vistas, and magazine and newspaper articles appeared in quick succession. The *London Illustrated News* ran
substantial articles on the fate of Sir John Franklin. The *Morning
Advertiser* depicted Jane clutching a miniature of her husband, declaring she would carry it to her grave. The *Times* demanded to know
what the government's plans were for future searches, and the *Daily
Telegraph* dubbed Jane "Our English Penelope"—referring to the
classical heroine who waited years for her beloved to return.

Having seen no sign of the promised assistance from the White
House, Jane composed a second impassioned letter to the president:

> Our brave countrymen, whether clinging still to their ships or
> dispersed in various directions, have entered upon a fifth winter
> in those dark and dreary solitudes, with exhausted means of sus-
> tenance, while yet their expected succour comes not! It is in the
> time, then, of their greatest peril, in the day of their extremest need,

that I venture, encouraged by your former kindness, to look to
you again for some active efforts... and [to] add to the means of
search... It is only by the multiplication of means, and those vigorous and instant ones, that we can hope, at this last stage, and in
this last hour, perhaps, of the lost navigators' existence, to snatch
them from a dreary grave.

In London she took a suite of apartments at 33 Spring Gardens, a
stone's throw from Admiralty House. Her presence was keenly felt.
Some nicknamed her headquarters "the Battery," but Jane played
down her role, mindful of the accusations of interference she had
endured in Tasmania.

Those who dealt with Jane found her energy and persistence
either admirable—a "truly feminine yet heroic spirit"—or exasperat-
ing. But none could ignore the fact that she had done her homework.
Sophy noted, "[Jane] grasped the details with a force and acuteness
which surprised those to whom Arctic exploration was familiar...
She mastered technicalities in order the better to throw herself into
the subject." Presidents, emperors, prime ministers, lords of the
Admiralty and captains of industry were sent streams of persuasive
letters. In 1850, no fewer than thirteen ships sailed for the Arctic in
search of her husband. All were driven forward by her indomitable
will.

ON AUGUST 27, 1850, the first shouts of excitement during the entire
five years of Franklin's absence rang out among the frozen inlets of
the Canadian North. "Graves, Captain Penny! Graves! Franklin's
winter quarters!" On tiny Beechey Island, rescue parties discovered
the remains of what had clearly been one of Franklin's camps. Strewn
over the desolate beach was a strange assortment of relics—a pair of
gloves neatly folded on a rock, a vast stash of tinned food—and nearby
were three graves marked by simple headboards. Mysteriously, there
was no cairn containing notes about where the men were heading. It
was an incomprehensible omission for a seasoned polar explorer such
as Franklin.

One by one the ships returned to their home shores with bare scraps of information. Jane had invested hope and a personal fortune in the search, but her efforts had gone unrewarded. Dejected, she took to her bed.

SEVERAL MORE RESCUE operations were launched over the next couple of years, though many people called for an end to the search, pointing out that other lives were being risked in the process. Jane soldiered on and organized more expeditions. Most resulted in no new information, and in one case there was tragedy, when the first officer, a Frenchman named Joseph René Bellot, drowned in the Wellington Channel. Jane was heartbroken. She had regarded Bellot as a surrogate son. The loss of such a courageous and spirited young man made the future appear bleaker. In a letter intended for her husband she wrote, "We are all growing old and shattered, grey-haired and half toothless."

The continued outpouring of public sympathy for Jane and her cause was tremendous. Whalers painted and chalked enormous messages on cliffs around the Arctic. Relief missions left food and clothing in caches; balloons were released carrying notes with locations of the rescue parties, and foxes were trapped and then released carrying messages on collars in the event that Franklin's men shot them for food. At home in Britain, Staffordshire pottery figures of Sir John and Lady Franklin were created; poems and stories appeared in local papers throughout the country, and "Lady Franklin's Lament" became a popular ballad.

> We were homeward bound one night on the deep
> Swinging in my hammock I fell asleep
> I dreamed a dream and I thought it true
> Concerning Franklin and his gallant crew.
>
> As I was musing on yon foreign shore
> I heard a lady and she did deplore

She wept aloud and to me did say,
Oh, my loving husband, he stops long away.

It is seven long years since three ships of fame
Caused my dear husband to cross the main
And a hundred seamen of courage stout
A northwest passage for to find out.

In Baffin's Bay where the whale fish blows
The fate of Franklin no one knows
I am afraid he is lost on yon foreign shore
Where he left his home to return no more.

Jane's willingness to finance her own expeditions caused tremendous rifts within her family. In May 1852, her beloved father, John Griffin, died, leaving what might have been Jane's sizable inheritance to his favourite grandson. The old man knew that, given the opportunity, his daughter would squander the family property and money in the search for Franklin. With the sole exception of Sophy, Jane's relatives believed that her quest to find her husband had become an obsession. More ships still would head north, but the hope of finding Franklin or his men alive after an eight-year absence was extremely slim. Franklin had granted his wife power of attorney over his resources—including the estate left by his first wife, which should have gone to his daughter—and by 1853 the coffers were almost completely empty.

By the time of the Franklin searches, Eleanor was a confident young woman, anxious to be free of the control of her critical stepmother. She was betrothed to the Reverend John Philip Gell, a gentle and intelligent man who had been chosen by the Franklins as the principal of their college in Tasmania. On their marriage in 1849, Jane had granted the newlyweds a small allowance, which was regarded by her stepdaughter as insultingly low. Eleanor feared Jane was exhausting the fortune that by rights was hers.

Her concerns prompted an ugly feud. Sophy claimed that Eleanor *"hated"* Jane and resented the closeness Sophy shared with her aunt. Philip Gell complained that Jane was behaving as if she were the only one suffering from Franklin's disappearance; any differences between the two women could have been resolved years before if Jane had had but a "spark of right feeling left towards Eleanor." In an extraordinary spectacle, the private exchanges between Jane and the Gells suddenly became public with a battle of letters in the broadsheets. "The painful part of all this to me," Eleanor wrote sadly, "is that the family affairs of such a man as my dear Father should thus be dragged before the world." To add to their distress, on December 12, 1853, the *Times* reported that the Admiralty was to remove the names of Sir John Franklin and his men from its books the following year. Eleanor grieved. Jane was furious.

Jane considered the Admiralty's decision "presumptuous in the sight of God, as it will be felt to be indecorous, not to say indecent . . . in the eyes of men." Surely Franklin and his men deserved that their country at the very least ascertain their fate. She refused her widow's pension and compiled a twenty-two-page summary of why the men might yet be living. The timing of the Admiralty's announcement was suspicious, she stated. One of the rescue expeditions, led by Robert McClure, had claimed the discovery of the Northwest Passage after an arduous and almost fatal journey on foot. McClure declared that, in the process, he had proved that the passage was unnavigable. In the light of his claim, Jane suspected that there was no incentive for the Admiralty to send further ships to the North.

Jane knew that her cause did not stand a chance without public sympathy. Image was everything. Since the moment the *Erebus* and the *Terror* seemed lost, she had taken to wearing nothing but black. It was a powerful symbol of her fear for her husband's life. Now she threw off her signature widow's weeds in defiance of the Admiralty's decision and appeared in public wearing brilliant shades of pink and green: "It would be acting a falsehood and a gross hypocrisy on my part to put on mourning when I have not yet given up all hope. Still less would I do it in that month and day that suits the Admiralty's financial convenience." Eleanor was dismayed and confessed, "I tremble for her mind."

ON OCTOBER 22, 1854, sensational news swept through London. John Rae, while on a Hudson's Bay Company expedition in the Arctic, had encountered a party of Inuit who were in possession of numerous relics from the Franklin expedition. Among the artifacts were several pieces of silver cutlery inscribed with the initials of officers from the *Terror*. Rae set up camp at Repulse Bay and offered large rewards for information. Before long he had collected a gold cap band, broken watches and Franklin's Hanoverian order of knighthood. He determined from interviews with the Inuit that a large party of Franklin's men had abandoned their ships off the coast of King William Island in Victoria Strait and had perished while trying to make their way to the mainland of North America.

No documents were found to give further clues. However, a tragic tale emerged which placed "the fate of a portion (if not all) of the then survivors of Sir John Franklin's long-lost party beyond a doubt; a fate as terrible as the imagination can conceive":

> From the mutilated state of many of the corpses and the contents of the kettles, it is evident that our wretched countrymen had been driven to the last resource—cannibalism—as a means of prolonging existence.

Rae's terrible discovery, reported in confidence to the Admiralty, was never intended to be made public. To his amazement, and to the horror of Jane, on October 23, the *Times* published his text with all its grisly details. Rae's revelations ripped through the genteel veneer of Victorian England and thundered through the civilized world. It was unimaginable that British gentlemen would stoop to such savagery. Horror and incomprehension gave way to denial. The *London Sun*, among other newspapers, was soon awash with outrage:

The more we reflect upon the fate of the Franklin Expedition the less we are inclined to believe that this noble band of adventurers resorted to cannibalism. No—they never resorted to such horrors... Cannibalism!—the gallant Sir John Franklin a cannibal—such men as Crozier, Fitzjames, Stanley, Goodsir, cannibals!

At Jane's request, Charles Dickens stepped into the fray. In *Household Words,* the weekly magazine he edited, Dickens challenged his readers to step beyond the sensationalism: "Heaven forbid that we, sheltered and fed, and considering the question at our own warm hearth, should audaciously set limits to any extremity of desperate distress!" Franklin's men had served their country well, Dickens continued, and their memory should be cherished. Having primed his audience, the novelist deftly tore Rae's findings apart. It was to be remembered, he stated bluntly, that Rae's allegations came from no more reliable source than "the chatter of a gross handful of uncivilised people, with a domesticity of blood and blubber." Dickens claimed it was the Inuit—"covetous, treacherous, and cruel"—who were the savages, not the white man. His two-part analysis of Rae's claims, entitled "The Lost Arctic Voyagers," was a tour de force that shredded Rae's reputation.

Privately, Jane felt the ground had given way beneath her feet. Not only were the revelations excruciating; as she examined the relics Rae had brought back with him, she was confronted with the awful proof that her husband was dead.

A FEW MONTHS later, on April 24, 1855, Robert McClure submitted a request to Parliament for the reward of £10,000 (over £500,000 in today's money) for discovering the Northwest Passage. Jane was appalled at his impudence. Franklin's discovery of the passage was, she stated, "a fact beyond dispute." Two months later a select committee was appointed by the House of Commons to look into McClure's claim. Ingeniously, Jane then asserted that there was more than one Northwest Passage. McClure, she wrote to the award judges, was simply the discoverer of *a* passage, "because the *Erebus* and *Terror* under my husband had previously, though unknown to Captain M'Clure, discovered another and more navigable route. That passage, in fact, which, if ships ever attempt to push their way from one ocean to the other, will assuredly be the one adopted." It was an extraordinary example of wishful thinking. The committee brushed Jane's contentions aside. McClure was awarded a knighthood and designated the discoverer of the Northwest Passage.

Incredibly, once she had recovered her composure, Jane began agitating for yet another expedition. It was needed, she argued, to find the records of Franklin and his officers and to determine once and for all that there were no survivors. In early 1856 she drew up a petition calling for the government to "clear up a mystery which has excited the sympathy of the civilized world." It attracted the signatures of dozens of the most influential men in the country. She then wrote to the prime minister, Viscount Palmerston, urging him to authorize another expedition by ship, and not leave it to "a weak and helpless woman" to complete their work for them.

When her entreaties were refused, she continued to plow forward. In 1858, with the help of public subscription and her long-time supporter Henry Grinnell, Jane sent the *Fox* to the Arctic under the command of Leopold McClintock. It had been fourteen years since the departure of the *Erebus* and the *Terror*.

Jane's confidence in her Irish commander was well founded. After persistent searching on King William Island, his team found an abandoned ship's boat and the scattered bones of Franklin's men. In addition, they discovered piles of clothing, medicine and supplies and a solitary paper record placed within a canister and buried in a cairn. The record had been written in two parts. The first, dated May 28, 1847, stated that Sir John Franklin was leading the expedition: "All well." A fortnight later, Franklin was dead. Notes around the margin of the first note briefly told the tale:

April 25th, 1848—HM Ships *Terror* and *Erebus* were deserted on the 22nd April, 5 leagues NNW of this having been beset since 12th Sept. 1846. The Officers & Crews consisting of 105 souls under

the command of Captain F.R.M. Crozier landed here ... Sir John
Franklin died on the 11th June 1847 and the total loss by deaths in
the Expedition has been to date 9 officers & 15 men.

The message was signed by Captains Crozier and Fitzjames. The
last piece of information read, "Start tomorrow 26th for Back's Fish
River."

In the following days, the discoveries made by McClintock's
team became all the more peculiar. Cairn after cairn was located,
dismantled and found to be empty. There were no further reports,
no journals, not even the barest scrap of a written note to indicate
what had happened or where the men were. Another boat found by
Lieutenant William Robert Hobson on top of a heavy sledge contained two skeletons that looked as though they had been attacked by
wolves. This in itself was a grim find, but far more surprising was the
bewildering assortment of possessions that the men had been attempting to haul: books inscribed to Lieutenant Graham Gore from the
Erebus; watches, nails, saws, files, knives, toothbrushes, towels and
soap. And that was the least of it: the men had also been dragging
behind them "an amazing quantity of clothing" and twenty-six
pieces of silver cutlery—eight of which bore Sir John Franklin's
crest and the remainder bearing the crests or initials of nine other
officers. In addition, there were five watches, two chronometers,
two rolls of lead sheet, two loaded double-barrelled guns and forty
pounds of chocolate. In short, reported McClintock, they were hauling "a quantity of articles of one description or another astonishing
in variety, and such as, for the most part ... a mere accumulation of
dead weight."

Why had the men burdened themselves with silver cutlery and lead
sheet instead of essential items such as medicines and navigational
equipment? Only one thing was certain. The crew of Franklin's expedition had made an attempt to reach the mainland, presumably in the
hope that they might find game and, eventually, a way home. It was a
tragedy—a very mysterious one at that—but a date and a place could

now be attributed to Franklin's death, exonerating him and his men of the charge of cannibalism. Clearly, there were no survivors left to rescue.

Jane's position in the public eye reached its peak with McClintock's return. Queen Victoria expressed her sympathy, paying tribute "to the devotion and perseverance to [whom] alone their recovery is due." In May 1860 the Royal Geographical Society presented Jane with its Founder's Gold Medal "in token of their admiration of the noble and self-sacrificing perseverance in sending out at her own cost several Expeditions until at length the fate of her husband was entertained." It was a unique honour. As her brother-in-law claimed, "[Jane] now holds the highest position of any English woman."

There was still one mission left unaccomplished: Jane wanted a public memorial to immortalize her husband and his legacy. "It is my duty now to endeavour to have justice done to the dead," she declared, "as it was to try to save them when it was possible they might yet be living." With McClintock, Palmerston and Benjamin Disraeli among her supporters, Jane secured not just one but several monuments testifying to the heroism of her husband, including a statue in Waterloo Place beside her husband's club, the Athenaeum.

Once her husband's legacy was assured, Jane and Sophy began to travel again. They had started out even before the return of the *Fox*. "They have travelled more than we have," commented the astonished McClintock, referring to Jane's steam tour up the Danube and journeys through Crimea and several countries bordering the Mediterranean and the Black Sea. Jane and Sophy then set off again to the United States. At Niagara Falls she learned of the sudden death of her stepdaughter; Eleanor had died from scarlet fever while nursing her second son. While saddened by the news, Jane kept on travelling.

After touring Canada, Jane went to New York, then on to Brazil. Now in her seventies, she rode in bullock carts over a mountain road in Chile, encountered wild horsemen in Patagonia and then sailed to British Columbia, where she was paddled in a canoe under an enormous banner announcing she was entering Lady Franklin Pass.

Her marvellous adventures reached an apogee in Hawaii, where she was met by the royal carriage and liveried footmen and presented at a gala reception as if she were royalty. Ever tireless, Jane continued on to Honolulu, Japan and India and travelled through the Suez Canal three years before it officially opened. In Sitka, Alaska, where she and Sophy lived for two months, Jane was closer geographically to the Northwest Passage than she would ever come.

On July 18, 1875, aged eighty-three, Jane, Lady Franklin died. Her gravestone in Kensal Green Cemetery, which she later shared with ever-faithful Sophy, is remarkably modest, given the impact she had on her age: a simple, weathered stone cross among a thousand others.

Jane Franklin's contribution to polar exploration is her legacy. The decade of searches for Franklin cost the equivalent of approximately £41 million in today's money. The Admiralty parted with a staggering £675,000; the U.S. government invested $150,000, and the American Henry Grinnell contributed over $100,000. Jane raised and spent a good £35,000 on ships and crew. Even if very little had been discovered about the chain of events that led to the end of the Franklin expedition, more than forty thousand square miles of new territory had been covered by sledge, and eight thousand miles of coastline had been mapped and examined. Perhaps the most fitting tribute was that of the *Aberdeen Journal:* "What the nation would not do, a woman did."

18

Jo Peary

THE PRICE OF FAME

I must confess to becoming a little weary of this publicity and
sometimes I ask where I belong in this affair at all.

JO PEARY

J O PEARY returned to the United States from her year-
long ordeal in the Arctic with Frederick Cook's damning assessment of her husband's condition ringing in her ears. The
doctor may have had his own motives for undermining Peary, but his
appraisal was disturbingly accurate.

Since Jo's departure, Peary had become overwhelmed by grief and
doubt. At night he would wake, heart pounding, from dreams of the
Windward being smashed against the rocks and sinking with his wife
and daughter trapped inside while he watched, helpless on the ice. At
the end of April 1902, after tackling the most crippling conditions
he had yet experienced, Peary came to a standstill. "The game is off.
My dream of sixteen years is ended," he recorded miserably. At Fort
Conger he noted, "Forty-six. Too old for this work." Later he added,

"The goal still remains for a better man than I, or more favourable conditions, or both."

> Now a maimed old man, unsuccessful after the most arduous work, away from wife and child, mother dead, one baby dead. Has the game been worth the candle?... As I think of the last four years and what I have been through; as I think of all the little petty details with which I have been and am still occupying myself, it all seems so small, so little worth the while that I could cry out in anguish of spirit.

That summer Jo and Marie came north again to bring him home. Marie recalled that her father boarded the *Windward* a "discouraged man," but Jo, as always, revived him. By the time they had reached the United States, the explorer's ardour had returned. Still, he would need all his strength to face his homecoming. The *New York Times* marked his return with the headline "Peary Failed to Reach the North Pole." Other press followed suit, some quoting statements from the disgruntled men of his previous expeditions and claiming that Peary was a "weather-beaten old fanatic"—a man who should be "pitied more than derided."

In 1899, during Peary's absence, Morris Jesup had formed the exclusive Peary Arctic Club of wealthy patrons. Although some of his supporters remained unquestioningly loyal, the damning press coverage, the fact that Peary had undergone yet another operation to remove his two remaining toes and Peary's failure to bring back significant new information were all disappointing. With Frederick Cook and Thomas Dedrick claiming Peary was a broken megalomaniac, the prospect of further funding seemed uncertain.

Remarkably undaunted, Peary began lobbying influential friends and associates to mount another expedition. To her amazement, Jo learned of his intentions through a report in the newspapers. Marie flew into a tearful rage, then wrote her father a letter: "I have been looking at your pictures ... and I am sick of looking at them. I want to see my father I don't want people to think me an orphan. Please think this over." This time, Jo let her daughter speak both their minds.

Jo and Marie were not the only ones who expected Peary to stay put for a while; his leave had expired and the navy also had a claim on him. Reluctantly, Peary reported for duty once again, only to find he was faced with jealous peers and a routine that was unfamiliar. He bore the initial discomfort well, knowing that he still had friends in high places, including President Theodore Roosevelt. With Roosevelt as his champion, Peary could be assured of special treatment, and he did not have to wait long. Within two months of his return from the Arctic, he was promoted to commander. Furthermore, although he had conspicuously failed so far to reach the North Pole, he was awarded two gold medals, and in 1903 he became the president of the American Geographical Society. But all of this was not enough. Robert Scott was in the Antarctic on his *Discovery* expedition, potentially securing the South Pole for Britain, and Peary could not accept the notion of anyone but himself claiming the North Pole for the United States. Roosevelt felt the same way. On September 5, 1903, exactly a week after the birth of his son, Robert Peary Jr., Peary was advised by the secretary of the navy that he had been granted another three years of leave:

> The Attainment of the Pole should be your main object. Nothing short will suffice. The discovery of the poles is all that remains to complete the map of the world . . . Our national pride is involved in the undertaking. . . In conclusion, I am pleased to inform you that the President of the United States sympathizes with your cause and approves the enterprize.

Jo knew that she would have to release her husband again. Already he was rarely at home, and she had to deal with any domestic problems on her own. On Valentine's Day 1903 her telegram to him had been one not of love but of fear. Marie was very sick: "Temperature still rising typhoid almost certain . . . Am frightened to death." Peary was too preoccupied with future plans to take much notice of his daughter's illness or his wife's unhappiness. With Jesup, Bridgman and the Peary Arctic Club shoring up his publicity campaign, which included two benefit performances in the style of a Buffalo Bill extravaganza, as well as a ship being built to his own specifications, he felt invincible. Even though Jo and the children had moved into a hotel near the shipyard to be close to him, they saw him becoming only more and more distant. On October 25, Jo wrote plaintively, "For the last six months or longer you have never had a nice thing to tell me & have been away from me more than with me."

The situation only deteriorated as Peary pushed forward with his plans, and by February 1905 Jo wondered if they had any future together at all. In return for her years of support, her husband had disregarded his promises and plowed on in search of fame and the Pole without a backward glance. After several sleepless nights of caring for her feverish children, she came to the end of her tether.

> While everything has been going your way I have had everything the other way. I did not write you, well why should I cloud your horizon with my woes, but now I must tell you... I am half dead & terribly disappointed & I think we might as well call the whole thing off. The sooner we make up our minds that we must each go our own way the better it will be for us.

But by now even the possibility of losing his wife barely checked his pace. Peary's obsession was absolute. At lectures he declared in sizzling oratory that he would sacrifice anything for the prize of the North Pole. If souls had still been a marketable commodity "like the good old days," he announced, he would sell his to the devil. As always, Jo eventually put her feelings to one side and took her place beside him. On March 23, 1905, at the dockyard in Verona, Maine, she smiled at the cameras and christened the completed ship *Roosevelt* with a bottle of champagne encased in ice. Just over three months later, the *Roosevelt* was in New York, its decks full of potential patrons enjoying a promotional day cruise aboard Peary's new Arctic vessel. "Every boat in sight, from the ocean grayhounds to the shabby little tugboats, gave three blasts for the Roosevelt, as she passed by," reported the *New York Tribune*. Just in time, Peary secured enough funds for his next assault of the North. On July 16, the *Roosevelt* steamed down the Hudson River before sailing to Nova Scotia, and on to the Arctic.

THE *ROOSEVELT* STEAMED northward from Etah with more than two hundred huskies and over fifty Inuit men, women and children camped on the decks. Peary was in familiar territory. The ship encountered the ice they were dreading, but Peary exulted as they surged farther north: "The forward rush, the gathering speed and momentum, the crash, the upward heave, the grating snarl of the ice as the steel-shod stem split it as a mason's hammer splits granite, or trod it under, or sent it right and left in whirling fragments, followed by the gathering for another rush, were glorious." The *Roosevelt* finally docked, battered and twisted, in Cape Sheridan: "We were deep in that gaunt frozen border land which lies between God's countries and inter-stellar space."

On February 28, 1906, Matt Henson set out from the ship to cut the trail. Peary began following his tracks on March 6. Hacking their way through broken, constantly moving ice, Peary's team stretched out across the Arctic Ocean. Their slow progress was unbearable. Hardly able to sleep, Peary found his mind wandering through the possibilities of failure and how it would affect him: "Will it break my heart, or will it simply numb me into insensibility?" His family and their private sanctuary of Eagle Island, in Maine, seemed so far away that he began to wonder: "Do such things really exist on this frozen planet?"

Since his departure, Jo had been defending his corner almost continuously. Among other difficulties, she had discovered that in his absence some members of the American Geographical Society had deposed her husband as their president, claiming that they needed an "active" man in the role. She had promptly written to all the primary members, reminding them it was *they* who had urged Peary to take the position, in the full knowledge that he would be in the Arctic for up to two years. In view of their established custom of retaining their presidents in office until removed by resignation or death, she continued, "I take the liberty of pointing out to you how severely the contemplated action of your Society would reflect upon my husband." Bluntly, she concluded:

> To wait until he had taken his departure & was beyond the lines of communication before striking him in the back is a method of procedure which should erase from your Society maybe the word American.

> That such action should be taken against one who has devoted as much of his time & labor & has contributed so much to the science & knowledge to which your Society is presumably devoted is sufficient to blot out the adjective Geographical & leave nothing to hold you together but the word Society.

After speaking her "plain truths," Jo reported to her husband that she had ensured he would be re-elected, but there were some who would continue to make life difficult for him.

> Oh, I pray you will return in safety to your ship & come home. Think of it *home* and to *stay* for I shall not let you go away again. You probably smile but I mean it this time. I have waited in vain for you to show me some consideration, now I demand it. I can't live this way any longer, besides your children have some claim upon you also. My Husband, my sweet heart. I want you so much. Just think life is nearly over and we have missed most of it.

On April 21, 1906, Peary noted a new farthest-north record of 87°5' N but could go no farther. Exactly seven months later, the *Roosevelt* limped back into Nova Scotia. Even before the tug had moored, Peary sprang onto the wharf into his wife's arms.

JO WAS HOPEFUL that her husband's quest was over; however, she was mistaken. The Pole must be claimed for the honour and credit of the United States, Peary insisted, and he was the only man who could do it. His fervour was heightened when he heard that Frederick Cook was encamped in the Arctic and contemplating a dash to the Pole.

Peary consoled himself that his rival was nothing but an amateur. No matter that Cook had served as surgeon with a Belgian Antarctic expedition from 1897 to 1899 and had subsequently won acclaim for his reported pioneering ascent of Mount McKinley in 1906; doubt was already being thrown on the accuracy of his Mount McKinley claim, and besides, Cook had stated that his next expedition to the Arctic was nothing more than a hunting trip with a wealthy sponsor. As Peary remarked to a fellow explorer, Vilhjalmur Stefansson, he could not conceive that "his" loyal "Eskimos" would help another white man toward a goal that clearly belonged to him. Publicly Peary complained that Cook was appropriating Inuit and dogs that Peary had trained for his forthcoming work and utilizing routes that Peary had pioneered "for the admitted purpose of forestalling me."

Life at home was soon more unsettled than it had ever been. With the attacks on Peary becoming more frequent, though, Jo did whatever she could to help. She knew that with Cook in the North, the Explorers Club had found itself without a president. The position had been tentatively offered to Peary, and Jo urged him to accept. If he was the club's president, surely its members would have to show some loyalty toward him. "Whatever you do," she urged, "do it in a dignified manner as becomes the *greatest Arctic explorer of the age.*"

She still beseeched her husband to see a future beyond the Arctic, but her entreaties came to nothing; Peary was fixated. For the next few months, any notes he wrote to his family were hurried; even his usual address of "My Darling" was abbreviated to "M.D." Desperate to save what was left of their marriage, Jo telegraphed Peary from their home in Washington while he was on a business trip in New York: "We need each other, will you come or will I?"

ON JULY 6, 1908, Peary left New York once more to a salute from President Roosevelt. "I believe in you, Peary," Roosevelt boomed, "and I believe in your success—if it is within the possibility of man."

With Jo and his children, Marie and Robert E. Peary Jr., at his side, Peary was in high spirits. "Surely no ship ever started for the end of the earth with more heart-stirring farewells," he later wrote. Henson, however, remembered the mood of their departure as intense, with gamblers placing wagers on their success or failure, and women weeping beside the quay. Eleven days later, Jo and the children disembarked from the *Roosevelt* at Sydney, Nova Scotia, then watched as the ship steamed away. "Another farewell," Peary reflected, "and there had been so many! Brave, noble little woman! You have borne with me the brunt of all my Arctic work. But somehow, this parting was less sad than any which had gone before. I think that we both felt it was the last."

Once in Arctic waters, all thoughts turned to the rival's whereabouts. At Etah, Peary was met by one of Cook's men, Rudolph Franke, who was suffering from scurvy and exhaustion and was desperate to return home. Franke begged to be allowed to join Peary's supply ship, the *Erik*. Peary agreed to give Franke passage home on the condition that he hand over Cook's cache of blue fox skins, bear skins, and narwhal and walrus ivory. On February 21, 1909, almost exactly a year after Cook had left Cape Sabine for the Pole, Peary prepared for his own quest. "This was my final chance to realise the one dream of my life," he wrote. "The morning start would be the drawing of the string to launch the last arrow in my quiver." He left the *Roosevelt* anchored at Cape Sheridan and followed the hard-packed trail of his depot-laying parties northward, knowing that failure was not an option.

On April 1, 1909, one month after the expedition had left land, Peary's right-hand man and chief navigator, Captain Robert Bartlett, calculated that Peary, Henson, Bartlett and four Inuit hunters, Egingwah, Ootah, Seegloo and Ooqueah, were 133 nautical miles from the Pole, although surprisingly, Bartlett had neglected to take an observation for longitude to assess their lateral drift, which is imperative to calculate a precise position on the Arctic Ocean. Peary advised Bartlett that Bartlett would not be joining him on the final marches to the Pole. He shook Bartlett's hand and watched as the disappointed man turned and began the long trek back toward Cape Sheridan. Peary's plan of using relays to break the trail had worked, but he was unwilling to "divide the spoils" with Bartlett. He would undertake the final march with his loyal companion Henson and the four Inuit hunters, none of whom he believed would expect to share in the ultimate glory.

As soon as Bartlett had left, the speed of the party increased exponentially. Obstacles that had relentlessly confronted them now appeared to be magically removed from their path. Up to Bartlett's departure they had encountered wide, open-water leads, treacherous rafting or pressure-ridged ice, and the ever-present subtle polar drift that would imperceptibly change their direction. According to Peary, the pressure ridges, while still "stupendous" in size, were now "easily negotiable either through some convenient gap or up the slope of some huge drift." (Henson, on the other hand, recalled having to use pickaxes to laboriously carve a path through the maze of ridges.) Peary recorded that the sledges were now going at such a lick that he was obliged to ride on one or else sprint to keep up. Their average speed was almost three times faster than his usual averages in similar territory. The smell of success was lodged in his nostrils, Peary exclaimed.

Since March 26, Peary had been making notes to himself regarding the accolades and the administration of the international celebrity status he could expect on his return:

Have Borup take a 5" × 7"... portrait of me in deer or sheep coat (face unshaven) with bear roll, & keep on till satisfactory one obtained. Have Foster color a special print of this to bring out the gray eyes, the red sun burned skin, the bleached eyebrows and beard, frosted eyebrows, eyelashes, beard...

Mark 1. monument for Mausoleaum? Faced with marble or graphite, statue with flag on top, lighted room at base for 2 sarcophagi? Bronze figures Eskimo, Dog, Bear, [Musk Oxen],

Walrus, etc, etc or bronze tablets of flag on Pole & suitable inscription. Bust... Senior Rear Admiral on retired list (with full pay?)
R- Ad- pennant with diagonal white bar.

On April 6, Peary ordered Henson and the Inuit to make camp.
As they did so, he pulled a small packet from beneath his coat and
unwrapped the silk taffeta flag that Jo had made for him several years
before. "This, my boy," he told Henson, "is to be Camp Morris
K. Jesup. The last and most northerly camp on Earth." With that,
he attached Jo's flag to a staff and planted it firmly on their newly
completed igloo. Peary then took an observation. After Peary had
noted down his calculations, Henson removed his glove and went
forward to congratulate the expedition leader—surely they must be
at the Pole? Avoiding Henson's proffered hand, Peary pressed his
hands to his eyes, stumbled toward the igloo and told his companion
to let him sleep for four hours. Henson was mystified. According to
Peary, on waking he wrote in his diary:

> The Pole at last!!! The prize of 3 centuries, my dream and ambition
> for 23 years. *Mine* at last. I cannot bring myself to realize it. It all
> seems so simple and common place, as Bartlett said "just like every
> day." I wish Jo could be here with me to share my feelings. I have
> drunk her health and that of the kids from the Benedictine flask she
> sent me.

These now-famous words were written on a loose leaf of a
different kind of paper, undated and slipped into his original journal,
which suggests this entry may have been written at a later date. It is
almost certain Peary knew he was not at the Pole. At 6 PM Columbia
meridian time, he set out with two Inuit companions and "pushed
on an estimated distance of ten miles." He made observations before
returning to camp and doing the same there. He then set out again, at
right angles to his previous course, and travelled a farther eight miles
before returning. Henson observed Peary on his return:

His face was long and serious. He would not speak to me. I quietly learned from the boys accompanying him that he had made observations a few miles further on.

"Well Mr. Peary," I spoke up cheerfully enough, "we are now at the North Pole, are we not?"

"I do not suppose that we can swear that we are exactly at the Pole," was his evasive answer.

"Well, I have kept track of the distance . . . " I replied, "and I have the feeling that we have now just about covered the 132 miles since Captain Bartlett turned back. If we have traveled in the right direction we are now at the Pole. If we have not traveled in the right direction then it is your fault."

In his published writings, Peary described making a beeline for the Pole on a course that "was nearly as the crow flies, due north, across floe after floe, pressure ridge after pressure ridge, headed straight for some hummock or pinnacle of ice which I had lined in with my compass." Henson, on the contrary, recorded that they "followed the lines of least resistance . . . frequently . . . going due east or west in order to detour around pressure ridges, floebergs and leads." George Borup, who had been part of the expedition in its earlier stages, also recorded, "We guessed and groped with many a twist and turn." It is impossible to travel on the Arctic Ocean for any considerable distance without having to make detours. Even if Peary and his men had been fortunate enough to cover the distance they recorded, it is possible they went in the wrong direction.

Although there is no entry in his original diary for the next two days, according to Peary's book *The North Pole* the party headed home on April 7. Peary was shattered. After the first two marches southward, he was forced to ride the sledge. "He was practically a dead weight," Henson noted later. When he returned to the ship he gathered his thoughts and wrote two loose-leaf memos. One of them includes a crucial gap: "Captain [Bartlett] came in from 87° 47' in 24 days. Self came in from——in 20 days (18 marches)."

BACK IN THE United States, as usual, Jo had borne all manner of challenges during her husband's absence. An unwelcome and surprising development had been the re-emergence of Minik, the now-orphaned Inuit boy Peary had brought to the United States twelve years earlier. Minik had grown into a disoriented and bitter young man of nineteen. In 1908 his guardian, William Wallace, had written to Peary asking him to take Minik back home to Greenland. Peary had refused, saying that his ship was already too crowded. Minik took his case to the press, and on May 9, 1909, the *San Francisco Examiner* ran a sensational feature headlined "Why Arctic Explorer Peary's Neglected Eskimo Boy Wants to Shoot Him." To Jo's dismay, the article was illustrated not only with a gruesome sketch of the boy recoiling in horror at the sight of his father's grinning skeleton from a glass case but also with a photograph of her daughter Marie, the Snow Baby, dressed in furs. Minik was quoted as saying, "I can never forgive Peary, and I hope to see him, to show him the wreck he has caused." Americans, Minik declared tartly, were "a race of scientific criminals" who would never discover the North Pole.

Herbert Bridgman was making arrangements for Minik to be taken back to the Arctic. Quickly Jo wrote to Peary to ensure that the boy did not land any firearms or ammunition without his consent. On no condition, she added, must he allow Minik to ever return to the United States.

There were other pressing concerns, too. The return of the *Erik* to the United States with the empty-handed Rudoph Franke on board had prompted accusations that Peary had stolen Cook's supply of furs and ivory and sent them as presents to his wife and the president. Bridgman reassured Jo that the Peary Arctic Club was prepared to fully vindicate her husband. It was a comfort to have such loyal support, but even so, by July matters had come to a head. While at the family summer home, Jo discovered that Cook's wife and her two children had taken up residence in the nearby village of Harpswell. "Perhaps," she wrote grimly, "she thinks she may find out if the $5000 worth of furs which she says you stole from her husband have been sent to Eagle Island." From this point on, both Dr. and Mrs. Cook were lodged firmly in the minds of the Pearys.

Meanwhile, Peary had encountered the Inuit who had travelled with Cook. In no time he was satisfied; according to Cook's companions, they had never been out of sight of land. To Peary's delight, he also came across Harry Whitney, to whom Cook had entrusted his "instruments, notebooks and flag" on the assumption that Whitney would return to the States ahead of him. In the event, Whitney's relief ship had not arrived, and as he had done with Franke, Peary agreed to give the man passage home on the condition that he leave all of Cook's property behind.

With Cook's "proofs" lost somewhere near Etah, and having heard the damning testimonies of Cook's Inuit companions, Peary was confident that the threat would disappear. Not so. On September 2, 1909, Cook's sensational claim that he had reached the North Pole the previous April, telegraphed from Lerwick in the Shetland Islands, made the front page of the *New York Herald*. The following day the news appeared in all the main newspapers around the world. In Copenhagen, Cook was given a tumultuous welcome and received by the king. Jo was dumbstruck. Over the past couple of weeks the strain had begun to tell on her. Frequently she was crippled with headaches, and Marie heard her pacing up and down restlessly during the night. On the afternoon of September 4, Jo retired to her room, incapacitated with a migraine, and asked that the children not disturb her.

Marie was sitting and reading on the front porch when she noticed a motorboat pull into the cove. "Another newspaperman," she thought impatiently. The reporter came to the screen door and asked for Mrs. Peary. Marie replied that her mother did not want to be disturbed. "I guess she will be glad to be disturbed for this," he said. "This is a telegram to the Associated Press from your father saying he has discovered the North Pole." Marie pulled the man by his lapels into the porch and pounded up the stairs. Jo immediately emerged.

Trying to appear unflustered, she read the telegram: "To the Associated Press, New York City. Have nailed the Stars and Stripes to the Pole. Peary." She thanked the man graciously for his time and trouble in delivering it, but, wary of it being a hoax, added, "If this is true, then there will certainly be a personal message to me from my husband." Moments later another boat pulled into the cove, and the storekeeper from South Harpswell scrambled directly up the cliff, arriving red-faced and breathless, clutching another telegram: "Have made good at last—I have the D.O.P. [damned old Pole]. Am well. Love. All Well... Bert." Within hours the island was besieged. "It was one of the most exciting days in my life," Marie recorded later, "and half the pleasure was to see Mother positively blooming, the drawn look gone from her face and the worried little puckers from between her eyes."

The relief did not last long. Incensed by Cook's gall in claiming the Pole, Peary wired a stream of statements pronouncing his rival a fake: "Don't let any of Cook's lies disturb you. I have him nailed." To the editor of the *New York Times*, he wrote, "He has not been to the Pole on April 21st, 1908, or at any other time. He has simply handed the public a gold brick." The reaction to Peary's fit of sour grapes was swift and ugly. Peary was roundly denounced for his attacks, which some proclaimed the words of a despot. Jo rushed to temper him:

> Sweetheart after all your privations & sacrifices now when you should be showered with honors & have everything your own way, this miserable creature causes a disturbance which can't help but annoy you & take from the pleasure of your success... If you only can keep still & not discuss this creature until you have had an opportunity to see what he & others have said, it would be far better.

Opinion quickly divided between those who supported Peary and those who believed Cook. Whereas Peary appeared arrogant and mean-spirited, Cook was reported to be like "a naïve, inexperienced child." The newspaperman W.T. Stead commented that Cook may have been mistaken about reaching the Pole but he was "both too honest and too limited to have conceived so colossal a fraud." This was a battle of personalities, and there were many who considered Peary undeserving of so great a prize.

Peary finally succumbed to the demands of his supporters that he withdraw while they attempted to repair his damaged reputation. He retreated to Eagle Island for several months, refusing to make public appearances. Peary's children were delighted to have their father home. Likewise, Jo's happiness was clear. "We have been married twenty-three years," she commented to a journalist; she added, "We have lived but three."

The reason for Peary's disappearance from public view was more serious than Jo would ever admit. According to their family friend Vilhjalmur Stefansson, Peary had suffered a breakdown. In confidence, Stefansson later admitted to the science editor of the *New York Times* that Peary's condition, which in those days would have been considered a disgrace, was kept secret. As the editor commented, "Much of the subsequent controversy would have been prevented had Peary's illness been acknowledged, but Peary's wife had extracted a promise of silence from Stefansson in her lifetime, and... her daughter Marie 'practically exacted the same pledge.'" Eagle Island, far from prying eyes, was the best remedy for a tortured soul. It was their sanctuary—seventeen wild acres crowning a rocky promontory, growing thickly with maple, beech, birch and spruce and hundreds of foxgloves planted by Jo's hand.

As Peary recuperated, the controversy swallowed up pages of newsprint. It became clear that if he was to be pronounced the discoverer of the North Pole, his claim had to be reviewed officially. On the polite insistence of his friends at the National Geographic Society, Peary agreed to submit his records for verification. His "house of friends," although conceding that the North Pole observations could have been faked, relied on their "belief in the personal honesty of Peary" and decided in his favour. By the end of November, Cook had assumed a disguise and gone into hiding. Six weeks later in Copenhagen, Cook's North Pole claim was overruled, and he was declared a "deliberate swindler." Three days later the

Explorers Club of New York stripped him of his membership. To top it all, in 1923 Cook was sentenced to more than fourteen years in jail for fraud in connection with an oil promotion. He blamed his spectacular fall from grace on Peary who, he claimed, had smothered him with a "leprous blanket of infamy."

With Cook satisfactorily removed from the arena, Peary and Jo hoped to bask in the hard-won glory. This they did, for a time. Peary received personal congratulations from President Taft and was made a rear admiral, his rank and pension backdated to April 6, 1909. He was awarded gold medals by several geographical societies that felt it unnecessary to check his proofs. One of these, a medal awarded by the Royal Geographical Society, had been designed by Kathleen Scott. But though the tributes poured in, there remained dissenters who called for Peary's proofs to be reviewed by an independent scientific body. The result was a congressional hearing. On March 3, 1911, after a good deal of manoeuvring and anxiety, a bill was passed by the House of Representatives stating that Peary had deservedly won his honours. Five years later a bill was introduced to repeal the earlier one; to the Pearys' relief it was dropped when its main proponent, Henry Helgesen, died.

During this time Peary had been diagnosed with pernicious anemia. Unconcerned, he reassured his wife, "Jo, we have won many fights. We are going to win this one." Anyone could see that he was becoming extremely ill. Most of his last summer was spent lying on a muskox rug laid out on the lawn on his beloved island. On February 19, 1920, Peary fell into a coma, and early the following morning he died. Jo was devastated: "The sparkle and the radiance went, never to return." She became a recluse, focussing purely on her family. But as Marie recalled: "Those of us who knew her best realized that while the love we gave her was a happiness to her, nothing could make up to her for the love she had lost. It was as if the mainspring were broken."

Jo and Peary had been married for almost thirty-two years, and Jo would live for a further thirty-five. In her later years she reflected that she had lived three separate lives: "The life before Bert, the life with Bert, and the life after Bert." The life with Bert was by far the most colourful, although she would gladly have done without his obsession for fame. In an interview with the *Boston Daily Globe* in December 1909, she remarked:

> I question whether any woman unless she be tremendously ambitious, a regular Katherine the Great or some such type, would select fame, with all the stings and heart aches and disappointments which it brings so close, rather than a peaceful, prosperous life with all her dear ones around her hearthstone. When a man goes out off the beaten track he possesses qualities which separate him from the mediocre, and when he blazes a new path and writes his name in big letters on his times, then every-one must concede he is neither commonplace nor conventional.
>
> But his wife, if he has one, is generally patterned after womankind in all times and ages. She loves her home and her husband, and fame purchased at the cost of imperilling both does not as a rule appeal to her... I do not claim to love home or domestic pursuits any more ardently than most women... [but] my supreme thought [when] my husband had reached the pole was not that of jubilation, though I did rejoice over that, but of deep thankfulness that, having attained the goal of his ambition, such perilous trips would no longer be necessary.

Those who met Jo Peary had little doubt that she had been a tremendous source of strength for her husband, and her daughter was keen that she receive some of the applause. Aged ninety-two, Jo was awarded the National Geographic Society's gold medal for her assistance in her husband's polar work. In an acceptance speech on behalf of her mother, Marie enthused: "I have always felt that my father would never have discovered the North Pole if it hadn't been for my Mother... She could have said 'We are only young once; why should we be separated?' Instead of that, Mother sent him off each time with colors flying, with pride and belief showing in her face for everyone to see, saying, 'Of course you'll do it.' And when you send a man off like that, he just can't fail."

19

Kathleen Scott

NO HAPPIER WOMAN
EVER LIVED

Let me maintain my high,
adoring exaltation,
and not let the contamination
of sorrow touch me.

KATHLEEN SCOTT

O N MARCH 6, 1912, rumours began that Robert Scott
had beaten Roald Amundsen to the South Pole, and
Kathleen Scott found herself at the centre of a media frenzy. "Reporters
began to flock and telephones began to ring," she wrote in the diary
that she had been keeping since her husband left. The next day "came
the clash and turmoil. Cables right and left to say 'Amundsen arrived at
Hobart states Scott has reached the Pole.'... whilst the posters shrieked
'Scott at South Pole—Brilliant Victory' etc."

Kathleen was certain there was something wrong. Surely if her
husband had reached the Pole first, he would have returned to Hobart
before Amundsen. Also, none of the cables were from the Norwegian
explorer himself. The news spread far. In New York, Robert Peary
commented to his friend Thomas Hubbard, "I sincerely hope we shall

hear soon that Scott got there, and got there first. That route was his, and he deserves to win the Prize. Whatever may be said, Amundsen's action in secretly entering Scott's field of work was not honorable." Others had similar feelings and wasted no time in communicating them. Then, sailing over the tide of conjecture, came the truth of the matter. It was Amundsen, not Scott, who was the victor.

Nansen immediately contacted Kathleen, saying his thoughts were with her. "Am sure that now you are bothered by all sorts of people, and all sorts of questions," he wrote. "If only I could be there to shield you, dear, good friend—tho' you are brave and strong enough to defend yourself." Kathleen responded, "Hurrah for Norway in spite of all." Her son, Peter, also tried in his own way to comfort her: "Amundsen and Daddy both got to the Pole. Daddy's stopped working now."

Just as with Jo Peary three and a half years before, Kathleen's quiet moments were filled with crippling headaches and awful thoughts about what her husband would be going through. The only remedy was to fill every moment with Peter, work and meeting friends. Remembering that her last birthday, on March 27, 1911, had been blessed with good news from the South, she again threw a large party and danced until 2 AM, every minute hoping that the phone would ring. A call came four days later from Central News to say that Scott was staying another year and that on January 3 he had been 150 miles from the Pole. The news was already out of date: unbeknownst to anyone outside of the expedition, Scott had died within days of his wife's birthday. His last journal entry was dated March 29.

It would be almost another year before the world learned that Scott's expedition had come to a tragic end. In the meantime, Kathleen had decided that she would go to New Zealand to greet the returning party via a journey through the United States. Her vagabond spirit had not been indulged for some time. After an emotional parting with Peter, she travelled to Liverpool and, on January 4, 1913, set off by ship to New York, carrying flowers and a promise from her inventor friend Guglielmo Marconi that she could send unlimited Marconigrams free of charge.

Having barely set foot in New York, she took tea at the Plaza, had dinner at the Ritz and then went to the Winter Garden and Martin's, where she found herself in the elevator with Robert Peary. Amundsen, she discovered, was being honoured at a dinner in one of the rooms above. Intrigued, later that evening she sneaked a look at the banquet: "It looked dull, *dull* . . . Poor [Amundsen] looked unspeakably bored."

New York was glorious fun, but Kathleen longed to see the great country. On January 22, she arrived at New Orleans, marvelled at the hordes of men unloading coffee from the large ships on the quay, then went into the desert with a companion: "Miles of desert, such desert & such wonderful light, & the most unbelievable mirage I ever saw."

Before long she was riding a train toward El Paso. She had acquired a letter that allowed her to ride in the engine car throughout the entire railway system of the United States, and she was having the time of her life. "Since my first flight in an aeroplane I have never been so thrilled, rushing through the prairies of Mexico at 120 kilometres an hour on a giant engine, throwing off & killing with the cowcatcher any cattle that were too slow getting off the line!" Still the thrill was not enough; she asked the engineer if she could ride on the front of the train, but he wouldn't allow it. After spending a night in a frontier town she galloped through orange groves to catch her next train, pulling off oranges as she rode past. She left her horse on the platform as the train pulled away.

On the recommendation of a friend she and her companion made their way through wild cattle country to the isolated Diamond Box Ranch. She climbed a small mountain alone, carrying a revolver in case she met bandits or wild beasts, then returned to camp to share meals of stewed corn eaten off black tin plates beside a large cedar-wood fire. She slept under a tree festooned with saddles and harnesses, listening to her chaperones and their horses stamping and snoring. The cowboy lifestyle suited her perfectly: "Sunshine, exercise, health, mountains, so many horses! So many men!" The following day she visited an observatory, where she discussed gravity and magnetism with scientists.

News of the deaths of Scott and his team had reached London on February 12, a week after Kathleen left Liverpool for the United States. Their bodies had been found by a search party the previous November, along with the expedition's records. But no one knew how to find Kathleen. On Valentine's Day, a memorial service was held for Scott and his men at St. Paul's Cathedral. A crowd of ten thousand gathered, and in an unprecedented act King George, dressed in the uniform of an admiral of the fleet, led the grieving masses. The *Evening Standard*'s reporter wrote, "[I doubt if St. Paul's] ever contained a congregation so profoundly moved as that which gathered here today," before reminding readers of the "one who is still ignorant of the frightful tragedy, that hapless woman, still on the high seas, flushed with hope and expectation, eager to join her husband and to share in the triumphs of his return."

Four days after the memorial service, Kathleen was in Tahiti, full of energy and expectancy. She woke at 6 AM and went to the river to bathe. The following day, February 19, she heard the news.

> Got my wireless. I was sitting on deck after breakfast not feeling very well. The captain came and said he wanted to speak to me in his room. It didn't occur to me in the slightest what he wanted but I went. Poor old chap's hands were trembling when he said "I've got some news for you but I don't see how I can tell you." I said "The Expedition?" and he said "Yes." "Well," I said, "Let's have it" and he showed me the message which ran "Captain Scott and six others perished in blizzard after reaching S Pole Jan. 18th." I remember I said without the least truth "Oh well, never mind, I expected that—thanks very much—I'll go and think about it" and I went downstairs.

Her defence against overwhelming emotion was to find a distraction. She requested that the captain not inform the other passengers, then immediately attended a Spanish lesson, went to lunch and discussed Australian politics. The following day the ship arrived in

Rarotonga. Desperate to get away, Kathleen went ashore with a young South American man, "as he speaks no language I understand but just quietly worships me." They sat on rain-soaked coral watching the breakers curl in over the reef and returned to the ship by moonlight, wet to the skin.

Kathleen longed to hide or have someone she could talk to; instead, she spent the next day on deck, occasionally writing in her diary.

> My god is godly, I need not touch him to know that. Let me maintain my high, adoring exaltation, and not let the contamination of sorrow touch me . . . Loneliness is a fear that I have never known. Had he died before I had known his gloriousness, or before he had been the father of my son, I might have felt a loss. Now I have felt none for myself. Won't anybody understand that?—probably nobody. So I must go on with this tedious business of discretion. Must even the greatest visions of the heart be blurred by discretions?

Before Scott left, Kathleen had urged him not to hold himself back for the sake of her or Peter. Scott had carried away with him this note from her scribbled in pencil:

> Look you—when you are away South I want you to be sure that if there be a risk to take or leave, you will take it, or if there is a danger for you or another man to face, it will be you who face it, just as much as before you met Doodles [Peter] and me. Because man dear *we can do without you* please know for sure we can. God knows I love you more than I thought could be possible, but I want you to realize that it won't [crossed out] wouldn't be your physical life that would profit me and Doodles most. If there's anything you think worth doing at the cost of your life—Do it. We shall only be glad. Do you understand me? How awful if you don't.

Kathleen spun between excruciating loss and admiration for what her man had achieved. To keep sane she "read violently." She had no details about what had happened, and this was more unbearable than anything else. Late one night she was called to the ship's wireless room as messages streamed in. For almost four hours she watched as the operator scribbled constantly: "A ridiculous thing happened. Messages of condolence (lovely messages) kept coming through, coming and coming without ceasing, thus blocking the line . . . Without knowing it my kind friends (and so kind some of them) were baulking my news and keeping me absolutely in ignorance except of the main fact." Then a ghostly message came through from beyond the grave. It was from Scott, written in his last hours, appealing to his country:

> We are weak, writing is difficult, but for my own sake I do not regret this journey, which has shown that Englishmen can endure great hardships, help one another, and meet death with as great a fortitude as ever in the past. We took risks, we knew we took them; things have come out against us, and therefore we have no cause for complaint, but bow to the will of providence, determined still to do our best to the last. But if we have been willing to give our lives to this enterprize, which is for the honour of our country, I appeal to our countrymen to see that those who depend on us are properly cared for.
>
> Had we lived, I should have had a tale to tell of the hardihood, endurance and courage of my companions which would have stirred the heart of every Englishman. These rough notes and our dead bodies must tell the tale, but surely, surely, a great rich country like ours will see that those who are dependent on us are properly provided for. R. Scott

The telegraph enflamed Kathleen's admiration: "That was a glorious courageous note . . . If he in his weak agony-wracked condition could face it with such sublime fortitude how dare I possibly whine. I will not. I regret nothing but his suffering."

Finally Kathleen arrived in New Zealand, where she heard first-hand how the party had been found. Scott had been the last to die.

What agony it must have been in those last hours. Oates was dead somewhere in the snows; Bowers and Wilson were dying beside him. In the weak light from a makeshift spirit lamp, with his strength fast ebbing, he wrote letters to his companions' loved ones.

On March 29, 1912, he made his last diary entry:

> Every day we have been ready to start for our depot *11 miles* away, but outside the door of the tent it remains a scene of whirling drift. I do not think we can hope for any better things now. We shall stick it out to the end, but we are getting weaker, of course, and the end cannot be far. It seems a pity, but I do not think I can write more. R. Scott
>
> For God's sake look after our people.

When the bodies were found on November 12, Apsley Cherry-Garrard wrote: "Scott had thrown back the flaps of his bag at the end. His left hand was stretched over Wilson, his lifelong friend... We never realized how strong that man was, mentally and physically, until now."

Kathleen was presented with Scott's diaries in New Zealand. She locked herself away and immersed herself in her husband's words. With the diaries was a letter addressed to her that had been written in stages, both while Scott was travelling and then as the team were dying off one by one in the tent. Mid-letter he sometimes paused: "You must understand that it is too cold to write much." His thoughts were for home, where he longed to be. "To My Widow" he began:

> Dearest darling—we are in a very tight corner now I have doubts of pulling through... I take advantage of a very small measure of warmth to write letters preparatory to a possible end—The first is naturally to you on whom my thoughts mostly dwell waking or sleeping—if anything happens to me I shall like you to know how much you have meant to me and what pleasant recollections are with me as I depart.

By the next paragraph, Titus Oates was dead, and the men's strength was deteriorating. The inevitability of death was all too apparent.

> Well dear I want you to take the whole thing very sensibly as I'm sure you will—The boy will be some comfort. I had looked forward to helping you to bring him up but it is a satisfaction to feel that he is safe with you ... I must write a little letter for the boy if time can be found, to be read when he grows up. The inherited vice from my side of the family is indolence—above all he must guard, and you must guard him, against that. I had to force myself into being strenuous, as you know ... My father was idle and it brought much trouble ... Make the boy interested in natural history if you can ... Try to make him believe in God, it is comforting ...
>
> Dearest heart you know I cherish no sentimental rubbish about re-marriage—when the right man comes to help you in life you ought to be your happy self again—I wasn't a very good husband, but I hope I shall be a good memory. Certainly the end is nothing for you to be ashamed of and I like to think that the boy will have a good start in parentage of which he may be proud ...
>
> I think the best chance has gone we have decided not to kill ourselves but to fight it to the last for that depot but in the fighting there is a painless end so don't worry.

By now it was -70°C, and the men had nothing but the shelter of the tent. Sadness crept in: "You know my thoughts have constantly dwelt on you and oh dear me you must know," he wrote, "that quite the worst aspect of this situation is the thought that I shall not see you again—The inevitable must be faced—you urged me to be leader of this party and I know you felt it would be dangerous—I've taken my place throughout haven't I? ... But oh what a price to pay—to forfeit the sight of your dear dear face."

The letter was agony to read, but Scott's request that Kathleen should boldly face the world and have no regrets made her adore him even more. "Any more magnificent invigorating document I have never read," she wrote. "One would be a poor creature indeed if one could not face one's world with such words to inspire one . . . My Peter has now a great birthright and we must be proud and happy and make our gratitude drown our pain at the thought of his terrible mental suffering."

Britain was keenly feeling the loss of its hero. When the last of Scott's rescue party returned to England, Cherry-Garrard wrote: "We landed to find the Empire—almost the civilized world, in mourning. It was as though they had lost great friends." The headlines ran bold: "A Nation's Tribute to Its Heroic Sons Dead in the White Wastes of the Far South." Stories dripped patriotism: "The calamity has its consolations in that it has proved once more the inherent heroism of British men of action. Like other great deeds it will brace the moral nerve of the nation." A record 1.34 million copies of a special memorial edition of the *Daily Mirror* had been sold on the day of the service at St. Paul's Cathedral, and the press continued to find new ways of elaborating. "It is a splendid tragedy," crowed the *Daily Mail*. "A splendid epic, written . . . in a language which every creed and race and tongue of man can understand."

All those who had been to the Arctic and the Antarctic felt a connection in some way with Scott's death, but perhaps none more than his rival for the Pole, Amundsen: "I am unwilling to believe the report is true. I was reported to have perished, so was Shackleton . . . I am grieved beyond measure."

Had Scott made it to One Ton Depot, which would have saved him, the fact remained that he was second to the South Pole; he would have returned as the loser of the "Great Race," with a debt of £30,000 as a reward. Now, such was the sympathy that some £74,500 was raised to cover the debt of the expedition and to support the families of the dead (approximately £3.4 million in today's money). The surplus went toward building an imposing memorial for Scott and his men in Devonport and setting up the Scott Polar Research Institute in Cambridge. Kathleen sculpted a number of busts and two memorial statues of Scott, one of which is located in Christchurch, New Zealand, and the other in Waterloo Place opposite that of Sir John Franklin.

Unlike Lady Franklin, Kathleen did not need to work at immortalizing her husband—the nation did that for her. A bloody war was looming, and those who were to be sent to the trenches needed a British hero. The press encouraged the public to believe that the bravery of Scott and his men was such that death was acceptable only under their own terms. The country owed honour and gratitude to Captain Scott and his companions, the *Times* wrote, for showing that "the solid stuff of national character is still among us, and that men are still willing to be 'killed in action' for an idea."

Kathleen had to accept that she was now known primarily for being the widow of the nation's hero. She was also now Lady Scott: the honour of Knight Commander of the Order of the Bath had been conferred posthumously on her husband. She remained the focus of intense media scrutiny, as did Peter. "Because of the Antarctic story," Peter wrote in his autobiography in 1957, "I was, even as a small child, regarded as 'fair game' by the press photographers and reporters . . . My mother made great and, on the whole, successful attempts to protect me."

Kathleen's approach to grief was unorthodox, and some, even among her closest and most open-minded friends, found it hard to understand. George Bernard Shaw wrote that Kathleen did not seem to feel any loss at all. It was a matter of pride for her not to grieve, yet she suffered continuously from a "ghastly head," which one doctor advised was caused by lack of weeping. Her outlet was her work. Years later, it was Peter who would confirm it was his mother's principle of living life to its fullest that had made her who she was: she "could never have tolerated any kind of continuing tragedy. She was one of the gayest people I have ever known."

Kathleen enthusiastically volunteered for the war effort, transporting cars and ambulances to France and working at a hospital. While in France she demanded, and was granted, an interview with the French war minister, Alexandre Millerand, to discuss the positioning of mobile surgeries at the front. She was not at all bothered by rank; after all, she was travelling with the daughter of her close friend the prime minister, Herbert Asquith. On her return to England she worked alongside other women making electrical coils at the Vickers factory in Erith.

Her circle of friends was more richly coloured than ever. Peter Scott recalled hiding with the dancer Madame Marie Rambert in the cupboard under the stairs at their little holiday cottage in Sandwich during an air raid. Madame prayed continuously for their safety, then, as soon as they were safe, taught him to do cartwheels. Kathleen made it a point to dance herself three or four times a week, sometimes during her lunch hour. Lords, politicians, writers and artists remained an essential part of her weekly social rituals. George Bernard Shaw read *Heartbreak House* to her aloud and sang in a "charming baritone voice"; in return, Kathleen taught him to dance. On summer nights Shaw, Kathleen and Apsley Cherry-Garrard slept out on the lawn under the stars. Cherry-Garrard, she noted, sang in his sleep. Several times a week "the most endearing of creatures," Prime Minister Asquith, would visit Kathleen and Peter; their home was a "haven of refuge" to him.

As an artist Kathleen could disengage from squeamishness and instead see the broken bodies of war as sculptural forms. In October 1918, as the war ended, she was drawn to Ellerman's Hospital "to fix about modelling hurt faces." Sir Harold Gillies, the leading British facial plastic surgeon of the time, had put out a plea: "Surgery calls Art to its aid." New techniques were required to rebuild the shattered faces of those evacuated from the front, and sculptors were recruited to make models of patients' faces, recreating a nose that had been blown off or forming a chin where there no longer was one. Using putty flaps on the model, as if they were flesh on the patient's face, allowed surgeons to experiment before touching the actual wounds. One day Kathleen sculpted a chin for a soldier, a peculiar but uplifting task that made her "feel terribly like God."

Once the war was over, Kathleen was possessed by a new-found energy for art; she even modelled small babies out of clay as she was out walking. Commissions rolled in for war memorials, medals and portraits of war heroes. In between commissions she began to sculpt friends again.

As had been the case throughout her life, Kathleen was never short of male attention. Nansen was still an ardent admirer, and in a wild moment she considered bolting to New York to marry him. Logistics prevented her from going, and she decided that she must finally put a stop to his hopes. After all, she was in the prime of life, a widow in her mid-thirties; Nansen was almost seventeen years her senior.

Then along came a wounded hero who inspired both Kathleen and Peter to feel "like a couple of radiant drunkards." Edward Hilton Young had been a journalist, a barrister and a naval officer before becoming an MP. "He has one arm, but is very clever about it," Kathleen wrote. "He was an amazingly gallant fighter." He intrigued Kathleen, particularly because he was one of the few men she had ever met who did not pursue her.

Hilton was wonderful with Peter. They talked endlessly about birds and nature, and it looked as though Scott's wish that his son should be interested in natural history was coming alive through this gentle and witty man. On January 18, 1922, Kathleen wrote in her diary, "At 10 H came and now we are going to marry each other. How absurd." They married in the crypt of the House of Commons on March 3, then disappeared to Hilton's "wretched little cot" in Wiltshire, where "great rest and peace were upon us."

No matter that she would be Baroness Kennet and would have another son with her second husband; Kathleen would be known as Scott's widow for the rest of her life. She remained fiercely protective of him. Ever since news of the failure of the expedition had broken, detractors had been lining up, gleefully rubbing their hands at the catalogue of mistakes they deemed the expedition to have made. The "debunkers" continued to dismantle his pedestal. Scott was described by some, on the whole unfairly, as an arrogant, elitist, bumbling leader so convinced of his superiority in the field that he had refused the advice of pioneers such as Nansen and Peary.

Friends of Kathleen also had their opinions, though these were rarely shared with her. Although Nansen did not publicly question

Scott's decisions, privately he confessed to Sir Clements Markham: "I was very sorry that he would not listen to my advice to take plenty of good well broken dogs and to trust to them and not to ponies... Had he done what I would have him do, we would still have had him among us. [His] equipment... was not adequate to the task." But other, more surprising detractors did go public, among them Apsley Cherry-Garrard. Kathleen was deeply wounded by the criticisms of her husband in Cherry-Garrard's book, published in 1922, which she described as "very offensive."

George Bernard Shaw had privately encouraged Cherry-Garrard to write his no-holds-barred account. Shaw had never been a fan of Scott, and after Kathleen's death, while he was trying to write about her, the playwright no longer saw any reason to conceal his feelings. Scott's "best right to celebrity is that he induced her to marry him," Shaw wrote to Kathleen's second husband in 1947. "How to do justice to Kathleen without debunking Scott is the problem... There is only one way of sparing him, to leave him out of her story altogether, which is possible, as he had almost no part in it." Shaw mistakenly believed that Kathleen's reluctance to air her grief about Scott meant their marriage had been a sham. Hilton politely defended her, and in just two sentences revealed what Shaw should have known: "If she did not seem to feel her loss, that is only seeming. Joy was her principle, and she would not let what she felt be seen and make her friends less joyful."

Kathleen lived life robustly until her death from leukemia in 1947. She had helped to mould Robert Scott into a hero, then loved him as her "god." She had brought "marvellous sunshine" into many other lives. Her "tiny" gravestone, as she had requested, bore the following inscription: "Kathleen. No happier woman ever lived."

20

Emily Shackleton

REJOICE MY HEART

On the strength of some of those tender letters,
our love was so complete in every way.

EMILY SHACKLETON

RNEST SHACKLETON returned from his failed Imperial Trans-Antarctic Expedition in 1917 to find the world changed. The war that had been announced on his departure in 1914 was still raging, and he had been unable to shake off the guilt of leaving for the Antarctic when so many other men were being sent to the front. Now he wanted to make some reparation by bolstering the war effort.

On March 20, he gave a rousing speech to eleven thousand people, which was later printed by the Australian government as a recruiting pamphlet. "To take your part in this war is not a matter merely of patriotism," he declared, "not a matter merely of duty or of expediency; it is a matter of the saving of a man's soul and of a man's own opinion of himself ... This summons to fight is a call imperative to the manhood within you."

Shackleton had been away from home for two years and eight months, and Emily feared that the peaceable life she and the children led in Eastbourne would bore him. In his absence she had developed her own interests; she was a competent golfer and an advocate for the Girl Guides, but she worried that such things were cheerless pastimes for a man recently back from the Antarctic. Her concerns were short-lived. There were pressing issues enough to keep Shackleton occupied on his return. The debts of the expedition had to be met, and Shackleton keenly felt his obligation to his country. His hopes that he might be deployed to Russia to advise on a winter invasion of Germany and Hungary came to nothing. Instead, he was posted to South America to assist in spreading British propaganda.

Leaving Emily and the children prompted a wave of regret and loneliness. It was always on leaving that he realized how important Emily was to him.

> I miss you more than ever I have done before Sweeteyes... I was happy really happy this time when all was right between us... I think darling that you are wonderful in many ways and the more I think about you the more I see what a wonderful wife you have been to me: I suppose darling that I am a funny curious sort of wanderer but take this [from] me I have been far happier at home these last few months than ever before: and the work I am doing is I hope going to be of permanent help to the country.

He returned a few months later to another round of job searching and frustration. He was, after all, a difficult man to place. To Janet Stancomb-Wills he confessed: "I am being as tactful as I can but bitterly restless now and hear the guns booming on the other side and also see this great German advance. My place is out in the war." Knowing that thirty survivors of his expedition had already enlisted amplified his impatience. Emily felt powerless to help. "He is getting very restless—& is chafing to be off," she confided to a friend, "so for his sake I shall be glad when he gets his billet, as I quite understand how he feels ... As soon as he goes I shall settle down again to the domestic duties I am neglecting shamefully—but the children are well & happy—& the servants very good—they all know I am having the time of my life just for these few precious weeks." Once in a while Emily and her husband took a flat in Queen Anne's Mansions in London for a week at a time. In those few snatched moments she had him entirely to herself. "Oh! *how* I loved being alone there with him," she recalled later. "It was bliss."

At last, in 1918, Shackleton received an order from the War Office. He was to travel to the North to assist with transportation and supplies for a small but vital force uncomfortably camped at Murmansk near the Norwegian frontier with Russia. It was, he wrote, "a job after my own heart ... winter sledging with a fight at the end." In October Emily received a telephone call from her husband. Having been loaded with supplies, his ship was to put into a Scottish port for a few hours—perhaps she would like to come north for dinner with old friends? Pressing her children into the arms of family, she rushed to catch the next train. Emily remembered it as one of the happiest leave-takings she had experienced.

Shackleton's small expeditionary force included four of his "own" men—Leonard Hussey, Alexander Macklin, Joseph Stenhouse and Frank Worsley. As they arrived in the Arctic, Worsley recorded that they were all as "happy as sandboys." They dreamed of driving their dog teams over the snow into Berlin just as "the victorious British, New Zealanders, Yanks & French troops burst in from the Western Front." But before long Shackleton was despondent. He was well over a hundred miles from the conflict, and his job was far from stimulating. His official title said it all: director of equipment, clothing, rations and transport of the mobile columns and director of clothing for the Syren Force. He was bored and lonely, and feeling increasingly frail. Earlier in the year, while in Norway, he had shown signs of a minor heart attack but had refused to allow a doctor to examine him. Now his thoughts were constantly of home. Trying to make up for lost time, he sent letters to the children that were filled with stories, jokes and drawings, yet his letters to Emily showed his vulnerability: "I have not been too fit lately. I am tired darling a bit and just want a little rest." He had begun to find comfort in drink, which only exacerbated his sense of frustration and failure. "Sometimes I grow restless and feel any part of youth is slipping from me and nothing matters: I want to upset everybody's calm and peace of mind when I meet calm and contented people. I feel I am no use to anyone unless I am outfacing the storm in wild lands."

A drinking spree at Christmas upset his equilibrium, and he realized that he was in danger of losing himself entirely. "I am strictly on the water wagon now," he reassured Emily. "It does me no good and I can tell my imagination is vivid enough without alcohol— it makes me extravagant in ideas and I lose balance . . . If I had not some strength of will I would make a first class drunkard." Only the thought of Emily brought him round: "I think you are a wonderful girl and woman to have stood my erratic ways all these years: I think you understand me more than all the people I know put together." In April 1919 Shackleton returned home to Eastbourne for four days: "the longest time at home for the last five years." Even when he was in England there were constant demands on his time. Emily found the continued separation almost impossible to bear: "The waiting was so long and weary. I used to dream he was back & that I said 'tell me, this isn't a dream' but it always was."

Meanwhile, Shackleton continued to stumble from one bad investment to another. The few times his prospects improved, his generosity ensured that there was little to bring home. The first showing of the film about his expedition, *Endurance,* in the Albert Hall that December was a sellout success, but he gave all the proceeds to the funds of the Middlesex Hospital. He embarked on another ambitious lecture tour, which included a season at the Philharmonic Hall of twice-daily lectures, six days a week, for five months. Talking about his exploits and actually living them were very different. If Emily could be sure of two things, it was these: her husband's need for her love and support was as strong as ever, and before long he would dream up another adventure.

She did not have to wait long. Shackleton had hoped to lead an expedition to the Beaufort Sea in the Arctic, but when finances forced him to change tack, he decided to return to his old territory. This time he would attempt to complete a circumnavigation of the Antarctic continent and to map and claim uncharted subantarctic islands.

The *Quest*, named at Emily's suggestion, left St. Katherine Docks on September 18, 1921. Emily was unnerved by this new expedition. She was convinced that her husband was concealing a serious health problem and had insisted that he be examined by a specialist before the expedition departed. According to one of the expedition doctors, Dr. James McIlroy, Shackleton had examined the specialist, instead of the specialist examining him. Emily constantly reminded herself that he was a sailor, and that this was his job. Nevertheless, it was agonizing knowing the dangers he would face and acknowledging her powerlessness to keep him safe.

To his men, there appeared to be something different about Shackleton on this trip. According to McIlroy, Shackleton had been convinced by an old woman in Ireland that he would die at the age of forty-eight, so it was no wonder he was behaving strangely: he would turn forty-eight during the expedition. McIlroy recalled that as they sailed out of Devonport Harbour and heard a bell buoy tolling mournfully, Shackleton turned to the harbourmaster and said, "That's my death knell." At Rio de Janeiro, Shackleton suffered a significant heart attack. Again, he refused to be examined.

By the time the ship reached St. Vincent, several on board were feeling uneasy about Shackleton's health. He wrote to Emily that he was not feeling at all well, "but I think in a couple of days I will be my old self." It had already been a tough journey; the ship was not well suited to the rigours of the voyage south, showing weakness long before they hit the ice-choked waters. One of the party observed that Shackleton was having "a hell of a time." The ship, in particular the engine, was in terrible shape. The Boss "smiled to everyone, and to a certain extent made light of what was the matter. But I knew he was worried to death."

Shackleton urged Emily not to worry; it was just that he felt the eyes of the world upon him, which made life so much harder. "Please God," he continued, "I come out of the work and can run home for even a month or two next May." As a postscript he wrote: "Darling I am a little tired but all right you seem always young... P.P.S. You are rather wonderful."

On January 4, 1922, Shackleton was in a pensive mood. The *Quest* had anchored at Grytviken, and together with Wild and Worsley he had relived the final episode of the extraordinary journey from Elephant Island, the open-boat journey of the *James Caird* and the struggle across the rugged interior of South Georgia. That evening he wrote in his diary, "In the darkening twilight I saw a lone star hover, gem-like above the bay." At 2 AM Macklin was summoned by whistle to Shackleton's cabin, where he found the Boss in considerable pain. Shortly after, Shackleton suffered "a very severe paroxysm" and died. He was forty-seven years old. Emily would learn of her husband's death through the British press.

ON JANUARY 29, Shackleton's coffin, adorned with red and white roses from the garden of the military hospital, was carried through Montevideo, flanked by a hundred marines and privates of the Uruguayan army. After the president of Uruguay had paid his private respects, the coffin, draped in both the Union Jack and the Uruguayan flag, was slowly taken through the crowded streets on a gun carriage flanked by a squadron from the cavalry regiment. Eighteen hundred troops were turned out on parade with reversed arms as the cortege made its way to the harbour, where a ship was waiting to take Shackleton's body back to South Georgia. On March 5, 1922, at Emily's request, Shackleton was buried at Grytviken in the company of whalers and sailors.

Three days earlier a memorial service had been held in London at St. Paul's Cathedral. The simple yet moving ceremony, attended by several members of the royal family and by representatives from many nations, culminated in the last post being sounded by the boys of HMS *Worcester*. Emily received hundreds of messages of sympathy, including a note from Kathleen Scott, which touched her deeply. Other letters of condolence were an indication of the broad appeal of her husband. Amid those from members of royal families throughout Europe were heartfelt messages from everyday folk, including a London cabbie who commented that "he was to us the man of men." For all his apparent failures, Shackleton was on course to become a legend.

Ten years later, while unveiling a commemorative statue, the president of the Royal Geographical Society, Admiral Sir William Goodenough, declared that had Shackleton "lived in the gold age [he] would have been a Drake or a Raleigh; of one among those men whose names encircle this hall as they themselves encircled the world; of one to whom adventure was an inspiration, death an incentive." Such heroic comparisons were compelling. Although Emily had simply loved her charismatic, complicated but boyish Ernest, like Jane Franklin she worked to ensure that her husband's legacy was built on a positive foundation.

In early April 1922, she paid a visit to the publishers Heinemann to ask if they would be interested in a book about her husband. When they agreed, she advised them that there was only one man she could trust to write a sensitive portrait: Hugh Robert Mill, a close friend of Shackleton, who had also been to the Antarctic. Emily was delighted when Mill agreed to take on the project: "Your kind letter rejoiced my heart."

Gathering material for the biography was a cathartic process for Emily, and over the next few months Mill became her closest confidant. Shackleton's closest benefactors were kind and sympathetic. Dame Janet Stancomb-Wills sent Emily a large packet of her private correspondence with Shackleton. "They were very confidential," Emily confessed to Mill, adding generously, "It was a beautiful friendship." Mill was courteous enough not to question Shackleton's fidelity, and Emily would naturally not want such things published. But these letters to another woman from her husband about his hopes and disappointments were heartbreaking for Emily to read. Revisiting love letters Shackleton had written to her made her utterly desolate. Yet shining throughout them all was his tireless optimism that one day he would make a fortune to keep her and the children in comfort.

In fact, Shackleton had left almost £40,000 of debt—£850,000 in today's money. Emily had a modest income of £700 a year from her father's estate; after taxes, liabilities and other expenses there was barely anything left for her and the three children to live on. A friend generously offered to pay the school fees for Cecily and Eddie, but she was still forced to take their eldest son, Ray, out of Harrow. Knowing her plight, Mill proposed that the proceeds of his book should go to Emily. But while his gesture was much appreciated, additional funds would still be needed to provide for Shackleton's mother and two sisters, who had been reliant on him financially for several years. In May 1922 a committee was formed to raise money for a Shackleton Memorial Fund to help support Emily and the children. Emily was used to living frugally, and she decided that the greater part of the income from the fund should go to her mother-in-law. Unfortunately, her offer inspired a keen sense of entitlement in her in-laws.

Emily's role as defender of Shackleton's reputation put her under yet more strain. When her son Eddie was given a new edition of the book *Scott's Last Expedition*, based on Scott's journals, to read as homework over the holidays, Emily found to her distress that a passage criticizing Shackleton's careless abandonment of the hut he built in Antarctica had been retained in the book, when Shackleton had expressly asked for it to be removed.

Maintaining due care of huts in the polar regions is enshrined in the unwritten code of conduct of explorers. There is no knowing when such shelter could save the lives of others. However, completely weatherproofing a hut in areas of high winds and frequent blizzards is not always possible. Shackleton had repaired the windows of the hut in question before leaving but had no time to fully board it up, as his ship was in danger of being trapped by the ice. When Scott subsequently discovered that Shackleton's hut had been badly affected by storms and snowdrifts, his disdain was clear. It seemed unfair to Emily that her husband should be so harshly judged:

> I can't bear to think of all the boys and girls who are reading it and thinking Ernest had failed in "civilized human sentiment". It has been pain to copy it, and I wept bitterly over it on Sunday when I read it . . . I thought of writing to Mrs. Hilton Young, but she is so hard about Ernest . . . I feel it all so much, and my pen rushes on, as if I were treading on red-hot lava! . . . I say to myself that Christopher Columbus would have thought it petty of Scott to write like that, but it doesn't comfort me, because I hate to think such a wrong impression is given of Ernest.

By November the matter was still burning in Emily's mind. Mustering all her courage, she wrote to Kathleen Hilton Young asking if she might be allowed to visit a few days later. There was no reply. The lack of response from Kathleen was bewildering, given the letter of sympathy that Emily had received from her.

With her husband gone and no one to speak for him, Emily keenly felt the responsibility to defend him. She also heard that Sir Francis Younghusband was spreading rumours that Shackleton had earned large sums from lecturing and had gambled the money away. The ugly insinuations, she wrote in distress, were "very unkind and also untrue, and it has done me great harm." It was important, she stressed to Mill, that Shackleton's biography state clearly that he had refused to profit during the war and that whatever funds came in went to pay off expedition liabilities or toward good causes.

Mill steadied her with his kind and straightforward manner. "It is such an untold consolation to me to feel that the world will have a true story, and that much unfair and unkind criticism of Ernest will be answered," she confessed. It was also some comfort that the loyalty of Shackleton's men was as strong as ever. Emily valued their love and devotion to the Boss above everything, because they had experienced the peaks and troughs of life with this extraordinary man.

The realization of how much time they had spent apart and how much the children missed their father was one of the hardest things for Emily to acknowledge. Even more painful were the memories of the difficult times she and her husband had shared.

> He always said each expedition would be the last. Can you wonder that I believed it? On the strength of some of those tender letters, our love was so complete in every way, it is agony to body, mind, and spirit to have lost him.
>
> I am enclosing these letters separately... You will understand the pain of them. I think I will burn them after I have them back. I must have failed him somehow—perhaps I was too sure. I want to remember that he used to call me his "blessing" each year.

For countless years she had believed that one day he would give up his restless life and come home to be the husband and father she longed he would be.

Emily would champion the many-faceted, vulnerable, romantic and courageous man she had married until her death on June 9, 1936. Unassuming, kind and dignified, Lady Shackleton maintained the respect of explorers such as Nansen and Amundsen, of members of the European royal families and of Shackleton's men. Frank Wild, James McIlroy and Frank Worsley, among others, adored the gentle Emily, or "Honey," as they called her.

For Emily, Shackleton's true legacy was the effect that his energy and selflessness had had on others. Shackleton the polar explorer was a flawed but generous husband, father and friend. Emily wanted the man, not just the hero, to be remembered. Her modest dedication to him in Mill's biography, *The Life of Sir Ernest Shackleton*, offered this: "To Those Who Knew Him Best Because They Loved Him Most." Yet as Shackleton often said, it was Emily who knew him best, sometimes better than he knew himself. She was his comfort and his conscience.

Emily Shackleton has often been pictured as the epitome of the long-suffering polar wife surrendering her ambitions for those of her husband on his great undertaking; bound to a brilliant but restless dreamer, who yearned for home when he was away but was often distant when he returned. Gentle and devoted she may have been, but there can be no doubt that when compelled, Emily was a formidable force.

On the eve of his departure for the South in 1908, Shackleton penned a love letter to Emily, to be handed to her in the event that he did not return. In it, he wrote these words: "Think kindly of me and remember that if I did wrong in going away from you and our children that it was not just selfishness... Your husband will have died in one of the few great things left to be done." Yet he added a sentiment that would have been appropriate for any polar explorer writing in tribute to his remarkable wife: "I want to tell you beloved that wherever I may have been, all the time I have loved you truly. You have been an angel of light and an arm of strength to me."

AFTERWORD

O N JUNE 12, 2007, while I was in the middle of writing this book, my father passed away. Though he had been ill for some time, the sudden loss was devastating. I felt uprooted, bewildered and strangely unprotected. As Marie Peary had said on the death of her father, some of the sparkle of life was gone.

When I was able to return to my writing, I was struck more than ever by the relationships between these pioneers and their families. I knew that just as I had mourned, so had Marie Peary, Eleanor Franklin, Cecily Shackleton and all the other children; as I saw my mother's pain at losing her soulmate, I understood the sorrow that Jo, Emily, Kathleen and Jane had felt.

This book is not a definitive study of polar exploration; it is simply a collection of human stories. What sets them apart is the intensity of experience and emotion: love was profound; anxiety and loneliness became crippling; journeys were epic ordeals, at times almost mythic. Fear and hope accompanied every stage of these relationships. These heroes, it is important to remember, were fathers, husbands, sons and brothers and, like the rest of us, wanted to find their place in the world. My father used to say, "Tell the truth, but always be kind," and in my writing I have tried to stick to this principle.

This book has always been as much about the women as it is about the men, and I hope that it sheds some light on who they really were: warm-blooded, courageous women. I hope I have done them justice.

My mother and father always joked that my sister and I had chosen them to be our parents. If this is true, then I chose extremely well. My mother's wisdom, energy and empathy continue to be an inspiration to me. Her sweetheart, my dad, was an instinctive explorer and a gifted writer and artist. More important, he was an exceptionally warm and generous family man and an utterly loyal companion. "The thing about Wally," friends have since told me, "was that he lifted something up in you." They are absolutely right. I am immensely proud of these qualities in him.

In the days after my father's death, I was asked whether I thought my father was a hero. In retrospect, I am sure many other "snow babies" would have given the same answer: "Everybody thinks their father is a hero. Yes, he was my hero, but more than that, he was my very loving dad."

ACKNOWLEDGMENTS

T HE IDEA for this book first came in a tent on the east coast of Greenland, over thirty years ago, when my father and his companion Allan Gill were attempting the first circumnavigation of Greenland. Both lovers of literature, they took their minds off the imminent dangers by discussing their favourite books. On one of those occasions, Allan recalled reading a book about women who had fallen in love with the explorers of the Far East. Knowing my father's guilt at putting his family through such a difficult time, he added, "Someone should write about the wives of polar explorers. They put up with so much." My thanks go skyward to Allan for this thought, which was passed along to me many years later at my parents' cottage in the Highlands as we sat by the fire, enjoying a glass of wine and the usual conversation about books and dreams for the future. It is hard for me to put into words my thanks to my parents for a lifetime of love and encouragement.

The woman who has helped to bring all these stories into sharper focus has been, of course, my mother. She is an exceptionally strong and joyful woman, and her light brightened my father's darkest days and nights, both at home and away. Her wisdom and spirit have been an enormous inspiration to me over the years, and it is due primarily to her that I have been able to get under the skin of some of my trickier subjects.

It is fair to say there is one woman, apart from my mother, whose story has had the strongest impact on my life: Josephine Peary. When, aged ten months, I was taken to live with a small tribe of polar Inuit, our home was just a few miles from the spot where Jo gave birth to her daughter Marie. Some of my closest childhood friends were the descendants of Marie Peary's playmates.

By the time I was fifteen, the Peary family had an even more significant role in our family life. Toward the end of 1984, my father was asked by the National Geographic Society to assess Peary's 1909 diary and astronomical observations, papers that had been hidden from the public eye in the U.S. National Archives for some seventy years. For the following five years, it was as though we were living with the Peary family. The study of Peary's life and work became almost an obsession for my father, as well it might have, for he had the utmost respect for the polar traveller and his descendants. He was deeply anxious about the responsibility placed upon him by Peary's patrons to "prove" that the American explorer had priority to the North Pole. This weighty task had a lasting effect on our family, not least because of the regard my father had for the unwavering loyalty of Peary's remarkable wife, Jo, amid controversy and betrayal; her love gave Peary his strength. We all share a deep and lasting admiration for this courageous woman.

Having taken five years to complete this book, I am indebted to many. Sincere thanks go to Kieren Phelan at the Arts Council and to the Society of Authors for providing essential grants for this project. Thanks also to my editors, Anya Waddington and Barbara Pulling, for their valued help.

Wherever possible, I have gone to original sources for research. I am particularly grateful for the assistance of Naomi Boneham and the staff at the Scott Polar Research Institute, Cambridge, U.K.; Cally Gurley at the Maine Women Writers' Collection, Portland, Maine; and Margaret Walsh and staff at the Athy Heritage Centre, Kildare, Ireland; and I thank Lord and Lady Kennet and Louisa Young for allowing me access to family papers at the Cambridge University Library. I owe much to other writers and collections, and I offer my thanks for the generous support and assistance of the Alexander Turnbull Library, Wellington, New Zealand; the British Library, London; the British National Archives in Matlock, U.K.; the Cambridge University Library, Cambridge, U.K.; the National Maritime Museum, London; the Royal Geographical Society, London; the Royal Naval Museum, Portsmouth, U.K.; the State Library of Tasmania, Australia; the University Library of Oslo, Norway; and the U.S. National Archives at College Park, Maryland. Permission to quote from these superb collections, or to feature their images, is greatly appreciated.

Kind permission to reproduce the photographs in this book was granted by the Scott Family Archive; the Gell Collection, British National Archives; the Athy Heritage Centre; the National Library of Norway; the W.L. Crowther Library, Tasmanian Archive and Heritage Office, for the photographic reproduction of Lady Franklin, 1816 (art original, chalk, 159mm × 133mm), which is in the collection of the National Portrait Gallery, London; and the Herbert Collection.

This book would not have been possible without the help of a number of people. I am enormously grateful to Doug Wamsley for opening his private collection to me; to Kenn Harper for our energetic conversations about Jo Peary and Minik; to Professor Andrew Lambert and Professor Russell Potter for illuminating discussions about Lady Franklin; to Alexandra Shackleton for her thoughts on her grandfather; and to Seamus and Frank Taaffe, Kevin Kenney and others at the Shackleton Autumn School in Athy, Ireland. Special hugs also to "Uncle" Joe O'Farrell and Frank O'Brien for their good company and hospitality.

Dear friends who must be remembered include Allan Gill and Fritz Koerner, my father's travelling companions, who both sadly passed away during the writing of this book. My heartfelt thanks go to the Alderton family, Shane and Nigel Winser, the Bilton family, Geoff Renner, and Edwin and Suzie Mickleburgh for their tremendous kindness over the years, particularly during the hardest times; to Hal Robinson, my mentor in publishing, for his ongoing support; and to my many long-suffering friends, whom I have neglected terribly in these last years of writing: their understanding, love and well-needed shoves in the right direction have been vital to the completion of this project. Lastly, a whole world of thanks to Huw and to Nell, who light up my every day.

CHRONOLOGY

1786   April 16, John Franklin born in Spilsby, Lincolnshire
1791   December 4, Jane Griffin born in London
1795   July 14, Eleanor Anne Porden born in London
1805   October 21, Franklin participates in the Battle of Trafalgar
1818   Easter, Franklin departs on his first Arctic expedition on
        the *Trent*
1819   May 23, Franklin departs on his Arctic overland expedition
1822   Franklin returns from his overland expedition
1823   August 6, Eleanor Anne Porden marries John Franklin
        in London
1825   Franklin returns to the Arctic; February 22,
        Eleanor Franklin dies of tuberculosis
1828   November 5, Jane Griffin marries John Franklin in Stanford
1837   Franklin becomes lieutenant-governor of Van Diemen's Land
        (Tasmania)

1845   May 19, the *Erebus* and the *Terror* sail for the Arctic under the command of Franklin to search for the Northwest Passage

1847   June 11, Franklin dies in the Arctic

1848   May, the search for Franklin's expedition begins

1850   The search for Franklin continues; a four-ship naval flotilla discovers his camp on Beechey Island

1854   October 22, John Rae returns with Franklin artifacts and news that the bodies of white men had been seen by the Inuit; his report suggests the Franklin crews resorted to cannibalism

1856   May 6, Robert Edwin Peary born in Cresson, Pennsylvania

1858   December 7, Eva Sars born in Christiania

1859   Leopold McClintock returns with proof of Franklin's death and news of the discovery of bodies and boats

1861   October 10, Fridtjof Nansen born at Store Frøen near Christiania

1863   May 22, Josephine Cecilia Diebitsch born in Washington, D.C.

1868   May 15, Emily Dorman born at Sydenham in Kent; June 6, Robert Falcon Scott born in Devonport

1874   February 15, Ernest Shackleton born in County Kildare

1875   July 18, Jane, Lady Franklin dies

1878   March 27, Kathleen Bruce born in Carlton-in-Lindrick, near Worksop

1879   U.S. Army Lieutenant Frederick Schwatka searches King William Island for Franklin relics and discovers a skeleton at Victory Point; he names Starvation Cove

1882   Nansen departs on first journey to the Arctic

1888   July 29, Nansen departs for the Arctic and completes first crossing of Greenland ice cap in September; August, Jo Diebitsch marries Robert Peary in Washington

1889   September 6, Eva Sars and Fridtjof Nansen marry

1891   June 6, the Pearys sail to northwest Greenland on the *Kite*

1893   June 23, the Pearys sail to northwest Greenland aboard the *Falcon;* June 24, Nansen leaves aboard the *Fram* to attempt to cross the Arctic Ocean via the North Pole

1895   Nansen sets a new farthest-north record

1897 October 2, Peary returns to the United States from the Arctic
with a group of Inuit and the world's largest known meteorite

1900 July 21, Jo and Marie Peary sail to the Arctic and are imprisoned
for the winter in the Arctic by ice

1901 British National Antarctic Expedition (*Discovery* expedition)
commences with Scott in command

1902 December 30, Scott and Edward Wilson attain new farthest-
south record; Shackleton is left behind in a tent

1903 March, Shackleton is invalided home from the Antarctic

1904 April 9, Emily Dorman marries Ernest Shackleton in
Westminster

1905 July 16, Peary sails on the *Roosevelt* to the Arctic

1906 April 21, Peary records a new farthest-north record;
Nansen becomes the ambassador for Norway

1907 October 21, Shackleton embarks on the British Antarctic
Expedition (*Nimrod* expedition); December 1, Eva Nansen dies

1908 July 6, Peary leaves again for the Arctic; September 2, Kathleen
Bruce marries Scott in the Chapel Royal at Hampton
Court Palace

1909 January 9, Shackleton records new farthest-south record;
April 6, Peary records that he has reached the North Pole;
September 2, news is telegraphed around the world that
Frederick A. Cook reached the North Pole on April 21, 1908;
September 4, Peary's competing claim is announced;
September 13, Scott announces another South Pole expedition

1910 July 16, the Scotts leave England bound for New Zealand, then
discover that Amundsen is also planning to go to the South Pole;
November 29, Scott leaves for the Antarctic on the *Terra Nova*

1911 December 14, Amundsen reaches the South Pole

1912 January 17, Scott and his party reach the South Pole;
March 9, news that Amundsen has reached the South Pole is
announced; March 29, Scott writes his last entry in his diary;
November 12, the bodies of Scott and his men are discovered

1913   January 12, the news of Scott's death reaches London;
        February 14, memorial service for Scott held in St. Paul's
        Cathedral; February 19, Kathleen learns of her husband's
        death while on a ship near Tahiti

1914   First World War begins; August 8, Shackleton leaves England
        to begin his Imperial Trans-Antarctic Expedition

1915   February 21, Shackleton's *Endurance* is beset in ice;
        October 27, Shackleton gives the order to abandon ship

1916   April 15, Shackleton and his men reach Elephant Island;
        May 10, Shackleton and companions reach South Georgia
        in the *James Caird;* May 20, Shackleton, Worsley and Crean
        reach the whaling station of Stromness

1917   January 10, Shackleton rescues the remainder of his men
        from the Ross Sea party

1918   October, Shackleton trains and supplies troops on the
        Norwegian-Russian border; November 11, armistice is declared

1920   February 20, Peary dies; Nansen becomes a representative
        for the League of Nations

1921   September 18, Shackleton departs on his final expedition
        in the *Quest*

1922   January 5, Shackleton dies off the coast of South Georgia;
        March 3, Kathleen Scott remarries; Nansen is awarded the
        Nobel Peace Prize

1930   Fridtjof Nansen dies

1934   October 24, Wally Herbert born in York

1936   June 9, Emily Shackleton dies

1939   Second World War begins

1943   May 25, Marie Walpole born in Dublin

1947   Kathleen Scott dies

1955   December 19, Jo Peary dies; in December Wally Herbert
        sails aboard the royal research ship *Shackleton* for Hope Bay
        in Antarctica

1956   Herbert sledges and maps the Graham Land Plateau;
        he surveys and maps Livingston Island, South Shetlands

1960   Herbert makes his first Arctic expedition, then returns to the Antarctic where he lives and travels for a further two years

1967   Herbert retraces Cook's journey across Ellesmere Island to Devon Island

1968   February 21, Herbert and three companions, Allan Gill, Fritz Koerner and Ken Hedges, begin the British Trans-Arctic Expedition from Point Barrow, Alaska

1969   April 6, the British Trans-Arctic Expedition arrive at the North Pole; May 29, the expedition arrives in Spitsbergen, successfully completing the journey; December 24, Marie McGaughey (Walpole) marries Wally Herbert in London

1971   Herbert family travel to northwest Greenland, where they live with a small hunting community for two years; Herbert's book *Polar Deserts* is published

1973   Marie Herbert's first book, *The Snow People,* is published

1977   Wally Herbert is awarded the German State Literary Prize for his book *Eskimos;* start of the British North Polar Expedition, the attempted circumnavigation of Greenland, with Allan Gill

1978   Wally Herbert's book *North Pole* is published

1981   Owen Beattie and James Savelle find evidence of lead poisoning in Franklin's men on King William Island

1989   Wally Herbert's book about Peary, *The Noose of Laurels,* is published

2007   June 12, Wally Herbert dies in Scotland

SELECT BIBLIOGRAPHY

Amundsen, R. *My Life as an Explorer*. London: William Heinemann, 1927.

Bain, J.A. *Life and Adventures of Nansen the Great Arctic Explorer*.
London: Walter Scott Publishing, 1925.

Bartlett, R. *The Log of Bob Bartlett*. New York: Putnam's, 1928.

Beardsley, M. *Deadly Winter: The Life of Sir John Franklin*.
London: Chatham Publishing, 2002.

Beattie, O., & Geiger, J. *Frozen in Time: The Fate of the Franklin Expedition*.
London: Bloomsbury, 2004.

Berg, K. *Fridtjof Nansen: Og Hans Kvinner*. Oslo: Schibset Forlagene,
2004.

Berton, P. *The Arctic Grail*. London: Viking, 1988.

———. *Jane Franklin's Obsession*. Toronto: McClelland & Stewart, 1992.

Blakey Smith, D., ed. *Lady Franklin Visits the Pacific Northwest, 1861
and 1870*. Victoria: Provincial Archives of British Columbia, 1974.

Bomann-Larsen, T. *Roald Amundsen*. Stroud, UK: Sutton, 2006.

Bryce, R.M. *Cook & Peary: The Polar Controversy, Resolved.*
　　Mechanicsburg, PA: Stackpole Books, 1997.

Cherry-Garrard, A. *The Worst Journey in the World.* London: Picador,
　　1994.

Cook, F. *My Attainment of the Pole.* New York: Polar Publishing, 1911.

Crane, D. *Scott of the Antarctic.* London: Harper Perennial, 2006.

David, R.G. *The Arctic in the British Imagination, 1818–1914.*
　　New York: Manchester University Press, 2000.

DeArmond, R.N., ed. *Lady Franklin Visits Sitka, Alaska, 1870.*
　　Juneau: Alaska Historical Society, 1980.

Dodge, E. *The Polar Rosses: John and James Clark Ross and Their
　　Explorations.* London: Faber, 1973.

Fiennes, R. *Captain Scott.* London: Hodder & Stoughton, 2003.

Fisher, M., & J. Fisher. *Shackleton.* London: Barrie Books, 1957.

Fitzpatrick, K. *Sir John Franklin in Tasmania, 1837–1843.*
　　Melbourne, Australia: Melbourne University Press, 1949.

Fleming, F. *Barrow's Boys.* London: Granta, 2001.

———. *Ninety Degrees North.* London: Granta, 2002.

Franklin, J. *Narrative of a Journey to the Shores of the Polar Sea in the Years
　　1819, 20, 21, & 22.* 1823. Reprint, New York: Greenwood, 1969.

Gell, F.M. *John Franklin's Bride: Eleanor Anne Porden.*
　　London: John Murray, 1930.

Green, F. *Peary: The Man Who Refused to Fail.* New York: Putnam's,
　　1926.

Harper, K. *Give Me My Father's Body: The Life of Minik, the New York
　　Eskimo.* Frobisher Bay, NWT: Blacklead Books, 1986.

Herbert, K., and H. Lewis-Jones. *In Search of the South Pole.*
　　London: Conway, 2011.

Herbert, M. *Healing Quest.* London: Rider Books, 1996.

———. *The Reindeer People.* London: Hodder & Stoughton, 1976.

———. *The Snow People.* London: Barrie & Jenkins, 1973.

Herbert, W. *Across the Top of the World.* New York:
　　G.P. Putnam's Sons, 1971.

———. *Eskimos.* London: Collins, 1976.

―――――. *The Noose of Laurels: The Discovery of the North Pole*. London: Hodder & Stoughton, 1989.

―――――. *Polar Deserts*. London: Collins, 1971.

―――――. *The Polar World*. Cornwall, UK: Polarworld, 2007.

―――――. *A World of Men*. London: Eyre & Spottiswoode, 1968.

Huntford, R. *The Last Place on Earth: Scott & Amundsen's Race to the South Pole*. London: Abacus, 2000.

―――――. *Nansen*. London: Gerald Duckworth & Co., 1997.

―――――. *Shackleton*. London: Hodder & Stoughton, 1985.

Huxley, E. *Scott of the Antarctic*. London: Weidenfeld & Nicholson, 1977.

Jones, M. *The Last Great Quest: Captain Scott's Antarctic Sacrifice*. Oxford, UK: Oxford University Press, 2004.

―――――, ed. *Robert Falcon Scott Journals: Scott's Last Expedition*. Oxford, UK: Oxford University Press, 2005.

Kane, E.K. *The U.S. Grinnell Expedition in Search of Sir John Franklin: A Personal Narrative*. New York: Harper & Bros., 1854.

Keegan, J. *The Price of Admiralty: The Evolution of Naval Warfare*. New York: Viking, 1989.

Kelton, R. *Edward Steichen*. New York: Aperture, 1978.

Kennet, Baroness (earlier Kathleen Bruce Scott). *Self-Portrait of an Artist*. London: John Murray, 1949.

Lamb, G. *Franklin, Happy Voyager*. London: Ernest Benn, 1956.

Lambert, A. *Franklin: Tragic Hero of Polar Navigation*. London: Faber, 2009.

Lansing, A. *Endurance: Shackleton's Incredible Voyage*. New York: McGraw-Hill, 1959.

Lewis-Jones, H. *Face to Face: Polar Portraits*. London: Polarworld and Conway, 2009.

Mackaness, G. *Some Private Correspondence of Sir John and Lady Franklin, Tasmania 1837–1845*. Sydney, Australia: D.S. Ford, Printers, 1947.

McClintock, F.L. *The Voyage of the "Fox" in the Arctic Seas: A Narrative of the Discovery of the Fate of Sir John Franklin and His Companions*. 1859. Reprint, Edmonton: Hurtig, 1972.

McGoogan, K. *Fatal Passage*. London: Bantam Books, 2002.

————. *Lady Franklin's Revenge: A True Story of Ambition, Obsession and the Remaking of Arctic History*. London: Bantam Books, 2006.

Mill, H.R. *The Life of Sir Ernest Shackleton*. London: William Heinemann, 1923.

Nansen, F. *Farthest North: The Voyage & Exploration of* The Fram, *1893–96*. 2 volumes. London: Archibald Constable & Co, 1897.

Nansen Hoyer, L. *Nansen: A Family Portrait*. New York: Longman's, 1957.

Noyce, W. *The Springs of Adventure*. London: John Murray, 1958.

Owen, R. *The Fate of Franklin*. London: Hutchinson, 1978.

Peary, J.D. *My Arctic Journal: A Year among Ice-Fields & Eskimos*. London: Longmans, Green & Co., 1893.

————. *Snow Baby*. New York: Frederick A. Stokes, 1901.

Peary, M. *Snow Baby*. New York: George Routledge & Sons, 1935.

Peary, R.E. *Nearest the Pole*. New York: Doubleday, 1907.

————. *The North Pole*. New York: Frederick A. Stokes, 1910.

————. *Northward of the "Great Ice."* 2 volumes. New York: Frederick A. Stokes, 1898.

Peary Stafford, M. *Discoverer of the North Pole: Story of Robert E. Peary*. New York: William Morrow, 1959.

Porden, E.A. *Cœur de Leon, or, The Third Crusade: A Poem in Sixteen Books*. London: G. and W.B. Whittaker, 1822.

————. *The Veils; or The Triumph of Constancy—A Poem in Six Books*. London: John Murray, 1815.

Ralling, C., ed. *Shackleton: His Antarctic Writings*. London: BBC Books, 1983.

Rawlins, D. *Peary at the North Pole: Fact or Fiction?* Washington, DC: Robert B. Luce, 1973.

Rawnsley, W.F. *Life, Diaries and Correspondence of Jane Lady Franklin, 1792–1875*. London: Erskine Macdonald, 1923.

Riffenburgh, B. *The Myth of the Explorer*. London: Belhaven Press, 1993.

————. *Nimrod: Ernest Shackleton and the Extraordinary Story of the 1907–09 British Antarctic Expedition*. London: Bloomsbury, 2005.

Robinson, B. *Dark Companion*. London: Hodder & Stoughton, 1948.

Rosove, M.H. *Rejoice My Heart: The Making of H.R. Mill's "The Life of Sir Ernest Shackleton."* Santa Monica, CA: Adélie Books, 2007.

Russell, P. "The Allure of the Nile: Jane Franklin's Voyage to the Second Cataract, 1834." *Gender & History* 9 (August 1997): 222–41.

———. *This Errant Lady: Jane Franklin's Overland Journey to Port Phillip and Sydney, 1839.* Canberra: National Library of Australia, 2002.

Savours, A., ed. *Scott's Last Voyage: Through the Antarctic Camera of Herbert Ponting.* London: Book Club Associates, 1974.

Scott, J.M. *The Private Life of Exploration.* Edinburgh: William Blackwood, 1982.

Scott, R.F. *The Diaries of Captain Robert Scott.* Tylers Green, UK: University Microfilms, 1968.

———. *Scott's Last Expedition.* 2 volumes. London: Smith, Elder & Co, 1913.

———. *The Voyage of the "Discovery."* 2 volumes. London: Smith, Elder & Co, 1905.

Seaver, G. *Edward Wilson of the Antarctic: Naturalist and Friend.* London: John Murray, 1938.

———. *Nansen: The Explorer.* London: H.F. & G. Witherby, 1959.

Shackleton, E. *The Heart of the Antarctic.* London: Penguin Books, 2000.

———. *South: The Story of the 1914–1917 Expedition.* London: William Heinemann, 1929.

Spufford, F. *I May Be Some Time.* London: Faber, 1996.

Thomson, D. *Scott's Men.* London: Allen Lane, 1977.

Traill, H.D. *The Life of Sir John Franklin.* London: John Murray, 1896.

Weems, J.E. *Peary: The Explorer and Man.* London: Eyre & Spottiswoode, 1967.

Wilson, E. *Journey of the Discovery Expedition to the Antarctic 1901–1904.* London: Blandford, 1975.

Woodman, D. *Unravelling the Franklin Mystery: Inuit Testimony.* Montreal: McGill-Queen's University Press, 1992.

Woodward, F.J. *Portrait of Jane: A Life of Lady Franklin.* London: Hodder & Stoughton, 1951.

Young, L. *A Task of Great Happiness.* London: Macmillan, 1995.

Young, W. "On the Debunking of Captain Scott." *Encounter* (May 1980), 8–19.

Kari **HERBERT** began travelling at the age of ten months when her father, pioneering explorer Sir Wally Herbert, took Kari and her mother, Marie, to live among the polar Inuit on a remote island off the northwest coast of Greenland. Today, she is an acclaimed author, photographer and speaker. Her work has been published in magazines and newspapers all over the world, including the *Sunday Times*, the *Telegraph*, the *Independent* and the *Guardian*. Her memoir *The Explorer's Daughter* received outstanding reviews and was chosen as Book of the Week by BBC Radio 4. It has since been translated into Danish, Dutch, Italian and Polish.

Kari Herbert is the founding director of Polarworld, an independent publishing company that produces books and projects to bring an awareness of wilderness places to a diverse audience. She lives in Cornwall, England.